COLOR

Is the Suffering of Light

COLOR

Is the Suffering
of Light

A MEMOIR

Melissa Green

W. W. NORTON & COMPANY
New York • London

The text of this book is composed in Weiss with the display
set in Elizabeth Ann. Composition and manufacturing by
The Maple-Vail Book Manufacturing Group.
Book design by Charlotte Staub.

Library of Congress Cataloging-in-Publication Data

Green, Melissa.
    Color is the suffering of light : a memoir / Melissa Green.
       p.   cm.
    1. Green, Melissa—Biography.   2. Women authors,
    American—20th century—Biography.   I. Title.
    PS3557.R37525Z465   1995
    818'.5409—dc20
    [B]   94-11265

ISBN 0-393-03650-2

W. W. Norton & Company, Inc.
500 Fifth Avenue, New York, N.Y. 10110
W. W. Norton & Company Ltd.
10 Coptic Street, London WC1A 1PU

1 2 3 4 5 6 7 8 9 0

For Linda Emmetts,
and my family at Charles River,
with love and gratitude

Child, little child with the chestnut hair,

You have been lost here

In order to be saved far away.

THE LEAF-DIVINER
Odysseus Elytis

Author's Notes and Acknowledgments

I grew up in a household where the literal and figurative walls were awry, and nothing aligned with the horizon. When I began to read, I saw that, in literature at least, the world was a steady and secure place. Books became for me a measure of orderliness and desire—I wanted to live where things were level and plumb. The spines of my books established the vertical; typeface across the pages established the horizontal; and I discovered that I could step between the lines of prose the way one would crawl between the bars of a fence into a beautiful field, and I could find myself inside the story, behind its language. Like Alice through the looking glass, I passed through into another world where everything proved delightful and strange, and my real, disordered life receded.

I fell in love with the language of books because it was wondrous, thrilling, tactile, alive; words had texture, shape, color, taste, dimension, weight, each like a sweet in my mouth. I even loved the littlest, most overlooked words—"a" and "the"—because they could have been throwaways like me, but were never useless in books. Words that were spoken at home were flat, judgmental, punitive, and cruel. I was amazed that language had such power, that it could both hurt and heal so completely.

This memoir is more than the story of what happened to me as a child. It is about how I was saved by language. I opened Shakespeare at the age of nine and was electrified. I crept closer and closer to language for protection. I hoarded words like money. In a secret room in the most walled-off portion of my heart, I kept them like a treasure chest full of gold doubloons or pieces of eight. I depended on language to save me. And after many years of sorrow and illness, it did.

When I lived inside books, I was safe. When I lived outside books, I was not; but making myself as small and invisible as possible in order to listen to the lives of my family, I heard wonderful, horrifying, true, compelling stories that changed me as much as did my secret treasure-trove of words.

We become the people we are because of what happens to us and how our memory of it charges the rest of our lives with meaning. It is not only that we make metaphor; metaphor makes us. Language is what we own to be greater than ourselves.

I am deeply grateful to the Writers' Fund Committee at the Pen American Center; the American Academy and Institute of Arts and Letters; and the Author's League Fund for their generous support. Special thanks to William Wadsworth and the many people at the Academy of American Poets who contributed much-welcomed financial assistance at a time when the proverbial wolf was at the door.

Also, I am in the debt of my surefooted and splendid guides: Ann Katz, Nancy Davis, Dan Buie, Michael Mufson, Joseph Brodsky, Derek Walcott, Ann Kjellberg, George Kalogeris, Sharon Hogan, Karen Fritz, and Neal Winston; dear friends at the Winthrop Public Library; my knight in tarnished armor, Harry Ofilos; Herb Leibowitz, editor of *Parnassus*, who generously published some of these stories in an earlier version; Jill Bialosky, my editor at W. W. Norton, and my beloved first editor and now agent, Kathleen Anderson, whose handprint is on every page of this book like a watermark.

Prologue

"the unlived life, of which one can die."

—RILKE

We didn't think you would live until your fortieth year. How did you?

You wouldn't believe me, even if I could tell you, I replied. Writing this book, in part, has helped to heal me.

How did you come to write your memoirs?

I did not know how the book would turn out when I began it. There were stories I wanted to tell myself—the oldest, most familiar ones—I thought I would learn who I am and where I belong in the world if they were written down.

And did you discover who you are and where you belong?

I learned who I had been, but I am not the same as I was. Now I am discovering how I must go.

What was it like for you before you found your way?

Imagine a beautiful bolt of cloth laid out on a table where someone has cut out the pattern of a dress. I was neither the fabric nor the garment, but the place where the garment had been scissored out. Imagine a house that has all the appearances of being a home—lights are on, music is playing, curtains are blowing at the windows. But if you knocked all day, no one would answer the door. I was that empty house. Someone very close to me said I was like a tiny tree clinging tenaciously to crumbs of earth on the sheer rock face above the abyss. I could not have a life. It was all I could do to hang on to the earth.

But you did have a life.

Yes, but it was like a dream from which I couldn't be

wakened. There were days and days when I moved through a mist. My self was not present, my shadow stood in for me. There were afternoons when the sun was too bright, the leaf-fall too loud, and even the gentlest wind from the sea burned my skin. I could not bear the press of so much beauty. I would feel myself plummeting through an eternity of space, crumbling like a sand castle, grain by grain, until I was washed away by darkness. There was no one to hold me together, and I could not hold myself. I do not remember years of my life—not where I lived, who my friends were, how I dressed or wore my hair. There was only shattering and a rain of fragments—razor blades; sleeping pills; hospitals; needles; restraints; people sitting near my cot, holding my hand trying to give me the strength to come back from the dead; waking, not knowing who or where I was.

How many years were lost?

Most of them. Too many to count. Waves of sorrow would break over me, I was overcome by simply being alive. How can I make you see that it was painful merely to be? I would crawl onto dry land, get to my knees, and rise. Another wave would overwhelm me. I would struggle and rise. This went on and on until I couldn't stand up unaided. I was too frightened, too exhausted and weak, too much in despair. And when kind and knowing hands lifted me from the water, all I could say was, *Help me, I'm trying to be born.*

To be born?

Yes, to come into being as myself. I was not the person I'd been intended to be. In my heart, from the earliest days, I knew I was meant to write—which to me meant finding out what was true about myself and the world—but I was too afraid to venture much further than the front porch steps. I knew I would die if I couldn't discover the truth, and I knew I would die if I tried. To find the truth was more terrifying than dying. And yet to tear down the walls of my life as I had known it and rebuild myself cell by cell was the only way I could go on. I had to be born anew.

How was that accomplished?

Imagine a rowboat, washed gently by waves at the edge of the shore and a shadow holding onto the oarlocks, afraid to move. The shadow-woman looks at the world as it was taught to her and sees the falsity of it, the sagging beams and rotted underpinnings of a city with cardboard cornices, doors that don't open, buildings with false fronts, cobbled streets that turn in upon themselves and go nowhere, churches where no gods reside, shops that sell lies, vendors peddling food that cannot nourish, fields of wheat blasted by disease, fountains that trickle with rust-colored whiskey not water, gold leaf on the palace walls burning in the sun of the shadow-woman's gaze and turning to blood which pours down the pitted walls. She is weeping—all she has ever known and believed to be true has been a lie—her grief is the fiery grief of the exile who has lost her native land. Her eyes burn, and a white farmhouse bursts into flames. Her eyes burn, and the jerry-built piers lean and tumble into the sea. She cannot go back. The city of lies begins to collapse. The shadow-woman weeps to see it disappearing, though it has cost her so dearly to live there. It has been her home. Towers crash from their pediments and split the pavement where they fall. Fences come down, paling by paling, blackened windows blow out of their frames and fresh, new air courses through the structures. With every shingle that tears from its nails, every chimney that plummets to its hearth, the shadow-woman is becoming more visible. She is fiercely gripping the oars as if they were hands.

And now it's possible to see that someone is in the boat with her, someone very close to her who says, *I know you are in despair and cannot see where this journey will take you. I will hold the hope for you until you can hold it for yourself.* And the shadow-woman, weeping still, says in reply, *It's true. I have no hope. But I think I have the hope of hope.* And together they paint on the bow of the peeling rowboat its name, *The Hope of Hope.* The shadow-woman, growing more substantial by the moment, smiles a half-smile, as if remembering something from long ago. *There is something inside me that could not be crushed. It is private and sacred and untouchable. It has always been there, though I could not always feel it, but I know now it cannot be destroyed.* Do you know, she says to her beloved companion, *that in the Middle Ages, the people called stones that lay along the beach sostoros, the oyster, and they believed that every morning at dawn, the stones would open their mouths and drink in the dew and the rays of the sun and the moon and the stars. And those simple, ordinary stones, taking in so much beauty, day after day, could make pearls. That is what I must do now. Every morning at dawn, I must open my mouth and drink in the dew and the rays of the sun and the moon and the stars, and write the truth.*

The beloved companion smiles at the woman, no longer a shadow but radiant with life, and says, *Yes you always had that place inside. I could see it when you could not. It will never leave you and neither will I.* Come, she says, taking one of the oars, *I will help you row.* I ask, suddenly afraid, *But who am I now? And where are we going?* I, the shadow-woman, have found my true voice. *You are a woman on a journey of discovery,* my companion says. *We will have to see where it takes us. We may not know where we are going for a long time. But we will know it when we get there.* And together, each gripping an oar, we cast off from the shore of the world and set out for the open sea.

COLOR

*Is the Suffering
of Light*

GLASS

*Once upon a time there was a girl who wished to live for-
ever. For the first few years, everything went well, but
because she had asked for everlasting life and had forgotten
to ask for everlasting youth, she soon began to shrink and shrivel till
at last she could neither walk nor stand nor eat nor drink. And yet,
she could not die. At first they fed her as if she were a little child, but
when she grew smaller and smaller, they put her into a glass bottle,
and she hangs there still, as small as a mouse.*

I remember yellow chicks on a white nightgown before I
remember the face of my mother, the arms of my father, the
room where I slept; yellow chicks nestling softly in ruffled cotton—on the sleeves, on the apron, through the smocking—
bright sun-drenched chicks fluttering awake to the morning
with me, as if we had slept companionably together for a long
time and were just now damply emerging from the same dark
egg.

Suddenly, something was falling away from my eyes. I was
awake, I was alive, I had grasped the toffee-colored bars of my
crib and was standing! A window shade had snapped up
sharply while I'd been dreaming, and with it the long oblivion
of babyhood ended. Brightness and darkness, dividing, poured
themselves into shapes the way water fills pitchers to the rim;
brightness and darkness in lustrous pools spilled in vivid con-
vections; everywhere forms, dimensions, designs were ham-

mered out by light on the anvil of a shadow. Wedges, arcs, and spheres quickened with color, disengaging hand from hand and face from face into a row of Hummel figurines on the mantelpiece, the butter-bright infinity of my mother's room, and the white squares lashed to the curtain rods became muslin streaming with sun. A dazzling puzzle of azure lozenges fell into place all at once, and between the muntins of windows like glass above a chapel altar, the sky etched itself across each gilded pane, reflecting the shimmering upper branches and leaves of two-hundred-year-old elms, and young clouds frisking like April colts in a meadow of blue.

Coming into the room with their pastel Easter coats and bright hair, adjusting the blossoms of their spring hats in the mirror until the whole room seemed filled with flowers, were Nana Higgins and her sister Genevieve, pulling on their long white gloves before church. And though I didn't know them by name, I knew with delight that they belonged to me, and I held up my arms for one of them to embrace me—and here the memory ends as if a heavy velvet curtain had come down. Did one of them reach for me or lean over to touch my hair? And if one of them did, why couldn't I remember it, when everything else was so clear? In a flash, I thought I understood: I couldn't remember ever being held in anyone's arms.

I rode and plunged inside this moment of awakening all through my childhood. My intelligence gripped the handrail of a metaphysical seesaw, tearing my allegiance in two: the exhilarating flight upward of *I am alive*, the thrilling plummet through space of *I am alone*, and the turmoil of rising like a winged thing into the atmosphere, falling in my mortal body toward the earth. Both were well-thumbed and twin halves of the same haunting locket I kept tight in my fist: *I am alive, I am alone*. Afterward, whenever I closed my eyes to invoke that first stunning vision, its power overcame me. I knew I was a self and in the world, and that the perilous moment of my waking— the brightness and darkness dividing—filled me with recognition and joy. But in the next instant I was back in my nightgown with its yellow chicks, and the world was beginning to whiten, moving in a violent wave over my head, and I was crumbling into fine ash, into granules of light extinguishing like snow, growing smaller and smaller, dissolving into air, into dust, into nothingness.

I was born on the third of April the year before Jonas Salk discovered a vaccine for polio and spent the first six weeks of my life at Boston's Beth Israel Hospital where there was a neonatal unit for premature babies. My birth weight was 3 lbs. 13 oz. and my lungs would not clear, so I was placed in an incubator. My parents had been expecting a boy they could name Richard Winthrop Green III. Consequently, they weren't prepared to name a girl. The doctors insisted I be baptized immediately since my color was blue and they didn't think I would survive, so in haste, by some miracle of imagination, they called me Melissa, meaning honeybee in Greek. A specialist from Children's Hospital was consulted because I would not eat and my weight had dropped to 3 lb. 3 oz., but after three days of wavering between life and death, I finally took a little sugar-water and tried to live. At least, that's how the myth of my birth was told to me.

I was haunted by this ghost of my existence as some children are haunted by monsters in the closet or dragons under the bed. I imagined a tiny, formless child lying wrapped in white sheets in an incubator like some hothouse flower whose bloom would wither and die if touched by human hands, and who, already pale, would lighten to the color of snow. Fragile enough to be blown away by an exhalation of breath, this child had been placed in a coffin of glass, alone on a snowbank of linen. Crying unheard, she was a wisp, a dandelion at the end of summer, turning to puffs on currents of air being borne skyward; when she opened her eyes she saw a tiny, baby-sized box encasing her in ice, opaque and infinitely quiet. No one held her in their arms, no one stroked her deathly pale skin. She was alone in the universe.

There is a black-and-white photograph of my mother and

Flap, part farmhand, part uncle—whose name was always said with the sound of "ah," not "slap"—squatting in front of the chicken-wire dog run with their arms full of pups whelped by Flap's beagle Susie on the same day I had been born. I tried to imagine what my mother felt as she held all that young life in her arms when her own newborn was fifty miles away. There is no sadness on her face. The pups squirm happily while she and Flap look proudly at the camera, never suspecting that in a few short weeks all the pups but the runt of the litter would be dead of distemper, and the baby they thought might die would be home with them.

All through my childhood I thought of the runt as my dog, since the linking of his birthday with mine made me realize that we both had lived by only the wildest luck, the frailest grace of God, under the very real threat of death. The dog was called BooBoo because he would not learn: time after time he came home with his mouth full of porcupine quills. When I was big enough to straddle him on the ground, Flap would get the needle-nose pliers and while he pulled out the quills one by one, the dog would whine as though his heart were breaking. Then he would go to sleep next to the wood stove in the egg room on a worn leather armchair and snore like an old drunk. But when Flap said, *Sing, Booboo! Sing for your supper!* the dog would throw back his head and howl for all he was worth, the long OW-OOO of his note traveling the curve of the driveway, over the orchard in Rossbach's field, down the backside of Barker Hill Road toward the center of town. He howled as a way of earning his keep on hot summer days when the briar patch was full of berries, or on winter afternoons when child-sized icicles hung from the eaves of the brooder house. BooBoo was at the mercy of his master who could withhold food if the song wasn't to his liking, deny love if a command wasn't obeyed. The dog had to sing for his life, and his howl seemed full of sorrow, like a church bell tolling from some deep well inside him. His howling frightened me. I thought he

was crying for his mother, his brothers and sisters, long dead.
I'd throw my arms around his collar and howl with him, crying
for his hunger and grief.

All the animals on my father's farm were required to earn
their keep. In exchange for love and affection, the dogs
patrolled the woods and fields by day and stood sentinel at
night against foxes, porcupines, woodchucks, and raccoons,
which they would tear into pieces with their jaws. The biggest
dog, Butcher, was always chained to a tree because he couldn't
be trusted. He was there to frighten people who came up the
road, unknown or unannounced, and clearly could make a meal
of any child. Even Flap threw bones in the dog's direction without touching the dog himself because he was afraid.

We had five thousand hens that gave us meat and eggs for
which they were paid with fresh water and mash in rudimentary conveyor-belt feeders. But when I'd go in to gather the
eggs, lifting the roofs of the nests with one hand and scooping
up eggs with the other, I wasn't sure if it was fury or hunger
that made the roosting hens flap so wildly, pecking my hands
raw or flying into my face in a profusion of dust and feathers.

Ruby, the wild barn cat, who would hiss if I came too close,
caught mice and squirrels in exchange for a place in the sawdust on nights when the temperature fell below zero. The donkey, Rosita, kept the fields down and was moved every day to
mow another circular swath beneath the apple trees, beside the
cooper shop, along the stone walls, and behind the barn cellar.
She ate everything in sight, even sumac. Her reward was mash
soaked in molasses and vegetable peelings. Whenever I fed her,
I had to make sure my palm was flat and my fingers bent away
from her dove-velvet lip because she liked to bite me, nibbling
hard to take all the salt from my hand.

The farm had belonged to our family for five generations.
Once, oxen had dragged stoneboats through the fields. Now
the woods had taken over the cleared pastures, and my father
raised hens and sold eggs. The oxen were gone. The enormous

barn had been badly burned in a forest fire and had to be pulled down. Life on a New England farm, then as now, was a practical matter. During its violent seasons—its poverties and riches—animals were either strong enough to live or they were not, and if not, they were drowned from a riverbank or clubbed and thrown into the barn cellar's compost heap, coolly and without ceremony. Some animals were even led by the halter or collar to the edge of an open grave and shot there between the eyes.

Nothing on the farm could be wasted, not a blade of grass, not a drop of water. Summers, when the artesian well ran dry and every bit of water was rationed to save the chickens, days' worth of dishes would pile up in the sink, and we'd bathe naked in the Squanicook River at the foot of Barker Hill, rafting Ivory soap over the rocks and into our hands until a battery of mosquitos drove us in for the night. Indoor plumbing became a luxury again, and we'd take turns in the shingled outhouse with the quarter-moon-shaped window in the door, inhaling deeply with delicious disgust the matter-of-fact smell of pine trees, roots, dead leaves, moss, and manure.

Anything edible from the supper table was scraped into a coffee can and brought out to the pigs, Honeysuckle and Rose, who wallowed in their sty, getting drunk on the pomace of apples, corn cobs, and grain, rooting through the trough in a frenzy like the Gadarene swine. They would feed us next winter. The six geese that patrolled the dooryard and terrace with their unpredictable and ferocious trumpeting kept visitors in their cars by the flourishing of their wingspans. They picked at my toddling brother's suspender buttons with their hard beaks and pecked at the curls on his forehead until they drew blood. They would be holiday fare. On some cool autumn mornings when the mist still threaded the apple trees like smoke, deer would come to eat windfalls in the field and sometimes leap over the stone wall, grazing the lacework of tea roses and lilac in front of the kitchen window. But they'd pay dearly for their beauty and proximity to us at the end of the season, when the men in plaid shirts and bright orange hats would come from out-of-state with their guns.

One Sunday during hunting season when I was nine years old, I was sorting eggs in the egg room. It was a particularly warm Indian summer afternoon, the door to the egg room was left open, and the last of the fat flies were wobbling in and out. I could see Rosita grazing under the pine tree near the dying raspberry canes, and as I was idly scraping manure from an egg with sandpaper, I heard a bright whizzing noise, the high faint buzz of a furious insect. I dropped the egg back in the washing tub and flew out the door, running toward Rosy who was frantically tracing circles around and around the pine tree, the chain clang-clanging as it gathered itself tighter and tighter about the trunk. I screamed at the top of my lungs the words I had heard my father say, "Get the hell away from my house, you goddamned son-of-a-bitch bastard!"

Two disheveled hunters stumbled out of the woods, looking from the donkey to each other sheepishly, their rifles pointing at the toes of their boots in embarrassment.

"Does this look like a deer to you?" I demanded, and Rosita, her ears laid flat back, brayed loudly in derision. The hunters flushed as red as their hunting hats and made their way back through the briars to the road, started up their Studebaker, and drove off. I returned to the egg room, astounded by the stupidity of people, incensed that they needed a nine-year-old child to teach them the difference between a donkey and a deer. I pulled the wire basket of newly rinsed eggs out of the washer and hoisted it into the egg room where, under the watchful eyes of animals cut from the pages of *Fish and Stream*, *New England Farmer*, and the *American Kennel Club News* tacked to the wall above me, I turned on the grader's conveyor belt and patiently lined up the eggs in the troughs to be graded.

If you held an egg up to the light, a very strong light, the shell was almost transparent, and if you looked carefully, you could see the shape of the yolk and sometimes the chick itself. It was called candling. It couldn't be done with our eggs, of course. Something was put in the feed to keep the eggs from becoming fertilized—they were just eggs for eating, so there were no chicks inside, but it was a curious idea all the same.

The ratchets and sprockets of the grading machine whirred at the touch of a light switch. The eggs arranged themselves in the troughs and traveled along each track like an oblong ball in a bowling alley, taking an abrupt left turn and riding along until each of them was dropped by weight into areas of the bench marked Jumbo, X-Large, Medium, Small, and Pee-wee—thirty dozen brown eggs in each box, six dozen in each layer, until all the crates were full. My father or Flap would carry the egg boxes into the cooler—a room on the other side of the wood stove where the eggs were stored in air-conditioned space on racks like money in a safe.

I was three when I was first taken to the little brooder house to see the downy black chicks, the day after the moving-van-sized trucks had delivered them from another farm, cheeping and peeping plaintively under the rotundas of light that hung over the brooder stoves. My father held my hand and lifted me over the brooder-house stoop, sweet with the smell of mash and sawdust and kerosene, where under each roof of light encircled by a corrugated knee-high fence were thousands of chicks, opening their yellow beaks and peeping. Each of the corrugated circles fencing the brooder stoves and all their heat was called an incubator. I knew about incubators. Did I live under bright lights like these? My father lifted me in under the light and set me down among the chicks. It was warm there in the sawdust. The chicks huddled around my boots as if they could get heat from me. Each tiny feathered thing made the faintest sound, and yet when they all cheeped together, they made a tremendous noise.

My father reached into the swarm of feathers and brought a chick close to my face, where I saw its pink tongue like a shred of ribbon candy straining for air, for food. Its downy wing-spurs tried to fly. I took the chick into my hands and felt its heartbeat throbbing, a tiny heart like mine that longed only to breathe and be fed, and for a moment our hearts beat together; it made me laugh with delight. Then I held the chick close to my ear, listening, hoping to hear some mysterious answer in the rhythm of its heartbeat, some sea-swell, some understanding about the universe, and how I had come to be. As I brought the chick closer, letting it know that I wanted to love it, and holding my breath so I could hear more, the tick-tock stopped inside its delicate feathers, the little head lolled on its tiny broken neck, and its eyes stared past me into the dust of the rafters under the roof. The chick was dead and I had done it. I had killed it by holding it too hard. A terrible wind began to blow inside my head. I opened my mouth but no scream came out, just a tiny peeping, a sound of terror for which there were no words.

Sternly, silently, my father took me by the hand, hoisted me over the step of the brooder house, and we walked out into the late winter sunshine, blinding on the crusted snow. Ice was whispering on the birches, on the bent-over blackberry bushes, on the sumac. Our boots crunched in the snow all the way up the hill to the egg room. It was cold, and the vines kept tsk-tsking on the ice. My father stoked the wood stove, took off the stove-lid, and adjusted the damper. It must have been Saturday, because the bean pot was bubbling for supper. I stood shivering in my cold, wet boots. My father lifted me into the leather chair where BooBoo sometimes slept, cupped both my hands around the chick's little body, and brought them over the open stove-lid. I was crying in silence. I heard an icicle slide from the roof and shatter on the snow. My hands were like a shell, I was candling an egg, and I thought of the room of glass where a baby once lay, barely breathing. Inside her was a heart made of glass. Inside the heart of glass was a baby chick with a broken neck, and a child, growing smaller and smaller. The chick was let go into the fire, and the child inside shattered into thousands of shards, light, winking out, winking out.

One early May afternoon I was upstairs, supposedly napping. Sleep was a requirement for healing children's hectic lives and I hated it. I was five years old and there were too many interesting things going on to be in bed during the day—the buzzing intoxication of spring, the trees full of music, the boughs sashaying like hooped skirts above petticoats of apple and pear blossoms. Robins poured out their haunting melodies. Head on my arms, I watched their cat's cradle mating dance through the window, back and forth from limb to limb in free, ecstatic arcs, stitching the air with their needle-swift wings.

To an old crabapple, knuckled and gnarled, we tethered a lamb we named Mary. I could see her grazing in her bramble crown, patient as a stone saint as she endured my four-year-old brother's relentless beating of her head with the butt of his six-gun. Some mysterious animal knowing shone from her eyes—eerie with horizontal pupils of gold in brown iris. I hated having her tied. We had no fences and many acres of open pasture, but I was told that if she wandered off she might get lost or she might raid the vegetable garden, which was nearly a criminal offense. So she was always tied.

Then one day Mary did the unforgivable: my mother had invited several important ladies in town to play bridge for the afternoon and had scoured the rooms and the three of us like a madwoman. The house sparkled. We glowed. But when she went out back to greet her guests, Mary, who had gotten loose, slipped in the open door and ran through the living room, dropping a frenzy of raisins all through the pristine house. We howled, but it was not funny. From then on, she was always securely tied. I liked Mary. But try as I might, I could not find a way to unfasten the chain that ran flashing through the grass, its links resisting any wish I had to pull them apart or tear them away from the grooved wool at her throat, just as I could never comb the burdock out of her matted fleece.

Months afterward, at nap time, I was not dreaming of Mary. I had forgotten about her and her nibbling poverty, the richest grass always out of reach. I was drowsily watching the wind ripple the fields like some underwater sea, dreaming from my vantage point as from the prow of a ship that the Little Mermaid would not have to give up her beautiful tail, her tongue, her home. Just then a truck came roaring up the driveway, huffing like an old pipe-smoking grandfather in suspenders whose lifting days are over and who has forgotten it, again. A green pickup with a handmade truck bed and no writing on the side backed around and parked under the pear tree, bending its lowest branches until they dropped a bridal veil of blossoms. Two men, in work boots and dungarees with caps on their heads, got out of the truck. Strangers. I didn't like strangers. Some premonition pricked at the base of my scalp. I was afraid. My young father appeared from the barn in a sleeveless T-shirt, work boots, and dungarees, and the three men chatted like old friends, soldiers in the army of adults who ran the world. I rested my cheek against the window screen, but I couldn't hear a word they were saying.

The men laughed, one of them throwing back his head and removing his cap to wipe the sweat off his face with his forearm. The other, younger man turned so I could see his face and spat heartily into the grass. The three of them walked under the marriage canopy where the apple tree stood solemnly next to the pear. My father unhooked Mary's chain from the low bough. I heard the links drop to the ground, the chain still looped around the lamb's neck. She stood still, placidly chewing. They were about to let her go—up past the garden where the grass was waist high and bees swam in sleepy circles overhead! I thought of her delight in such an Eden of grass, her jaws working back and forth without fatigue, her impassible face revealing nothing. I loved my father for setting her free.

Instead he walked toward the truck with the chain in his hand until it stretched its full length, and Mary cautiously stumbled forward on her delicate black hooves. I pressed my nose harder against the screen, watching. My father pulled tight and long on the chain, and the animal balked. Then both men, one on either side of her, fell against her fat sides in a single motion, their huge hands on her buttocks, their fingers deeply and resolutely clutching her broad back. My father stood on the ramp of the truck supervising the two strangers who were pushing their full weight upon the lamb as she tottered fearfully up the ramp, some instinct making her resist. I pounded on the screen and tried to release the double catches at the bottom, but my hands weren't strong enough. Suddenly I knew what was happening. I ran downstairs to my mother, crying, "Where are they taking her? Don't let them take Mary away!" I wanted to run out and stop them, or tell them to take me instead, but my mother gathered me into her arms and calmly told me my first lie.

"They're taking her to another farm to be with her brothers and sisters," she said.

I stopped, mid-howl, my mouth open in astonishment as the weight of what she was saying hit me full in the chest. I couldn't believe the same mother who bathed me and fed me, sung and prayed with me, was telling me such a ridiculous and palpable lie, and the same father who held me over his head at arms' length, who tickled me mercilessly and blew his lips like a tuba softly into my neck, was conspiring with her. Did they think I was stupid? They were taking Mary to be killed!

And yet, nibbling my lip for a minute, I thought it might be true—that a perfect farm, where sheep would roam happily in a flock alongside the cheerful barking of a gentle sheep dog and the tender benedictions of a shepherd, where fields of fragrant clover extended as far as the eye could see, might actually exist. Then I was angry and frightened. Not only did I know Mary was going to die, something in me was dying too.

I drew back from my mother with my mouth agape. Thinking I had not understood, she repeated the lie in a soothing voice. *Mary was going to another farm.* I wailed inconsolably. I knew the lamb was lost and that in some way I was lost as well. I cried a child's desolate tears. If they thought I didn't know the truth, then my parents didn't see me clearly at all. I was a stranger to them. They didn't even suspect I knew they were lying—I was just a child who could be fooled.

It wasn't long before the lamb appeared one Sunday dinner, complete with mint jelly—made from mint I had obediently picked, not knowing what it was for. I began to tremble at the table, because Mary was dead and I knew they would make me eat her, even though I'd loved her. But what I wanted was unimportant. Tears ran down my cheeks as my father matter-of-factly slapped a piece of the pink meat on my plate. It smelled like death. Blinking, I felt for my knife and fork and tried to slice gently but I screamed when I cut right through one of her veins. My father in a fury stabbed at my plate and stuffed a forkful of meat into my mouth, vein and all. I ran upstairs in hysterics. There was nothing on earth I could trust.

I thought of my favorite fairy tales, ones in which the hero is given a magic cloak that makes him invisible so he can win the castle, the treasure, the hand of a beautiful princess. A cloak of invisibility that allowed him to move like light through the battlements, to walk undetected through the palace until he found the object for which he risked everything. I was already invisible. But there was nothing I sought, no enchantment from which a prince's kiss could wake me. I was not good. It was too late. In my world, where I was seen but not visible, the cloak I wore was a sign of disintegration, dissolving me. My carriage was turned into air, the armature of my bone into fog, my tissue into sea-spray, my skin into mist or light—not the shining mantle of saints, but ordinary invisible daylight. Yet, the wind blew, and I could feel it. I must be alive.

Sometimes my mother held me up before her face as though I were a looking glass, a gilt-edged mirror that would lie to her about her beauty and her age, a mirror in which she saw herself, forever young. I remember Granny leaning over me in my crib as though I were Echo Lake near Mt. Kearsage, and in the delicate reed-pale water of my face, she saw her own reflection. It was her hair that winnowed there, her cheeks floating, milk-white, just under the surface, her eyes lashed with unsmudgeable kohl.

I was invisible to them, submerged in their personalities, deeply drowned. I was Ophelia, not an oval-faced beauty crowned with garlands and Pre-Raphaelite hair, but a dead girl lying underwater. My voice, a susurrus of saints' robes brushing the heavens, made the faintest noise. My cries, my laughter, my despair flew against the high unfathomable wall of the Baltimore Catechism where every question had a brusque solution. Where was God? Did he see me, invisible and unhappy as I was, crouched by my bed, crying soundlessly into my hands? I woke from nightmares screaming for someone to come from the darkness and comfort me, for the frightening objects of lightlessness to reassemble into their harmless daytime selves. But no one came, and I began to doubt the power of my own voice. Not only could I not be seen, I was powerless to be heard. My voice was silence itself. I felt the magical shroud wrap tighter around me.

How could the prayer of a child whispered into the darkness rise above the world, past the stars, and into the ear of God? I was invisible; death was invisible. I knew I'd already been claimed, one shadow to another, by death, because I too was made of dampness and air. I no longer believed in the saints or eternal life because Mary the lamb had been led to slaughter. They had lied to me. Heaven must be part of the same lie. What could I believe when I'd lost Lucy, Agatha, Perpetua,

Felicity, and the God who could see the smallest sparrow, even me? The lamb had been led to slaughter. Jesus was the Lamb. I would die and be dead forever, lying in a glass coffin under the earth.

I finished my first novel at the age of seven. It was a ten-page, single-spaced story in eight chapters I had painstakingly typed myself on a monstrous Royal that weighed more than I did. I'd finished typing one Sunday morning before church, relishing the power of the final words, *The End.* Later, I fidgeted in a pew with all the other children at the front of the church where the whiskey priest could keep an eye on us. I was waiting for the incomprehensible drone of the sermon to stop, perspiring under the brim of my straw hat with the double navy grosgrain ribbons hanging down my back, white gloves clutched damply in my lap. Everything was stranger than it had ever been. Didn't my mother and father know what I had done? It hadn't changed a thing for them. I turned to look back at the congregation, but saw only strangers. I glanced to my right, to my left, seeing children I knew from school, feeling suddenly older and other than. They didn't know me either. I sat still, listening, understanding in the ache of a heartbeat that I looked the same as I had yesterday, that no one knew I had changed. I had written a book. Didn't anyone see what that meant?

I looked up to the tiny window above the wooden Christ and felt surprised because it had been broad daylight when we'd come down the aisle, and now the clear oval window was a beautiful midnight blue, a radiant Mary-blue, and it was infinitely quiet. And then I knew I was nothing at all, a dust mote, a bead of dew on a stem, and through the window a waterfall of stars cascaded down, rushing through me, a conduit for all eternity. A dazzling volcano of gold was falling down from the Chagall-blue window using my body as an aqueduct. I stood up in the middle of Mass, crying because the feeling was so immense, and stumbled down the speckled aisle,

votive candles flickering confusedly in my eyes, reaching out
with my arms for the blessed, ordinary daylight.

I was nothing and knew myself to be the same as the grass,
the leaves on the trees, the birds' nests, the flapping, withering
vines on beanpoles. God was not an all-embracing Father in a
white beard. He was darkness, immensity, the speed of light,
the milling of a thousand constellations careening through
Heaven, pouring from an ewer of ebony the fire of eternity
through my inconsequential child's soul, imprinting on my
mute tongue, *You are a falling star, death is always at your elbow,
write as fast as you can, time is passing.* It was a monumental secret.
I could not tell anyone what I had seen, that death was near,
that God was distant and immense and invisible. I was no one
and knew it, and yet, I had to find the words to say what I had
seen.

I learned what adoration meant the summer I was six, when
the dampness of dawn and the brightness of the hour merged
over the Squanicook River, as if time and temperature were
conspiring to hide some fugitive light that fled across the
morning fields. Thirty years later, I see that into those mists all
the hours of childhood's endless days had gone; every blue late
August morning had dissolved into a burning September and
taken with it the crucial shynesses and sand-pail tyrannies,
those seizures of goose bumps that came and went with each
cloud's passing. What did we mourn for then, that our teeth
chattered so violently there at the edge of the pond?

But my mind can only gather fragments of a simple summer
day, as though a mirror on the morning had shattered: the
placid, kidney-shaped pond under the pine trees, the gritty
back seat of a beach wagon opening over the noiseless carpet
of pine needles, the slap of our flip-flops as we struggled to run
a root-path down to the cold sand where a sunlit necklace of
bobbing, brightly colored corks rippled in the shallows. The
pond was little more than a swimming hole, a humble body of

water that cowered sheepishly near a cottage bought by the
Veterans of Foreign Wars. It had no name. If it was called
anything, it was called the VFW pond, though I never saw a
veteran there or even an American flag.

Body of water. I liked the way it sounded. Each lake and pond
and sea had unique boundaries, an individual animation, and I
wished that I had an icy, spring-fed body of water, that I was
a fluid, invisible being bubbling over stones, warm and pebbly
underfoot, swimming like a minnow, floating sunward, face up,
splashing furiously like an infant porpoise over the falls. Paddling where the water was up to my knees was heavenly, but
some kind of animal sonar reacted whenever I dove backward
into darker water and it suddenly dropped off into unimagin-
able depths. I was terrified I'd be pulled into a whirlpool, and
a wrenching desperation would pump through my fluttering
heart. Water had a mind of its own, an animus, a daemon, and
overpowered by its imperceptible undertow, I would be pulled
away from daylight into the void.

Every summer the town fathers paid a pair of high-school
students to teach the little ones to swim, and every year the
smallest ones were weaned away from shore, won over by
games, coaxed forward from the safety of their footprints
squelching in the sand and out toward the deep end where
their feet floated free and they learned to kick. Hair and water
in their eyes, the children would cross the finish line like little
terriers, paddling mightily out of the shallows into the bottom-
less waters of independence, their splashing feet displaying
their eagerness to prove themselves worthy of the sacred,
bewildering task of growing up. I was a slow child, timid and
terrified of things that moved too fast or too loudly and had
too much power of their own. I'd stand shyly on the playground near the teachers, afraid of the swings, the seesaw, the
merry-go-round, afraid of the velocity and pitch of other children's voices, their spinning games, their feverish animal activ-
ity—but I was most afraid of water. So when they insisted that

I learn to swim, my feet squelched in protest like anchors pulled from sand. I had no choice but to leap forward into time and grow up.

We were little girls in ruffled, one-piece suits, flowered rubber bathing caps, and Mamie Eisenhower bangs, draping our towels behind us like Princess Margaret, capes of orange terry cloth stitched with heraldic giraffes or winking starfish in cartoon anemones on a turquoise sea, scripted in red lipstick with our names: Jane, Jody, Marcia, Cindy, Linda, Marianne. Boys our age in baggy madras shorts snorkled and finned, shook water from their crewcuts as they ran, blue-nippled, in their piratical race to the raft set on oil barrels fifty feet from shore: David, Darby, Michael, Richard, Carl, their leaping electric bodies and gap-toothed faces mocking one another, uproarious, incredulous, never believing as they disappeared into the woods that it was into their own grown-up names they were running.

All summer our teacher held out her arms from the breast-high water, asking each of us to wriggle like tadpoles into her embrace, to shed our fear like a beach robe and paddle into the circle of her acceptance and affection as if it were a spotlight on stage. Her name was Bonnie, and she grew more beautiful every day, the sun lavishing its gold on her graceful arms, her dripping hair, her long legs as she bent to unlatch her sandals. When I would timidly dog-paddle toward the welcome of her arms, something about the gleaming hoops that caught the light as she threw back her head to laugh, the water beading on her lashes, about her absolute belief in her body and in mine, made me suddenly buoyant. I'd kick off the shape of a reluctant child and metamorphose into a fledgling mermaid. The strength in my arms was hers; if I could float on my back and squint into the bare sunlight, it was because her palms were buoying me up. I was no longer afraid, and every word of the swimming lesson fell on my forehead like grace.

Then, on one of those last late days of summer when the

skies were cobalt over the town pond, the shreds of a downed kite snapped like pennons in an elm, when elation had gone out of the trees, and the Squanicook had dropped to a trickle over the Grist Mill dam, the class arrived early to watch the Buick Roadmasters line up—end to end—like a funeral beyond the silvered picnic tables. Our parents had come to see all we had learned about buoyancy, about water, and being in over our heads. And we had gathered on the creaking dock around Bonnie, gabbling and shivering like a flock of ducks still downy with morning dew.

But I was not thinking about the water ballet that she'd shown us how to perform. I was thinking about graduating from baby class. Summer was over and I would never see her again. Soon I would be indistinguishable from a dozen other giggling, squirming little girls, showing off the places where a tooth had fallen out, and she would not know that I wanted to be just like her. Bonnie blew her red whistle and we all stood alert, water runneling into pools on the white dock.

"Who'd like to be the first to dive?"

Her voice rang out as clearly as a school bell. *Me, me!* clanged the silent clapper of my tongue, but I could not move. No one moved. I was afraid. I knew that I would fail her, that my body would forget what it had learned and return to its earlier, terri-fied splashing. Bonnie would be disappointed in me, and the brightness of her face would dim, and she would ask someone else whose limbs would not disobey, someone who could prove themselves worthy and cut the water like a knife. Still no one moved. The water was so dark, so deep, I could not look down.

But if no one dove, the parents in lawn chairs lounging in sunglasses and fanning themselves might sit forward and find her at fault. She would never be forgiven for not teaching us to swim properly. They would not see her beauty, how right they had been to trust her to teach us. I couldn't bear to watch her standing alone, quietly, unhelped. All at once my love was greater than my fear, and I dove in. The water was black and cold, a death in winter, and my heart sank to the bottom of the pond. I wasn't strong enough. I was going to drown. I would fail her after all. My eyes were open, but I could not distinguish darkness from darkness. There was no sunlight, no sound, only the beating of a death-drum in my ears, a hard thunder in my lungs. She would never know how much I tried.

Then a hand like the hand of God pulled me up by the hair and I was on the dock, choking, gasping for air that would not go into my gills. I could not understand why I was crying. Bonnie, the dolphin nudging Arion to shore, had jumped in to save me when I had been trying to save her. Wild sunlight buzzed around my head, the noise of children gabbled like ducks, parents were applauding, and Bonnie was smiling and saying my name. Swimming lessons were over. I had been promoted.

To graduate from the baby class was to fathom, for the first time, that things were required of us according to some mystical, preordained route. We were no longer the ones to be coddled and protected; we were members of something larger than ourselves. What had been formerly measured by our family's private yardstick, marked in pencil inside the cellar door, was now inspected by our principal, our teachers, the starched school nurse. We said our alphabet together in singsong unison; we lined up in pinafores to take our polio vaccines; we competed on the blacktop to master the complexities of Dodgeball and the strategies of Capture the Flag. We would never be the same again. At six, we learned to leave home, to be part of a class, learning lessons inherited from children the same age; we joined hands and moved ahead as a body. We sat in rows of war-scarred desks whose lids crashed over the same childhood clutter—fat, flat-sided crayons in primary colors wrapped like cigars in curious paper, yellow pencils that we used to practice penmanship, our names drawn out in enor-

mous letters on one-inch lines, readers with those silly characters, Tom, Dick, and Jane and their sillier dog, Spot, lunch
money, handkerchiefs, rubber bands, gum erasers that
squeezed when you bit down on them, well-punctured with
the points of our too-often sharpened pencils. There had
always been children at this school, at my desk, whose ghosts
disturbed my concentration. In earlier years, some pudgy,
freckled-faced volunteer fireman's son would have dipped my
braids into an inkwell, so who was I to be sitting there? There
was no I, only a girl sitting near the windows, third from the
front, with the smell of chalk like brimstone burning in her
nostrils, the smell of billowing chalk dust from the arc of felt
on the blackboard as the teacher erased her name.

All twelve grades attended our school together that first
year. Arranged by height and weight on the Glee Club risers in
the auditorium, starting with the first-graders up to the newly
mustached sons of farmers, undertakers, and ministers, I imagined the tallest ones marching down, step by step, like pages
returning to a calendar, until they stood young and frightened
in their knee pants on the bottom step, before I had even been
born. And then my imaginary game grew more complex,
because then their older brothers and sisters had to step backward into their younger selves. Girls stopped punching the
noisy buttons on their cash registers to put on the mohair
sweaters and pearls of graduation, their yanked-back hair of
young matronhood softened into bleached bouffants with
bows. Boys exchanged their wrenches and greasy coveralls for
suits with string ties, shirts pinching at the collar, shaved, without a cigarette behind their ears, slipping out of enormous,
pastel-finned cars. When I brought them slowly back through
the changes their bodies made, into the cotton undershirts and
flannel slips they had worn when their mothers sat beside the
radio knitting khaki socks on double-pointed needles and their
fathers tied their boots to reveille, I released them from the
pain of their first loves, first betrayals, and their faces grew

softer, pinker, less and more afraid. I knew then that the cycle
was endless.

I loved being one of the youngest girls. I felt safer somehow.
The disadvantage of being older showed itself when the air-
raid siren rang and we'd thunder together as a body to our feet,
line up in terror at the door, and in a massive wave of sound,
descend to the basement. The bigger ones could no longer
huddle beneath the wooden cafeteria tables with us. They had
to bend, froglike, against the wall. I worried about them, the
older ones; it seemed so sad, their sacrifice. Their shoulders
had grown so big, they had to take their chances in front of
the numbered lockers, like an infinite row of coffins down the
corridor. At least they had already grown into their bodies,
into petticoats and prom gowns and tuxedos. We would burn
as we were, crouched in the shadows of our grown-up bodies,
ash falling over our faces like snow. We'd cry because we knew
that we would hear nothing; the bombs would make no noise;
we would roast and turn to ash like the people at Pompeii, and
no one would come after us. We were the last of the least, and
I was one of the smallest ones there. I would always be six, and
too little to bear the enormity of so fierce a death. From then
on, every tiny twin-prop plane that flew over Spaulding
Memorial School seemed to carry death in its arms. Even the
name of our school had death inside it. Each plane became the
shadow of a hawk over baby ducks on the blacktop, and in our
games we would pile instinctively on top of one another in a
panic as if the whirr of a wingspan would be the end of us.

❧

I fell in love with Roger St. Cyr the day they let us out of
school on a snow day and Joe Luke the Pig Man gave us a
ride up the hill through the blizzard in his broken-down 1947
International truck. I was in first grade. Snow was falling outside Mrs. Chase's windows as big around as paper doilies, and
Danny Keefe, who sat in front of me, whispered that he'd seen
the twelfth-graders putting on their coats when he came back

from the Basement, which meant that school was about to be dismissed. Danny Keefe had a crewcut and seemed to know so much about first grade that I wondered if he'd been in it before. He taught me the proper way to pray the Pledge of Allegiance, how to carry my food and silverware on a tray into the lunchroom without dropping it, and most important, never to ask if I could pee; instead I must raise my hand and say, *I have to go to the Basement.* It was puzzling. There were so many things to learn about being in school, and none of them were nearly as much fun as curling up on the couch at home in the corner behind the living-room door and reading the Yellow Fairy Book. But today the fire whistle by the mill kept blowing the way it did every morning and evening at six, the school buses were lining up outdoors, the intercom crackled, the bell rang, and finally Mrs. Chase said we could go.

The room erupted into chaos with the crashing open of the cloakroom doors, chalk flying from the chalk trays as the louvres parted, and the mad scramble for coats and boots and hats began. I hated the jostling and shoving at the end of the day. I didn't like anyone helping me dress. In fact, I didn't like people touching me at all. The man in the shoe store had once tried to measure my feet for a pair of Mary Janes, and I had let out a terrible scream. Granny slapped me hard, the man held my foot in his vicelike grip, but I could not stop screaming. So I stayed at my desk while the turmoil continued in the cloakroom, squinting at the tops of the high windows, trying to follow a single snowflake between the spider legs of my lashes in its flurried, bewildering descent to the sill where it disappeared into the white flannel blanketing the bushes. I marveled that its journey could happen so slowly, and end so fast. Each flake was as lacy as an antimacassar on Granny's sofa. It was hard to concentrate on one flake all the way to the ground. How could so many things falling at once make no noise?

The classroom was empty as I pulled on my snow pants over my tights, my snuggies, my jumper, took my Buster Browns off the radiator, tied them on, and snapped my red boots over them. I looped the red scarf my mother made me three times around my neck, then put on my matching hat with the pom-pom, buttoned the funny frogs on my loden coat, shaking out of my sleeves the mittens that were clipped to the cuffs. By the time I got to the playground, I was astonished to discover that Bus Two had gone. Bus Two was as much a part of my self as my name, my classroom, my mittens made like twin raccoons. If Bus Two was gone, who was I?

Every morning while it was still dark, I ate a big bowl of oatmeal, brown sugar, and bananas before I bundled up and walked down the driveway to wait for the school bus to come roaring down from Moore's house and the turnaround to pick me up, my breath flowing out like a white scarf. I liked the morning routine—the way the bus doors squeaked open and shut like an old lady's purse, the same children flying up the steps to get out of the cold, in front of the same mailboxes with rusted red flags leaning off their posts. Roger St. Cyr and his older brother Billy would get on after I did, on the road past Rossbach's farm. Roger always sat in the way-back of the bus. He was eleven and the handsomest boy I'd ever seen. I had to act as if I was talking to somebody else in order to look at him at all, especially the beautiful part in his hair. After we had gone down the hill past Roger's house and the Retina Foundation and picked up four boisterous high-school boys, the bus bounced and slid over the icy back roads where the plow and sand trucks had hardly made a difference, and drove by the white birch trees on Rossbach's lower pasture leaning over the frozen Squanicook River at Dudley Road. When the bus turned the Dangerous Corner and stopped at Penny Bar-rett's house, my heart froze in my chest. Penny Barrett was so pretty. She had rhinestones on her glasses. I saw her once at assembly dressed in a long blue gown with a blue velvet bow in her hair, standing in front of the whole school to sing some-thing from the Congregational church choir. She was in Roger

St. Cyr's class and sat with him on the school bus every day, and every day I would turn away, pretending to be interested in the ash heaps of the dump, or in the trailer where the dwarf who ran the dump lived. But the scenery and the houses all went by in a blur, my eyes pricked with hot tears, and I nursed the knife in my heart.

Now Bus Two was gone, and I stood by the swing set with the flakes falling in front of my eyes, thinking how happy I would be to see even Penny Barrett with her blond ponytail and long blue stocking cap. The other kids had run onto their buses, laughing and joking, and were on their way home. I didn't even know the way to Barker Hill Road. I looked across the schoolyard at Dr. Goldfarb's house and could see the crumbling grandstand through the snow, the baseball field, and further along, the faintest outline of the little gray house under a tall pine tree where my best friend, Jody Hebb, lived. There was the library, the town hall, Churchville's huge brick octagonal house, Eastman Street, and the way to the dump. There, at the end of a two-house dead-end street was where Mrs. Bennett lived, but home? I had trouble with directions sometimes; I could picture where a road started and where it ended up, but I couldn't remember any landmarks in between—not a house, not a bridge, not a farm or field of cows.

It was starting to hail. The bricks and slate-roofed gables of the school were dusting over with snow like frosting on the Civil War headstones in the cemetery by the West Townsend Reading Room. Someone was turning out the lights, room by room, and I was standing alone in the deep ruts made by the buses, all because I was absent-minded and liked to daydream and had been lost in a world of my own. I would never get home because I'd been thinking of snow instead of keeping my mind on Bus Two.

"Hey, kid!" came a voice in my ear, and I jumped, then sighed with relief because I wasn't the only one who'd been left behind—Roger St. Cyr was standing in front of me. For years afterward, I would remember how he looked that day, shaking snow from his hair and smiling, his brown eyes shining bright as pebbles in the shallowest part of the Squanicook, and dark as the bottom of Damon Pond.

"We missed the bus," he said cheerfully, pulling on his hunter's cap with the army-plaid lining and ear flaps, buckling it under his chin. He seemed completely unconcerned. "I guess the only way to get home is to walk."

He seemed as tall as a grown-up, with the snow roaring around his face. He was so handsome I could hardly talk.

"Well," he said doubtfully, pointing at the road that led past the dump. "We live on the same road, you know. We could go to Mr. Quimby's office—" I blanched. I'd never been to the principal's office—"and call your mother and father on the phone. What's the number?"

That was one of the virtues of being eleven; I would never have thought of the telephone. At that moment I would have given anything just to be eleven and sit all day in Roger St. Cyr's class, anything to be eleven and be able to look at him all day when nobody was looking at me.

Somebody was shaking my shoulders. "Hey, kid," he laughed, rubbing my face with snow. "I'm talking to you. Wake up. What's your telephone number?"

I blushed to the roots of my hair—daydreaming, with him right in front of me, his skin as smooth as a porcelain cup and saucer. What was my telephone number? I was suddenly confused. We lived on a party line. I could pick up the phone and say, *131-W4, please,* for Dorrie Moore's house, and Marcia Mountain's number was 2-2, like Tutu, the name of our marmalade cat. Mama might say, *Mae, I'd like to speak with Mitzi for a minute. Do you know if she's home?* And the lady would reply over the crackling line, in a voice you could hear in the next room, *No, Anne, she and Bob have gone to Nashua for the day.* Then Mama would say, *Well, put me through to June Clark then.* And Mae's static reply would crackle through the kitchen, *She's over at Elsie Lowe's with Pomona Atherton.* What would I say to the operator whose name was Mae? Could I pick up the phone and say, *Is my mother home?* I imagined I was Alice in Wonderland and could hear Mae saying in the caterpillar's imperious tones, *Who-o-o is your mother, little girl, and who-o-o are yo-o-o?*

"I don't know my telephone number," I said finally, sitting down to dig snow out of one of my boots so I wouldn't have to look at Roger St. Cyr. How did he get so tall?

He shrugged his shoulders. "Don't worry, kid," he said, tucking my braids under my ear flaps and tying my red hat tightly under my chin. "I'll take you home." He held my mittened hand and said, "Come on. We'll walk. It's only five miles."

But before we'd even left the schoolyard, I stepped into a snowbank left by the plow and sank in over my knees. With my hands around his shoulders and his collar under my cheek, he picked me up and held me in his arms as though I were precious, as if he cared for me, and something began to hammer inside my chest. I knew I was going to marry Roger St. Cyr and love him for the rest of my life.

The wind was starting to howl. He carried me out to the street and set me down, brushed off the hem of my coat, and matter-of-factly took my hand again. We walked backward into the wind for a while because the snow was blowing hard, and I watched Spaulding School get lighter and lighter like a fading photograph. I had to squint to see the roof, then the top of the chimneys disappeared, and then I couldn't see anything any more—just the snow in front of my eyes and Roger holding my frozen hand. We followed the plow tracks until the snow had drifted over the scrapings and tire marks. We could barely see the edges of the road for the banks and banks of snow. How long was five miles? We hadn't even come to the little bridge yet. I was cold and wet. Snow in my face was making me cry.

Then we heard a rumbling noise grow louder and louder, like the big grain trucks that came up our driveway, bringing

tons of chicken feed to my father's farm. The noise came closer
and closer but we couldn't see anything because of the snow.
Suddenly two headlights burned into view, large and gold as a
dinosaur's eyes, and a huge rusting pickup truck lumbered forward with tiny windshield wipers squeaking back and forth,
clearing two little fan-shaped paths in the glass. An old man
with a hunter's cap in a plaid wool coat and not a tooth in his
mouth opened the door and shouted, "Get in!"

We ran around through the lights and I read the word "International" on the grille. Roger wrestled with the passenger door,
pulled it open, got in, and lifted me into the truck right over
the broken running board, and then slammed the door shut.

My feet didn't reach the floor. I couldn't see over the dash-
board. Where were we going? I looked up at Roger, who
winked and squeezed my hand. The man who was driving
smelled of manure and wood smoke. He wore a flannel shirt
with long winter underwear, black at the neck and wrists, the
cuffs of his dungarees flaked with sawdust. I'd never seen him
before in my life. I began to feel frightened.

"I know you," the man barked at Roger, grinning a toothless
smile and grinding gears with his hand, the truck bucking in
protest.

"You're Frannie St. Cyr's boy, ain'tcha? This storm sure is a
corker. Ayuh. Might have trouble gettin' up the hill."

I could hardly understand him. He said "stawm" and "cocka"
and opened the door to spit tobacco into the blizzard. His face
was all bristly. He looked like the bogeyman.

"I know where you live, too," he said loudly to me. "You're
Dick Green's little girl."

My mouth fell open in surprise. He knew Daddy? How? He
pushed his big black boot hard on the gas, and the truck shook
as he accelerated.

"Ain't gonna be able to stop at Dudley Road. Won't get
enough traction."

We flew through the stop sign at the blinding intersection

under the pine trees heavy with snow and bounced up the ice-
filled potholes until my head nearly hit the ceiling. The back
end of the truck, skidding loudly on ice, almost spun us into a
snowbank higher than the windshield. The snow swirled
around us until I didn't know if we were driving uphill or down.
The engine roared and the tires screeched around the big
curve. We swung back and forth to the scream of brakes, like
the Dodge 'Em rides I hated at Lincoln Park. I held my breath
for the crash, but it never came. We stormed past a terrible
snowman with white in his beard, on his coat, on the top of a
lantern he held in front of the Retina Foundation, and I recognized Linwood Hatfield, the man who ran the Foundation's
farm.

"Nobody's spearmintin' on rabbits' eyes and monkeys' brains
tonight," the bogeyman said, and giggled foolishly behind one
hand like a kindergartner.

Is that what they did at the Retina Foundation? I wondered.
Spearmint? My stomach went up in the air as we hit the roller-
coaster bumps just below St. Cyr's farm.

And then I remembered. All the darkened barns were full of
rabbits and monkeys in wire hutches and sawdust, shivering in
the cold and from operations on their eyes under ether. I saw
rows and rows of them, crouched in their sodden cages like
the zoo, except they had bandages over their faces and their
hind feet thumped in terror. One of the hateful Hatfield boys
would poke through the bars with a stick, laughing at all the
blood on the floor and the fear he could engender.

We came to Roger's house, and the truck barely slowed
down as he jumped out and slammed the door. I watched him
disappear into the white as we flew up the road, then held onto
the door handle for dear life until I saw Rossbach's red barn
and knew our mailbox was just ahead. How could it still be
daylight when it had gotten so dark? My voice sounded froggy
when I spoke.

"Who are you?" I asked the bogeyman.

"Joe Luke," he replied, opening his door to spit.

The Pig Man! I opened my door and fell out of the truck into the soft snow. I heard him curse to himself as I brushed off my coat. He slammed the door and roared off, skidding and sliding up the hill to Mason, one evil taillight disappearing into the darkness. And then I discovered I'd wet my pants all the way into my boots.

I stood for a minute under the elm trees. I'd never seen the Pig Man, but he knew me. How was that possible? I shivered. I'd never been to his house, but people *said*—I racked my brain, trying to remember exactly what terrible things I'd heard went on at the Pig Man's house, but nothing clear came to mind. He was so creepy. Whatever the rumors were, they must be true. But he gave us a ride home through the storm and let me off at my driveway, didn't he? He didn't take me to the Pig House. Even though he looked like a bad man, he had done a good thing. I puzzled it out as I trudged up the driveway, the snow up over my knees.

In all the years I loved Roger St. Cyr, my devotion never truly wavered, nor did my conviction that I would marry him when I grew up. I fell in love briefly and fiercely from afar with a dark-haired Irish priest whose musical brogue made me shiver in a transport of passion during Sunday School, but he soon went back to the Congo and I returned with fidelity to dreaming of Roger St. Cyr. The summer I was nine I often stood out under the dripping eaves of the porch, watching the roiling clouds across the valley and the trembling of heaven whose brow darkened with fury, the seizures of lightning, the moaning of the sky as it heaved and thrashed in its animal pain. But the storm would pass by and by, and the sun would tiptoe through the clouds like a girl in her first party dress, the long leaves of the tiger lilies bright and running with water, the birds beginning to sing tentatively again. The whole world seemed combustible and full of deep, inarticulable longing.

Something was trying to reveal itself, something that the world or the storm or I could never quite say.

Roger and his older brother Billy each had their own horse. I was so jealous. I'd wanted a horse of my own for years but Daddy always said no. We had a donkey, and that was good enough: Rosy, who brayed like a fishwife, refused to canter, and once tossed a tipsy John Nolan clear over her head into a pile of manure. St. Cyr's barn was dry and sweet-smelling with dust gently falling from the loft and the rafters, beams of summer light dividing bales of hay into gold and green. Billy's horse was a gentle russet mare named Buttons who would nicker absent-mindedly when we were around and then go back to munching in her trough as though we were but the faintest distraction from her ruminative lunch. I wasn't very interested in such a docile, well-mannered creature. I was much more entranced by Roger's horse, Sugar. He was a palomino the color of honey with a white diamond on his forehead and a long blond mane that I would help Roger brush out on a milking stool, where I stood two feet taller than usual. I felt grown-up and enormously important, so much higher than the hayrick or the watering trough. I was as tall as Roger then, Sugar whisking his tail on my dungarees as he ate his mash soaked in molasses. I could pretend that the five years between Roger and me were gone, that he could love me as a girl his own age.

When Sugar turned and hung his huge head over the stall door, I could see how little I was and would tentatively put out my hand, palm side up, so he could lick the salt off my skin the way Rosita did, with her soft velvet nose and appreciative nicker. But Sugar shook his huge head from side to side and argued, the muscles of his flanks twitched; and he stamped his hooves that seemed as big around as pie plates. I was afraid to stay on the stool and afraid to get down.

"He's too big," I cried, watching him butt his head when Roger tried to put on the bridle; but instead of taking me out of the stall as I wanted, Roger laughed and lifted me onto Sugar's back.

"No!" I screamed in fright, dropping the currycomb and grabbing for the just-brushed mane. Then Roger was up behind me, an arm around my waist, and we were trotting out of the barn bareback, blinking into the sunlight, the horse lifting his feet proudly as if we were in a Decoration Day parade. The brown dogs dozing on the grass each opened one eye to look at us, then went back to sleep. We clip-clopped along the stone wall toward Rossbach's field, the sun and shade dancing in patterns on the road, on Sugar's neck, on my hands holding onto the mane. I felt bathed in butter. Roger held onto my waist, dug his heel into the horse's side, and we flew past the ducks in the barnyard, past Ida Krüll's sauna, over the stone wall and into the pasture, where the cows stood up in alarm and started to run, until we came to the fallen-down shack of a house at Joe Arlen's place where pussy willows grew in the spring as tall as me. No one lived there now. No one even remembered Joe Arlen, but we still called it his place. The golden horse cleared the stone walls with effortless ease as we rode past the deserted house, and I knew that someday Roger and I would come back to this house, with newspapers rotting over broken windows, the front door off its hinges, the roof bowed into the letter V. I would be wearing a long white dress. Roger would lift me down from Sugar's back and carry me over the threshold, and we would live there together until we grew old, lying in each other's arms, too blind to see the crows in the berry patch or the frost flowers creeping up the window panes.

Later that summer my family went to one of the weekly Thursday-night band concerts on the Townsend Common. Christmas lights hung from the trees even though it was only July. Old people sat in folding chairs along the cast-iron rail like the one that circumscribed the cemetery. Kids from school ran by with balloons. Babies cried in strollers while their mothers rustled in full summer dresses and petticoats the way peonies grew, shaking their charm bracelets, talking and laughing out loud. Everybody wore their best clothes. Some people parked their cars side by side facing the Common and sat inside, so they could listen to the town band play and honk their horns when each march was over. There was popcorn and caramel apples, cotton candy, and pony rides for the littlest kids. The stocky gray pony was nasty and tried to bite us sometimes, but I thought it was because they made him go round and round the stupid ring behind the ropes and he never had a chance to run. I'd want to bite somebody too. They sold pies and jars of jam to buy the choir new robes. They gave away kittens and usually raffled off a bike or roller skates. That night, however, they were raffling a bride doll.

Standing on a table near the bandstand, on top of a box wrapped in birthday paper and ribbons, was the most beautiful doll I'd ever seen. A man in a white shirt was rolling up his sleeves and counting money into a cigar box. People gave him a dollar in exchange for a ticket he'd tear from a roll as big as my red wagon's wheel, then he'd put an identical ticket into a glass cookie jar. I couldn't take my eyes off the doll. I stood there, chewing my fingernails, thinking of the bride doll I had at home, but she didn't look as real as this one did. My bride doll didn't have a bouquet of pink flowers. She didn't have a veil you could draw down over her face and pull up over her crown for a kiss. This bride doll had big blue eyes and long, curly red hair. She had pearls around her neck and wrist. Her shoes resembled the roses on wedding cakes that Mrs. Farrar could make out of frosting, and I knew I was going to win her. This doll was mine. I gave the man all of my allowance and put the ticket in the cookie jar myself.

Mr. Talcott, the band leader, who looked as though he'd come over on the *Mayflower*, announced that the drawing for the bride doll was taking place and would everyone in the raffle please gather at the sodality table? I held my ticket tight in my hand as Father Mealey reached into the cookie jar. I already knew I was going to win. Then, nobody moved. He called out a number, and from the buzzing and rustling a man's voice lifted like a shot, "That's me!" People cheered and clapped and moved out of the way so he could get to the table.

I opened my mouth but nothing came out. Father Mealey had made a mistake. He meant to call my number. A man put his hand on my shoulder, trying to squeeze by. It was Bruce Lashua's father, who cut everybody's hair in the barbershop with the peppermint-striped pole. He was reaching for my doll. He held it up high and people whistled and stamped. The barber? Bruce Lashua's father? What was he going to do with a bride doll? He had five boys and no girls! Maybe if I could just talk to him, he'd see how silly it was for him to have the doll and give it to me instead.

But Bruce Lashua's father never saw me. He walked into the crowd and disappeared. I was left alone at the raffle jar, watching in disbelief as the man removed the white shelf paper and turned the table on its side to fold up its legs. I was dumbfounded. God had given away my bride doll to a barber who couldn't possibly appreciate it, and whose five boys wouldn't even notice that her dress was made like Queen Anne's lace or that her veil was as beautiful as spider webs shining with diamonds of dew.

I cried all the way home in the car, stormed upstairs, and slammed my bedroom door. I kicked the footboard of my bed again and again. It wasn't fair! My old bride doll with her crooked headdress lay face-down on the blanket. I hated her. I hated Bruce Lashua's father. I kept crying, kicking the bedstead. Roger St. Cyr wasn't going to marry me. He was going to marry Penny Barrett with the beautiful singing voice and the blue velvet bow in her hair. He would marry her and live in his father's white red-trimmed house on Barker Hill Road with the barn full of palomino colts and lots of brown-eyed, dark-haired children. I'd never carry a pink bouquet and walk down the aisle in a foamy white dress with pearl buttons down the back and a silk petticoat or shoes like wedding-cake roses. Even my stupid, blank-faced doll got to wear a beautiful wedding dress, but I would not. I tore her veil into shreds. It fell apart in my hands like spider webs. I tugged at the seam of her dress, and when it wouldn't give, I ripped it in half with my teeth. I held her by the feet and bashed her head against the radiator over and over, crying: *Nobody will marry me, nobody, nobody, nobody.*

I was afraid. Our school nurse, Mrs. Amiro, had telephoned my mother to report that I had taken the eye test and failed: I could not find the apple on the picnic table. I tried to see it, I willed it to be there, even half-believed I could see it in my imagination—a fruit out of fairy tales on a white plate, lustrous, tempting, polished ruby-red. But it was useless. I couldn't see the apple. I couldn't even find the picnic table.

My mother took me to the eye doctor two towns away. I hunched forward in the Chevy's big back seat and watched my mother's hands on the wheel as she drove, sneaking furtive glances out the windshield at all the people in the city carrying bundles and briefcases and bags from the Victory Market. What did they see that I couldn't and why did I see things differently? Some of them wore glasses. Maybe I would have to wear blue cat's-eye glasses like Janie Briguglio, my second-best friend. Glasses would be neat.

I was led into a dark room by a man in a white coat. He sat me in a high chair like Uncle Howard, the dentist, and turned off the lights. My mouth was dry. The man had soft, cool hands when he held me by the chin to shine his flashlight first in one eye, then in the other. He pushed a helmet down over my eyebrows until it rested on the bridge of my nose and told me to look out of the eyepieces at a wall on the other side of the room.

I saw a big E, then rows of other Es facing in different directions piled under it like a layer cake. With each line, the letters got smaller and smaller until they seemed to be crawling like ants. I pointed with one finger to show the doctor which way they were scurrying, wondering if this was a trick. If other people saw things I couldn't see, then maybe I saw things that weren't there.

Something black fell over my right eye, and suddenly the ants, the paper, the light, and the doctor were gone. I saw only shadows webbed with gray. *It was night. There was a hazy moon behind the clouds.* He told me to look for the Es again, but I couldn't see them. I couldn't see anything—not the chart, not the wall, not his hand in front of my face, not the fingers held up for me to count. I touched my cheek to make sure I was still there. I was. Only the world was gone.

He left me alone with the iron helmet over my face, hooded like a falcon, my hands gripping the armrests like claws, my left eye blinking away tears. My own hand, which I was waving back and forth in front of my nose, had also disappeared. I swallowed something stony in my throat. I heard the rustle of petticoats but could not turn my head. My chin was locked in an iron clamp, and I could not move. I heard my mother's petticoats ssh-sshing as she spoke to the doctor in the voice she used when she didn't want me to hear. I shut my eyes hard to concentrate on listening.

I heard a jumble of things that didn't make sense and took the sentences apart bit by bit like a biscuit. *Lazy eye. Good eye. Bad eye.* What did he mean? My left eye wasn't lazy. It strained open just as eagerly as the right; it wanted to see everything the other one saw. I could feel both of them moving together from side to side. It wanted to work, it was trying to work, it didn't mean to be lazy, it didn't mean to be bad.

The voices came closer. *Eyepatch.* The iron hood was taken off. I blinked, and my mother was frowning, not looking at me, and the doctor had his hand on my forehead. The shimmering pinwheels of the world were spinning together. But after a moment I heard the word *blind*. My heart stopped in its cage. The doctor tore open a paper and pulled out an egg-shaped bandaid, and the world went away as he covered my good eye again. I could see only dark shapes swimming here and there with the light. I strained to see through the adhesive. I was practically blind already. Suddenly I understood. I was going to lose my sight altogether. They were covering the good eye to keep it from becoming weak and useless like the bad eye, but little by little I'd go blind, until all I could distinguish were the shapes and shadows of things moving around me.

Every morning after that was a battle of wills, until all the days ran together, and the more fearfully I struggled, the more like quicksand they became. At bedtime my mother put medicine in my eyes, to help them rest while I slept. She plunged the glass dropper deep into a brown bottle and held it for a fraction over each eye until I could open them wide without blinking. Then I'd feel a single drop like water falling into a well. She'd tell me to keep my eyes closed until morning, but in those days when bedtime came before dark and after my mother would leave me to sleep, I would pad to the window above the lilac trees and the rain barrel to hear the whippoor-will sing and watch the light seep away from the day, until the grass and the garden and the shape of the carriage shed blurred together in the shadows. And sometimes the stars would come out over Barker Hill and the moon would rise through the laced arms of the elms, but however the day ended, I did not plead with God to help me. Neither wheedling nor bargaining could change the mind of God. I'd go blind no matter what I promised Him now. Instead, I vowed to keep one promise for the rest of my life: I would never forget what it looked like— the light, the world. I would remember all of it until the day I died.

In the morning when my father, who hated mornings, stood at the foot of the narrow stairs and boomed out his snarl of "Up! Up! Little daisies!" I would whisper into my hands squeezed together for a prayer, *Please don't let me be blind today*. And for a minute, the world was light, and I was in it and could see. And then the patch would go on, and my mother and father became gray shadows in the darkness. I blundered outside toward the brightness like a crocus blindly groping its way toward an April sun. I followed the shapes of my brother and sister down the long driveway, past the white blur of the cooper shop and the green flags of willows, and waited with them at the mailbox until the enormous yellow blur of the school bus lumbered down the hill from Mason and my daily mortification began.

I tripped on the school-bus steps nearly every day. I would stumble into my seat; someone would laugh and start whispering. At school, before Mrs. Minehan or Mrs. Ormsby rang the brass bell on the playground and we fell into an orderly assembly by sex and class, everyone ran squealing and shrieking in and out of their ordinary games, and I'd stand leaning alone against the swing set, squinting my eye until the edges of things dissolved; and instead of a bright patch of children, I'd imagine a beautiful oriental rug with fringe as long as a pony's mane lying on the schoolyard at my feet. I'd see myself step onto its colorful pile and sit cross-legged on red velvet pillows hemmed in gold lace. At the merest wish, the carpet would rise, high over the heads of my astonished classmates, above the hands of Mrs. Chase and Miss Brooks begging me to come back, up over the roof of Spaulding School, above the current of the glittering Squanicook like a phoenix rising over the earth, but not so high as to lose sight of the beauty below.

I could not see the chalk in my hand make a mark on the blackboard. I could not read the lines in my songbook. When the school day and the long bumpy ride up the hill finally ended, I would practice walking up the driveway with both eyes closed, tap-tap-tapping with a willow stick, pretending I was Helen Keller.

And then I was free, running into the woods away from the

house, the squabbling, the chaos, into the deep quiet of the pines and birches and moss. Where the brook welled up from a cold spring, before it raced for the quarry and into the Squani-cook, I would tear off the eyepatch in a fury and blink up through the silvery birches netting the sky. I'd look ferociously at everything and, with my hand on a tree trunk, say, "This is bark. Don't ever forget it." Then, bending down to the brook, I would scoop up a freezing fistful of pebbles and snap at myself, "These are stones. Remember them."

Through a blackberry thicket, between the rusting chassis of two long-abandoned cars, I would come to a stone wall and a clearing of land belonging to a neighboring farm. Standing transfixed by the moment, I'd watch the beauty of the after-noon, the changes since yesterday. I'd see and burn into my memory every freckle of shade on the clover, every glint of mica in the granite boulders that the frost had heaved down, the faint and sometimes deep-blue brush stroke of Monadnock behind the trees. I'd watch a monarch light on a day-lily's leaf and touch my lip with my tongue to remember its flight. When I had memorized the afternoon's mosaic, I'd replace the patch the best way I could, by a clumsy kind of Braille, and go down to the house for supper.

I hunched over my blue-and-white bordered plate, feeling the old chipped china scallops with my hands, tipping my head to get my left eye closer to the food. Aromas rushed into my face, but I was determined to identify what was before me by what little sight I had. A cloud of white—mashed potatoes. Red would be beets. Green—brussels sprouts or broccoli or spinach. Something mud-colored could either be bread or meat. I crisscrossed my knife and fork over and over the plate, in a mockery of cutting, until it all ran together.

Then, every night after the dishes were done, I'd sit at the kitchen table with paper and pencil and practice forming my letters with both eyes shut, so when the day came as I knew it would and I couldn't see any more, I'd still be able to write my stories in the dark. Over and over I'd draw them and feel my way to the edges of the page until I could write legibly without my eyes.

Several months later, my mother and I went back to the eye doctor. Patching the strong eye to strengthen the weak one had been futile. My vision would never change. I'd been saved from blindness, but I would never be cured of the need to see everything clearly. Or to remember it forever.

My mother's hair was as bright as copper pennies, each coin-shaped curl shook when she laughed, and on bath nights when steam fogged the windowpanes and erased our faces in the mirror over the sink, when she'd kneel by the tub on the green mat, her curls tightened with moisture, her cheeks flushed, and pour pink liquid bubbles into the water from a bottle foiled to look like expensive champagne, she seemed the most beautiful to me. I would sit by the faucets in the secondhand tub because I was the oldest, knew H from C, and could be trusted not to get burned. The ledge of porcelain was scarred a deep brown as big as my mother's hand, exactly in the shape of South America. My brother sat next to me, his small hands alternately cupping and freeing his fascinating and strange penis; my sister crouched on the far end. Splashing the feathery soap at each other, we took turns washing each other's backs with a terry-cloth rag, like some proud and simple ritual performed before an icon—my mother with a sacred towel over her shoulder tending to us like a priestess.

There was no shower—I'd never had a shower—but on the wall above our heads was a large mural of our farm painted on gypsum board when my father and Flap first moved there after the war, and before my mother had come and any of us had been born. It was a funny picture. A long road led up to the white house with green shutters, the old cat Blackie was stalking something by the cooper shop, and several Rhode Island reds were scratching in the sand under the maple trees, some of their feathers speckled with whimsical pink and yellow polka dots. Daddy in his dungarees, cowboy boots, and sleeveless T-shirt was running with a steaming cup of coffee and a copy of *Time* magazine up to the outhouse with the moon carved on the door. Down front there was Flap, complete with mustache, tattoos, and Chinese brush-stroke eyes squinted against the sun, dressed like my father and carrying a pail in each hand to Honeysuckle and Rose, the blissful pink and black pigs. *Green Acres* was written in big green letters over the top of the pine trees.

One by one my mother would pull us from the frothing water and stand us on the toilet seat, embracing us with the towel and scrubbing us dry with a fierceness that made our skin burn. Then she powdered us with a soft white puff, and powder showered everywhere. We laughed as we struggled into our Doctor Dentons, and only I could button the seat of my pants without help. Our hair still curling and wet, we tiptoed into the living room to say goodnight to our father, who was drowsing over his newspaper. On some nights he would pucker up his lips like a fish and buzz kisses onto the backs of our necks, but most of the time he would murmur goodnight in a drunken half-sleep. I would lift the wrought-iron latch carefully, shut it silently behind us, and turn to stand at the foot of the dark and narrow stairs. Then the three of us would race up to the "girls' room"—where my sister and I slept—and all pile into my bed under the ragged army blankets, waiting for Mama to come and read us to sleep.

It was a cold room on the north side of the house with two small windows and sloping eaves. In winter we could hear the squirrels scrabbling between the rafters, rolling their acorns back and forth in a frenetic game of ninepins, their ratlike claws scratching the walls, the wind rattling the cracked panes of glass. Our maple twin beds did not match, nor did the odd bureaus. Our closet was a horizontal pole nailed between two upright pieces of pine. An old ship's lantern with a dusty, dim

bulb hung in the center of the room. But Mama had made
green-and-white flowered curtains with flounces for the windows and matching bedspreads, and we both had a plywood
toy box full of grubby stuffed animals—one painted yellow
and the other pink—that Daddy had made one Saturday out
in the tool room.

My brother's room was across the hall, where his model cars
were partly assembled on his desk, the George Washington
bedspread hung down neatly, and all the drawers of his tall
pine dresser were closed, even though most of the drawer-pulls
were missing. In one corner of the room, a yellow rocker with
flowers painted on it stood next to a window that opened out
over the yard—the pear tree, the apple tree, snow wrapped
around the foot of each trunk like a sheet under a Scotch pine
at Christmas. My brother always snuggled up with us in my
bed so Mama could read to us there.

At last Mama would come in, shut the door, take off her
apron, and gather us into her arms. She smelled soft, of soap
and cigarette smoke, of lavender Bond Street, and I knew she
was the most wonderful mother in the world. Every evening
was different. We sang, we danced, we recited poems she had
taught us. She tickled us until we were in raptures of giggles,
we played Here We Go Loop-di-Loo or Ring Around the Rosy
on the rugless pine floor, and as we sang she told us about the
Black Death, the red-circled lumps of illness on the bodies of
plague victims which *ring around the rosy* referred to; *pocket full of
posies*, the nosegays people thought would protect them from
contagion; *ashes, ashes, we all fall down*, which meant that none
would be saved. So when we all fell down, we too were suc-
cumbing to the plague that had wiped out most of Europe in
the Middle Ages.

My mother read stories that were full of history. Nothing
existed merely as itself; it always contained some message from
people who had come before us. She taught us the Our Father
in Old English and when we recited it in that strange yet

strangely familiar tongue, *Faeder ure, thuthe art in heofonum*, I saw knights at Arthur's table dropping their chins reverently on their glinting hauberks by rushlight, heard the horses shake their shining bridles, and saw the Holy Ghost fly into the great hall, beating its wings like a sparrow, lighting on the rafters above the spears, the longbows, and the kneeling squires whose young lips trembled a bit before the battle they knew would be coming at dawn.

We learned to count to fifty in German, to sing "Sur le Pont d'Avignon"—beautiful words mingled with English that were the same and not the same, mysterious, unknowable treasures like sweets in our mouths. We saw Richard Coeur de Lion riding off to the Holy Land with his retinue in tow and colorful, heraldic banners of every duchy flaming behind him. We saw Hannibal with his elephants lumbering magnificently over the Alps. Mama told us how God had put his hand on a little girl in Domrémy, how the little girl saw visions of glory for the Dauphin that no one believed, how she saved France and was brought to burn at the stake for being a heretic. Our cold bedroom filled with the sounds of hoof beats, the slashing of swords against shields, the bitter weeping of widows and mothers who came to bear away the dead. The world was an older and more terrifying place than I had imagined. But when we snuggled together under the covers and Mama sat at the foot of the bed and opened the Yellow Fairy Book, I thought I would never be happier in my life.

I insisted on hearing the same stories over and over, though I wept inconsolably when the expected tragic endings came. I knew I was hearing the truth, truer than my name, my being, the fact that I was alive. The fairy tales showed me my life, how I would suffer later in order for my dreams to come true. The Little Mermaid would have to relinquish her beautiful tail, her green and glittering undersea, her unearthly and sweet singing voice, in order to marry the prince she loved. Rapunzel, who was given to the witch by her parents, would live in

a tower seeing no one, and when the prince came, they would
be parted, wounded, and lost because of forces that they were
too young and powerless to overcome. The Little Match Girl
would always starve to death in the cold, because her grandmother had died and no one else loved her. Her last match
guttering on the page burned in my heart, my stomach rumbled sympathetically, and I imagined I would die in the snow
under a window where an impossibly rich and unreachable
feast was laid, but not for me. I would wander with Elsa in the
Wild Swans through thickets of brambles and thistles, unable
to speak, knitting garments to save my seven brothers who had
been turned into swans. I felt the thistles tearing my hands,
bleeding profusely as I worked, and I did not say a word. As
the cart trundled to the fire where I was to be burned as a
witch, I'd fling the garments on my brothers' wings, with all
but one sleeve finished, and they would be saved at last. I
would speak again after years of suffering and being alone in
the forest with no one to help me.

Our mother read like an actress, emphasizing each story's
fits of passion or desperate pleas for amnesty, each conflict and
defeat. The room darkened when we entered the deepest forest. The bright heaped-up hay was spun into gold, the dwarf
laughed dreadfully, smugly, then had a tantrum when the girl
pronounced his name, Rumpelstiltskin. We heard the kind and
otherworldly voice of Jesus say, *Lazarus, come forth,* and saw Mar-
tha and Mary kneeling with awe as their dead brother struggled to sit up and walk out stiffly into the daylight in his grave
clothes, blinking in astonishment that he had been brought
back to life. As my mother read, her voice became the words
and the language flared and flamed in the room like Fourth of
July sparklers. Language became a holy living thing; listening
to her voice was like being in the presence of angels bringing
the word of God. All the words were His; He was just lending
us Heaven for a while until we could come home to Him.
Someday, I thought, my mother would read my books out loud

and hear the growling consonants, the purring, liquid vowels, and when she saw the world's colors wave across the page like wind through a field of rainbow-colored grass, she would love me as much as I loved her then. I hadn't met the people in my stories yet, but I knew they were waiting for me down the road, sitting patiently in their hats and coats on stone walls, knowing I was coming to meet them.

When Mama finished the story, she'd close the Yellow Fairy Book with a flourish, tuck us in and kiss our foreheads, leaving a trace of lipstick like a talisman to keep us safe through the night. The light would flicker in the ship's lantern as she went through the door, closing it gently and turning off the light from outside the room. It was dark. There were no stars. And yet when I shut my eyes, I'd see a thousand sparklers burning, the colored patterns of a kaleidoscope turning and changing their breathtaking designs. I'd go to sleep dreaming of a shelf in the public library where my books would be lined up in their hardback bindings and bright paper covers, my name printed across the bottom, and count them until I fell asleep.

Then one day, everything changed in a heartbeat. We ran home from school and Mama wasn't sitting in the kitchen window waiting for us. The back door was locked, so I had to stand on a box, turn the handle of the freezer in the breezeway, and lift the heavy lid to look for the key under the frozen venison. I took off my boots and coat and hat in the mudroom, helped the little kids store their galoshes in the cupboard under the window and green wooden awning where Mama put pine cones and juniper boughs in winter, and walked into the bright yellow kitchen. The fire had gone out in the wood stove. I stuffed in crumpled balls of the *Boston Herald*, laid down kindling, lit the forbidden matches, and when the fire had caught, put in a few small pieces of maple. I had discovered a few weeks before, when I'd turned seven-and-a-half, that I could finally reach the damper without standing on a chair. When the flames started to roar, we laid our wet mittens on top of the stove. The floor hadn't been swept, the dishes were piled in the sink, and the kitchen table still had the breakfast things on it. I washed the plates, my sister collected the silverware, and my brother put away the jam and butter. Where was Mama?

Her kitchen was a panoply of growing things—cactuses, ivies, philodendrons, hearts-on-a-string, pink and purple coleus, and a tall many-leaved sansevieria in a Mexican pottery wagon painted ochre, sienna, and light brown. That morning she had been wearing a flowered bibbed apron over a pretty full skirt. The great glass cookie jar in the pantry was filled with gingerbread men, sugar cookies, and Rice Krispies bars, reminding me of St. John's fall bazaar, where she ran the Penny Candy table with the long peppermint-striped tablecloth and dozens of cookie jars stuffed with fireballs, Tootsie Rolls, lollipops, mint juleps, gumdrops, red and black licorice whips, jawbreakers, caramels, and pinwheels. All the kids from school would gather around it because selling candy made us celebrities. We stood on wooden blocks behind the table and played with the change in the Dutch Masters' cigar box. It was thrilling. My mother was everyone's favorite the day of the church fair, and she was ours.

I wiped the green-and-white checked oilcloth with a sour-smelling sponge, brought out the Play Doh and cookie-cutters to spread on newspapers, and sat the kids down on the bench under the window, pretending everything was all right. The mail was unopened beside my father's place. I went to the corner of the kitchen under the telephone where the intercom was—a white box with a switch to call in the men from the henhouse—and pushed down the button, called for Flap and Daddy, then pushed up the button to listen. There wasn't a sound from the egg room, except for the scratching of static. Someone was always in the egg room.

Mama, I called out tentatively into the living room. Everything was still: the organdy curtains, a newspaper half-open on

the split arm of one of the leather chairs. An earring sparkled
on the braided rug. What was it doing there? I picked it up
and held it tightly in my palm. Mama's Marlboros and matches
lay beside the glass ashtray on the table lamp next to the
rocker where she sat nights, knitting—but her knitting things
were gone. She'd been working on two pullover vests in navy
blue, the backs plain, the fronts woven like a basket in gray,
pink, and pale blue. My father's was the only one finished.
Sometimes she measured my brother's vest against my back to
see if it was long enough, the colored balls of yarn bouncing
under my feet, her long hands yanking the half-made vest
under my arms, against my ribs. I turned, hearing an unexpected noise. On the mantelpiece between two brass candlesticks and a brass platter of men in a tavern in half-relief, lifting
their glasses of stout, their heads thrown back with laughter
and good cheer, was a small Seth Thomas clock ticking gently
above the cast-iron eagle on the fireplace. Why was it ticking?
My father hated the ticking sound, however faint. It distracted
him, and the pretty tinkling chimes at the quarter-hour could
drive him into a rage, so the clock was never wound and the
tiny brass pendulum hung still.

Mama, I called louder, struggling with the iron latch and the
door to the hall that swelled all year round and was hard to
open. The hall was empty, the front door bolted, and a pile of
laundry was waiting on the woven rush seat of the ladderback
chair for someone to take upstairs. The radiator was cold. I
knocked on Mama's door, then opened it slowly. Bright sunlight poured in over her jewelry box, her bottles of cologne
and hand lotion, the lace runner that fell evenly on either side
of the dresser. Hesitantly, I laid the earring down on the lace.
The old Singer was open—spools of thread clustered like my
teachers on the playground in their pastel spring coats—and
next to it sat a pile of woolen shirts that needed mending and
a bolt of creamy material with trellises of roses growing on it.
Tossed on the brown bedspread with the yellow flounce were

some of my mother's nighties, one thrown over the pillows as if she'd just pulled it off, silky pajamas wadded up beside lace panties, a pink flannel robe with a ruffled collar. A sleeveless shortie had slipped onto the rag rug and someone had stepped on it. I could see the imprint of a shoe. Where was Mama?

I crossed in front of the fireplace, the bookcase, the piles of ladies' magazines, and opened the door to the dining room. The latch rattled in my hand because I knew she would not be there. It had just been Thanksgiving. The dinner plates were ready to be put away in the narrow closet. The silverware was fanned out over the lace tablecloth waiting to nest in velvet racks inside the leather box under a velvet cloth hemmed in gold. No one but Mama knew where everything went.

I opened the door beside the pine blanket chest and was back in the kitchen. I called down into the dark cellar. The brooms and mops hung motionless. Horizontal lines laddered up inside the yellow door where Daddy measured us in pencil as we grew taller, the date carefully noted under our names and ages. Mama must be upstairs! I took them two at a time, calling out from the landing, but no one answered me. I came to Daddy's room first. Mama and Daddy had slept in the same room until I was born. But when they brought me home from the hospital and put me beside their bed in the old wicker clothes basket, my baby noises and crying disturbed Daddy so much that Mama moved me with her to the room downstairs. For years I thought that growing up and getting married meant you had a room of your own. Daddy's room was always dark, the shades drawn all day long. His clothes were flung over the backs of two wicker chairs, his clean underwear stacked on the dresser. He never put his things away. He liked to have them out where he could find them. A water glass on the night table had dust motes dancing in it. Behind the door was a Dew More Farms milk bottle half-full of pee. Everything looked normal, except his bed wasn't made. I'd get hammered if he came home and found it this way—I had forgotten to make it before I went to school that morning. I pulled at the old blankets, straightening the wrinkled sheets on the horsehair mattress, and plumped up his two pillows against the cannonball bed-posts, then shut the door tightly. Daddy didn't like fresh air either.

The attic! Maybe Mama had gone into the attic for some-thing. I opened the door but the narrow stairs were so dark that my heart skipped a beat. I crept up a couple of steps, calling her name, spider webs festooning the rafters, the trunks, the broken chairs, the stacks of paintings, the sleigh bells, the Revolutionary War flintlock and tin boxes of ammunition. A tall brass stand with a stuffed parrot on its perch, one dead black eye seeming to cross-examine me, towered at the top of the stairs. The parrot had lived for fifty-six years, the last stage of its life at Granny's house, until its incessant squawking so annoyed my drunken grandfather that he'd thrown his shoe at it, his aim so fierce and accurate that the bird dropped dead instantly like a stone. Granny had had it stuffed. It sat there, staring down at me, as if it were guarding the entrance to a pharaoh's tomb.

A door in my brother's room led to Flap's bedroom and the shed chamber under the eaves. I knocked on Flap's door and went in when I heard no answer. The cold air struck my face like an ice-wash. The room was without a radiator, so Flap never had any heat. All winter he burrowed in his shutter-green twin four-poster like a possum or a friendly half-grown bear cub, always in long johns and a flannel shirt and some-times with socks on his feet. Against the wall a bowing piece of plywood across two sawhorses held all his ham-radio equip-ment—aluminum boxes with buttons, levers, switches, wheels, and amplifiers—as well as a Prince Albert can full of pencil stubs and a pad of yellow paper under a gooseneck lamp. The shutter-green dresser drawers were overstuffed with long underwear and V-necked undershirts. In the corner a plywood closet, holding all his winter shirts, leaned precariously. His room was dark. The two windows on the floor, more like tran-soms than real windows, were covered on the outside with

creepers from the ivy and trumpet vine that ran along the edge
of the roof. They didn't open.

One more door led into the shed chamber which was
spooky and still and stacked with more piles of stuff that no
one used any more: old lamps, wrought-iron porch furniture,
shredded awnings, moth-eaten clothes, flower pots, dressers
with the drawers leaning against them, storm windows, broken
rockers, the spindles of a staircase from another house, an old
spinning wheel, an anvil, cardboard boxes chewed through by
squirrels, old fur collars pulled out and dragged across the
floor, dresses and our baby clothes torn into confetti. A wasp
nest occupied the windowsill at the far end. I shivered. Mama
was not there.

As I was bolting the lock, I heard a car come up the road,
followed by another. I ran into my brother's room and looked
out over the driveway. Daddy's green '51 Chevy was followed
by my grandparents' '56 Buick Roadmaster. As they drove past
the house to back around and park by the clothesline, I shut
all the doors behind me and flew down the stairs, through the
kitchen, the mudroom, the half-open red dutch door, and out
into the yard. *Mama! Mama!* I cried joyfully, pelting around the
woodshed, but I stopped short in shock at what I saw. The
Buick's doors were wide open and my grandparents were standing by my father's car, talking to him quietly. Daddy had his
head on the steering wheel and was sobbing like a child.

I didn't know what to do. I'd never seen my father cry. Tutu,
the marmalade cat, was rubbing herself against my knee socks,
purring for attention. I picked her up and held her against my
face, stroking her calmly as a tear slipped out of my eye and
into her ear. She leapt out of my arms like she'd been shot, ran
across the grass and over the stone wall.

"Where's Mama?" I asked Granny. She turned as though
she'd never seen me before, grabbed my hand hard in her
glove, and marched me toward the house.

"You shouldn't be out here without a coat. I'll make us some
tea."

She hung her coat, scarf, and pocketbook on the pegs beside the kitchen door. My brother and sister barely looked up from their clay. She had no use for them—I was the only child who mattered to her—which she often said out loud within their hearing. In fact, she never really understood why my parents had bothered to have two more children. It hurt me that she didn't love them, but I was only seven-and-a-half, and everything was stronger and older and more powerful than I. I put out the cups and saucers, brought down the sugar bowl from the shelf in the pantry, and got out the pitcher of milk. The kettle clanked on the faucet as she filled it and clanked again when she put it on the stove. Then, as she was spooning tea leaves into the old brown teapot, I said quietly, so the little kids couldn't hear, "Where's Mama?" She looked at me fiercely and said, "Your mother's gone away."

Gone away? What did that mean, gone away? Gone away where? When would she be back? My grandfather came into the kitchen, took off his coat, and then helped my father with his. The kids looked up from their cookie-cutters, but neither of them said a word. My grandfather took my father's arm and led him upstairs. I could hear the creak of the floorboards in his bedroom and the squeak of springs as he lay down. Was Daddy sick? My grandfather came down and sat at my father's place at the table and proceeded to pour his hot tea into a saucer and drink from it, both of his pinkie fingers held out, slurping every swallow. My tea was hot, mostly milk and sugar, almost too sweet to drink. What was wrong with Daddy? Where was Mama? We drank our tea in silence.

Granny was starting supper when Flap stomped into the mudroom, scraping his work boots on the mat, and squeaking them off on the bootjack under the window. He carried them over to the Windsor chair, where he sat down wearily, stuffed balls of newspaper into the toes so they would dry before morning, and placed them beside the stove. Taking his chair at the table, he brought out a red pouch of Prince Albert, filled his pipe, tamped down the sweet tobacco with a barrel nail, and sat silently puffing. I wanted to scream, but nothing came into my throat. I could barely catch my breath. Something was terribly wrong. No one was talking. Was Mama dead?

I helped the kids put away their clay and cookie-cutters and rolled the messy newspaper into the stove. I pulled down the plates, counted out the silverware—should I set a place for Daddy? Granny came to the table with an iron skillet of browned corned-beef hash, served herself and my grand-father, then set it by Flap's place. He helped himself and served the three of us on the bench under the window, while she returned to the pantry and brought back a poached egg for each of us, plopping it on the hash like some eerie yellow eye. Its jelly shook when she slipped it off the slotted spoon. My stomach turned over. Poached eggs always made me gag. How could I eat this mess, this accusing yellow eye, staring at me as if to say, *Your mother's never coming back and it's all your fault.*

We went to bed early that night. I knocked on Daddy's open door to say goodnight, then peeked in, but he lay on his side with his face to the wall and did not answer. Granny had tucked us in roughly and gone downstairs, but I got up again and whispered into my brother's room, *Get up, I'm going to read you a story*, and he padded across the hall and crawled into bed with my sister and me. I opened the Yellow Fairy Book and in my most grown-up voice began to read them a story I didn't know:

A little brother took his little sister by the hand and said, "Since our mother died, we've not had one moment of happiness. Our stepmother beats us every day, and when we come near her, she kicks us away with her foot. We get nothing but hard crusts of bread, just leftovers for food, and the dog under the table is better off. At least he gets a good chunk of meat to eat every now and then. Lord have mercy on us, if our mother only knew! Come, let's go off together into the wide world!"

But after the first paragraph, the three of us were crying. The Yellow Fairy Book fell to the floor, and we huddled together as if a great storm were rocking the room, sobbing for our lost mother, for what death might be, for being too young to understand, for our sick father, for our abandoned selves. We fell asleep there together, curled up under the ragged army blankets like a nest of baby raccoons.

Daddy did not get up the next day. My grandfather drove the Buick to work at the Boston Naval Shipyard. Granny and Flap joked all through lunch until she laughingly smeared peanut butter on his cheek, and everyone fell into hysterics. That's all I remember about the day. That night, when it was bedtime, I whispered to Granny that I wanted to stay up and read in Mama's room after the little kids went upstairs. She rarely refused me anything, so I crept into Mama's room in the dark, turned on the black lamp, and pulled the heavy gold-leafed wing chair closer to the fireplace. The fragile Hummel figurines on the mantelpiece were dusty, frozen children that time had stopped in mid-play. I felt small enough to sit up there with them, clutching my doll Maggie, and staring blankly over the room as if my mind were in the grassy fields of Germany, picking edelweiss in my lederhosen, the hot sun beating down on my kerchiefed head.

I pulled the crocheted yellow afghan off my mother's bed, careful not to disturb anything else, and huddled under it on the chair in my furry red bathrobe. I sighed, trying to get warm. The chair had been pretty once, but under the arms' lacy antimacassars, the fleur-de-lis fabric was greasy with use. I opened the book I had clutched in my lap and read aloud to my absent mother:

"Christmas won't be Christmas without any presents," grumbled Jo, lying on the rug.
    "It's so dreadful to be poor," sighed Meg, looking down at her old dress.

I read the entire first chapter of *Little Women*, stumbling over the biggest words, pausing to sound them out phonetically. It was a hard book, a grown-up book, but I wanted my mother to hear how well I could read without her, to hear the beautiful sounds and rhythms of the words as they filled the empty room, to conjure her onto the edge of the bed where she would be sitting with her legs crossed, smiling and humming softly to herself as she knitted a navy blue vest. I wanted the words and sounds and pictures to bring her back, the way things came to life when she read to us about soldiers and saints and princesses rescued from castles, the sound of running water, the smell of roses growing outside a cottage gate. If I read out loud in a strong, sure voice, she might appear in the room with me. I promised myself at the bottom of each page that I would not look up to see if she was there until the bottom of the next one. But no matter how many magical consonants and vowels floated through the air, her corner of the room stayed dark and my mother did not come. When I came to the end of the chapter, I lay my head on the open book and cried.

The next morning at breakfast, Daddy was sitting with his head in his hands. I stood quietly by his elbow, gently scratching my fingernail over one of the marks in the grease-blackened arm of his captain's chair, and said *Good-morning.* He didn't move. He hadn't touched his coffee. A cigarette with a long ash was burning in the ashtray. *Daddy,* I said, and hesitated, then kissed him lightly on his stubbled cheek. He jumped and put his hands on the table, then looked at me with bloodshot eyes as if he was puzzling out who I was. His eyes grew wide, filled with tears, and he grabbed me hard, his forearms wrapped so tightly around my shoulders and neck I couldn't breathe. Then he pushed me away, stood up, stubbed out what was left of his cigarette, and rushed upstairs. A few minutes later he was dressed in his best suit and chesterfield coat. He polished his shoes with a rag by the stove, fished for the keys in his pocket, went out through the kitchen door, and was gone.

I went into the bathroom and stood on the step stool to brush my teeth, taking care to get my new front teeth especially clean. Granny walked in without knocking, left the door open, and bunched up her skirts to sit and have a pee.

"Your turn," she said, wiping herself, "before I flush it."

I pulled down my pajamas and tinkled quietly into the bowl, hating her for standing there, watching me. She always watched me. I flushed the toilet and closed the lid. She grabbed a washrag, ran it under the cold faucet, and fiercely scrubbed my ears and face.

"Where's Daddy going?" I asked, as the icy water ran down my spine.

"He's gone to Boston for the week," she said, drying me off, then tore a comb through my tangled curls. "Stop squirming!" she snapped, and I stood like a statue while hanks of hair came out of my head and she threw them away. "Now go put on your clothes."

I jumped from the step stool and raced upstairs, pulling things out of my drawers in a frenzy, not knowing what would please her, afraid of wearing the wrong thing. Was Daddy leaving us too? Granny had already made his bed and moved her things into his room. His chairs were strewn with her clothes, the shades were up, and the window was open a crack. Would she be my mother now?

She made us sandwiches of bread and molasses for lunch and sent the kids for a nap as soon as they'd finished, then gave me little kisses on my neck, hugged me close, and said, "Now it'll just be the two of us." She smiled with her soft red lips. "You have to take the big blackhead out of my back right this minute."

I put down the rest of my sandwich and started to retch, but she went into the bathroom, got the alcohol, cotton balls, tweezers, a big needle, and laid them on the table. She unbuttoned her house dress, her huge breasts weighing down her camisole like two cantaloupes, and I laughed inside to see them so big as I draped the dress on the back of my mother's chair opposite my father's. My mother's chair! I swallowed hard. I hated this more than anything. I dragged out the step stool and stood behind her.

Granny had beautiful clear skin which seemed to stay milk-and-coffee-colored all year from the sun. But in the middle of her back was a blackhead that she thought was spoiling her perfect skin. I opened the alcohol, poured some carefully into the cap, and set the needle in it to soak. I took a cotton ball, splashed a little alcohol on it, and dabbed at the blackhead in disgust. I took the needle out of its bath, my hand trembling, and began to probe gently at the embedded dirt.

"Don't be afraid to hurt me," she always said. "Give it a good digging." And so she settled back comfortably, serenely, the way she did at Margaret Purdy's when she went to get a permanent wave.

I took the deepest breath I could. If I did this thing, I thought, I'd be able to read in Mama's room again. If I didn't, Granny might send me to bed as punishment. Tears blurred my eyes, and I had to blink them away before I could see what I was doing. As I dug at her back, I looked at her hands, a diamond on each of her ring fingers. Her nails were painted scarlet with half-moons left white at the cuticle. Her nails were perfect—one job I wouldn't have to do today. As the afternoon sun crept slowly through the window, over the table, teacups, newspapers, and all of Mama's plants on the sill, I tried to think about summer and being in the fields, away from this house, until I was done with the blackhead.

After supper, when I was wiping the dishes, the phone rang, and I could tell from Granny's cooing sounds that she was talking to my father. The dishrag went around and around the plate. She talked as if I weren't there, and I put the dishes in the cupboard very quietly so she wouldn't hear me and send me out of the room. She murmured uh-uh and clucked, and said some strange words—*uterus, hysterectomy*—that meant nothing to me, but when she said the word *cancer,* a coffee cup slipped from my hand and crashed in pieces on the floor. I got

the handbrush and dustpan out of the pantry, swept up the
shards, and emptied them into the wastebasket. I knew about
cancer. It was a disease that could kill you. Mama was going
to die. I took off my apron, hung it on the nail in the pantry,
and announced in a loud voice as though I'd heard nothing out
of the ordinary, "I'm going into Mama's room to read." Granny
just nodded me away.

I climbed into the gold chair with the afghan up around my
throat and *Little Women* clutched in my damp hands. I wanted
to cry, but my jaw was clenched so tightly I couldn't squeeze
out a tear. I'd never see her again. She was dying. She was
dead. She would never come back. I tried to imagine what it
would be like, but it was too big a thought. I opened the book
furiously and read to myself. There was no point in reading to
her any more.

Night after night I read like that in Mama's room, angrily,
hungrily, wrapped in the yellow afghan in the gold wing chair,
forgetting Mama and Daddy and Granny and cancer. I read
with a fury, wanting to be Jo who was headstrong, tomboyish,
temperamental, sturdy, imaginative, brash, daring, and bold;
wanting to be Beth who was best-loved, fragile, sweet-tem-
pered, and gentle. I loved the story, the way it went on and on
and every page was a surprise. The characters seemed not like
puppets or cartoon figures, but real people with dreams and
feelings and sadnesses of their own. Soon I came to the part
when Beth was dying, her family gathered tearfully at her bedside, loving her almost too much, and I knew their lives would
be dark without her brightness. I wept for them, for Beth who
was too good for this world, for the music that would not be
heard in their house any more. I cried myself to sleep, wanting
desperately to be dying too, my family gathered around my
bed, grieving for me, loving me best. If only I could die instead
of Mama, think how much they would love me then.

When I woke up it seemed very late. At the window, a sliver
of the new moon hung like a Christmas ornament in the elm
tree, and I felt stiff from having been curled up for so long in

one position. I moved my knees and *Little Women* slid to the floor, but as I retrieved the book, my heart stopped in my chest. A woman was sitting at the table in front of the fireplace, and she was writing. I could smell the black ink in her fluted inkwell, heard her tapping an extra drop off her pen point, and the scratching of pen on paper. She had a lace handkerchief at her nose and was sniffling slightly. She had a beautiful profile. Her shiny thick hair was coiled over her ears. Her dark lashes moved up and down as she wrote. She wore a brown gingham dress with three-quarter sleeves and lace running down the bodice and a ragged brown shawl over her shoulders. She stopped to dab the hankie at her nose, then dipped the pen in and out of the inkwell. She wrote and wrote. My hand on the page I'd been reading grew damp. I looked down at the words under my fingers and at the woman writing and knew it was Louisa May Alcott. She was writing *Little Women*, weeping as I had over Beth. Beth was dying, and she was making it happen. I read the passage again, and the ink seemed to be drying on the pages with each word. How could this be? Louisa May Alcott was dead. *Little Women* had been written a hundred years ago. How could she be writing it now?

Suddenly, I understood how you could live forever. People died, people had to die, but if you wrote a book, the book stayed written, and whenever it was opened by a new reader, the people in it were reborn and so was the writer. Louisa May Alcott was alive because I was reading her words, and with every page they were newly written. I was stunned. In her spidery hand, she wrote and wrote, the ink was still wet, and the story was new. I watched her dab at her nose with her hankie and stretch her shoulders from having been still for so long. Then she turned and looked quizzically in my direction, as if she were in her Concord room and I was a ghost in it. She smiled absent-mindedly and went back to work. The next time I woke up, she was gone.

I couldn't sleep any more that night. I kept thinking of writing a book, many books. I saw them all lined up on the library shelf, and knew that because of them, I would never die. It was exhilarating, my own secret.

Weeks went by. My brother and sister and I went to school, had snowball fights, helped Flap feed the animals. We sat in stony silence at the supper table and ate food we hated. No one mentioned Mama or Daddy or cancer. It was getting close to Christmas. Flap had cut down a tree and dragged it through the snow to the front porch where it would stay until Christmas Eve when we would trim it. The little kids kept asking about Christmas, but I didn't know what to tell them. It was all the same to me.

The day before Christmas we came home from school just as it was starting to snow. We were trying to catch the big flakes on our tongues as we walked up the long driveway from the mailbox. I wasn't paying attention to anything but the flakes falling in my face until I heard my little sister squeal and saw both kids head for the house like puppies tumbling out of their run. I looked in the kitchen window and stopped in my tracks. Mama was sitting in her chair as if she had never been away. I couldn't believe my eyes. I dropped my schoolbag in the snow and ran inside.

The little kids were nuzzling her like baby lambs at her teats. My father was standing by the sink, smiling. I kept looking from one to the other, my strange father and the woman sitting in Mama's chair. She was very pale, as white as a ghost. Deep lines were embedded in her forehead and beside her mouth. Jesus had said to her, *Come forth*, I thought, and she had struggled to sit up in her hospital bed, hung her legs stiffly over the side to step into her slippers, and my father had helped her into her robe because she'd found it hard to move her body again after being dead such a long time. She was holding my brother and sister, one in either arm, and staring at me, stretching out her pale hands. She was so white. She didn't say a word. Her white hands were reaching for me. I gazed into her eyes, and they looked like two snuffed-out candles.

"No!" I shouted, banging my hand on the table until the

teacups rattled. "No, no, I won't!" I ran upstairs and buried myself in my bed, the blankets pulled up over my coat collar, still wearing my snow pants and boots. She was not my mother. Something young and beautiful had gone out of her face. The mother I loved was gone forever, and she would not come back. I did not help trim the tree that night.

The next morning, under the lowest tinseled branches between the satin balls and shiny tin horns, was the gift I'd been dreaming of for what seemed like a lifetime, something more wonderful than a doll or a game or a toy. Mama had called an old friend at Liggett's where she had worked long ago and ordered it for me from her sickbed in the hospital.

It was the thing I most coveted in the world—a typewriter— a heavy, black, enormous 1936 Royal wrapped up with a fiery red ribbon and a tag that read, *For Melissa, who wants to be a writer, Love, Mama.*

It had been snowing all day. The blizzard prevented us from going to school, from even going outside with the sled or toboggan. After supper it was still snowing hard, but the wind had died down. Sometimes on nights like this, the temperature dropped to twelve below zero and the snow drifted under the kitchen window until it partly covered the panes, but tonight as I filled the sink with dishes and soap, the thermometer read twenty-nine. The blizzard came down while my brother and sister and I sat inside after a supper of beans, frankfurts, and brown bread, the wind howling through the ell, rocking the post-and-beams. Flap had gone away on an ice-fishing trip to Lake Winnepesaukee and Mama was in her room, lying down again.

Daddy pushed his chair away from the table and put on two wool shirts, socks, his heaviest boots, his hat with the fur ear pieces and chin strap, and went out to start the old truck with the welded-on handmade wooden plow. The driveway was always kept clear so the trucks could get up the hill to deliver

grain to the chickens, tons of soft yellow corn and mash roaring down the chute into bins. Soon we heard the old engine
crank and start, the truck throbbing against the snow like an
old man briskly rubbing his arms to keep his hands from going
numb in the cold. We heard the plow truck groan down the
hill from the brooder house, the blunt scraping of snow being
plowed forward, the grinding of gears as my father drove backward out of the drift. Over and over the snow was scraped and
pounded into banks as high as the roof of the carriage shed,
back, back, ground over ice and stones. Back and forth my
father pushed the snow away from the driveway, away from
the house, away from us. The engine coughed and wheezed as
he thrust the gears into forward and reverse.

Then the truck rumbled down to the road, its two small
lights barely cutting the blizzard, the windshield wipers frantically trying to erase the ice in little fans, my father hanging
out of the cab's open window, waving to us as he drove by.
With my hands cupped against the steamy windowpane, I
could barely see the words Forge Village painted on the door
as he flew past the house. We heard the plow choking, chaw-
ing, chewing, down by the mailbox, the raw scraping and
scouring as he backed away from the drift, the empty oil drum
in the battered bed of his truck banging, banging against the
truck's corrugated sides as it rocked into and away from each
snowbank. The truck turned and charged up the driveway once
more, as if the engine were willing itself up the hill in order to
help my father; the great treaded tires sliding and swerving on
the ice, past the cooper shop, the maple trees, and up past the
back door in the dark where the engine would idle, and the
clanging of pistons would knock and knock like something
trying to get in or get out.

When I looked outside again to see how hard the snow was
falling, my father was standing on the porch with his face at
the window, and I jumped a mile because I hadn't heard him
or seen him come up the steps. His face simply came forward,

disembodied, out of the snow like a ghost's. There was snow on his cap, on his eyelashes and mustache. I could see his breath in plumes, ice forming in his mustache before my eyes. My father seemed to be freezing to death—he didn't move, he didn't speak, he just stood there peering in, staring over our heads into the room as if there was something on the tip of his tongue, or something he couldn't quite remember, or something he was trying to forget. I sat there, aghast, as he looked past me, frozen in silence, into the warmth of the kitchen's light.

Suddenly his big glove reached out and rapped on the windowpane, and everything was all right again—it was the signal that meant we could all come out and ride in the truck with him while he plowed. We tumbled off the bench and into our snowsuits and boots, excited because there was a blizzard, excited because it was dark and we could be with him in the snow. He hoisted us up one by one onto the bed of the truck, slammed the back flap shut and fixed it with a chain. He jumped into the cab, the gears ground, and the truck lurched forward into the night with us aboard like prisoners, refugees, like workmen, thieves. We loved being with our father then, he in the cab of the plow, scraping and backing and pushing the snow away from the road, away from the house, with us squealing in the rocketing truck bed because it was cold, so bitterly cold, and so dark, so wild. My father is the bravest man in the world, I thought. Under the laden pine trees, midnight never seemed so black. With the engine rumbling and a shriek of gears, Daddy stopped the truck and we leaped from the rattling truck bed of the plow into the deepest snowbanks we could find, and he laughingly fished us out. We were all snowmen now.

The day after a blizzard, when the snow was so white and clean it hurt your eyes and the sky was cobalt and all the limbs of the trees were frosted with brightness, my father would bundle us up, put on his black-and red-checked lumberjack coat, his leftover army hat with woolen ear flaps, and drag the toboggan out of the woodshed for what we knew would be the ride of our lives. We trooped delightedly behind him, up the hill past the brooder house, carriage house, and egg room to the stone wall beside the outhouse door. From there we picked our way over bumps and furrows up a much steeper, very narrow path, the stone wall on one side, the heavily laden pine trees bending down their branches on the other. It was slow going, and so cold it made my teeth ache. At the top of the hill by the old well, the path flattened out, and my father positioned the toboggan heading downhill and sat at the very back. My daredevil brother leapt to the front, grinning like a monkey, my sister crawling after him and clasping her arms tightly around his coat. I burrowed against my father with tears in my eyes, half from the cold and half from fright, and held on to the steering ropes. The farm seemed like a doll's house below us, the brightness shone all around, and the day looked like a Christmas card, with snow on the roofs of the barns, smoke puffing across a deep-blue sky, the air so cold that the smoke hung perfectly still, feathered and stationary as a plume. It was a moment of pure joy. We held our warm breaths inside our cold cheeks, feeling scared, knowing a great thrill was coming. At those times, I thought, I could never love my father more.

The toboggan's nose pointed straight down as if we were heading for the center of the earth. We pushed off and suddenly we were flying—under the pine trees, snow whitening our faces, rushing past the outhouse, the egg room, the brooder house, and we were screaming, my father laughing hard, leaning left together to breast the curve by the maple tree and the woodshed, leaning right as we screamed by the house, crashing over bumps and furrows, leaving the ground with glee, past the cooper shop to the mailbox and out across the road, up a high snowbank where we all tumbled off, laughing and squealing like piglets, snow in our hair, in our boots, down the fronts of our plaid wool coats. *Again, Daddy, again,* we cried, and we dragged the half-buried toboggan out of the high bank, turning it toward another run. We could have gone up and down the hill forever.

At the end of one of the nights when Daddy took us plowing and then sent us in for the night, we ran into the mudroom, took off our snowsuits and hats, stuffed newspapers into the toes of our soaked boots, and put them by the stove. Then we ran upstairs with our wet hair and ju..ped into our flannel pajamas while the truck roared up the hill and parked beside the brooder house. The little kids went to bed, and I came downstairs to sit at the table and read a little before my father finished plowing. When Daddy came in, he stamped his boots hard in the mudroom, shook out his coat, and a cap of ice came off his head when he removed his hunter's hat. Ice melted from his mustache. He poured himself a shot of whiskey and sat in his captain's chair.

"What number am I thinking of?" he demanded. "Hurry up."

I slumped in my chair. I hated this game. My father insisted we could read each other's minds, that we were closer than anyone else, and every night he made us practice telepathy. Sometimes he thought of a number and I concentrated, trying to guess it, and sometimes he made me close my eyes and try to send him a number from one to ten across the table. But tonight my mind was blank. I shut my eyes and tried to feel for a number in the air. I counted numbers in my head, hoping one would light up, change color, seem warmer than the others, and be the right one. He hated it when I was wrong.

I took a deep breath and whispered, "Four."

"Right!" he said, triumphantly slapping the table. "Again!"

With my eyes closed, I heard the snow spitting against the kitchen window, the stove crackling, and Tutu, the marmalade cat, purring in the armchair next to it. I heard my father's intense breathing, smelled the whiskey in his glass. Number. Number. What number was he thinking of? When I didn't think I knew which one was right, I had to guess. I hated to

guess, and I often guessed wrong. What number was he sending me now? Seven? No. Eight? No. Nine. Nine?

"I think it's nine," I whispered.

"Right again, kid," he said, bringing the whiskey bottle to
the table, his eyes growing red-rimmed with the pleasure of
the game. "Now you try to send me one."

I swallowed. This was harder, sending. *Two,* I said to myself
quietly, *It's going to be two.* I sat still, staring at my father's face,
boring the number two into his brain, the number two, two
eyes, two ears, two hands, two, two, two. I traced the number
in my head as though my mind were a pencil, giving him
the shape of it, concentrating on the sound of the word,
spelling it to myself, t-w-o, t-w-o, sending him the number two
with all my will across the green-and-white-checked oilcloth.

He stared back at me and furrowed his brow angrily. Why
did this mean so much to him? What did it prove? That I loved
him best, understood him better than anyone else? It was a
stupid, dangerous game. I loved my father so much, but it
would never be enough. I had to try harder, so I willed two,
two, two, praying he would hear me.

He finished one whiskey and poured another, a gleeful look
on his face.

"I've got it," he said under half-closed lids. "You're sending
me the number three."

Should I agree, say, *Yes, Daddy, I am sending you the number
three?* It would be a lie, of course, but it would keep him calm.
I hesitated. Oh, if only he'd said two.

"No, Daddy, it was two," I murmured sheepishly.

"Goddamn it, you're not trying!" he growled. "Try harder!
Now do it again."

I bowed my head, determined to send my soul out to him if
I could. *Seven, seven, the magic number, seven,* I thought as clearly as
if I had spoken out loud. *Now, Daddy, concentrate. I know you can
get this. It's seven. It's seven. Seven. Seven. Seven.*

I looked into his bloodshot eyes, trying to help him hear me. *Seven. Seven. Seven.*

He drank his whiskey, his eyes never leaving my face. He coughed and put his palms flat on the table. On nights like this his gaze was ferocious, his eyes burned like two coals at the bottom of the stove. There was sweat on his upper lip. He stared at me, and I prayed that God would make him guess the number right. *Seven, seven, seven,* I w..iled frantically. *Daddy, it's seven. Please, say it. Say it and get this over with.*

"One!" he shouted triumphantly. "It's one, isn't it?" not waiting for my reply. "We've got something here, you and I, you know that? Goddamn, it's amazing! We can read each other's minds, do you hear me? It's goddamned amazing!"

I hesitated. How could I tell him he'd guessed wrong? It would be my fault for not trying harder, he would take it out on me. It would be so much easier to let him think that he'd guessed right. But I couldn't. It would be a lie.

"Daddy," I said in my softest voice, watching him finish his whiskey and fill the glass again. "It wasn't one. It was seven."

Suddenly he slammed his fist on the table in front of my face. Spittle hung from the corner of his mouth as he roared at me like some giant out of Grimm's, "I said it was one! It was one, wasn't it, you lying little bitch?"

His pupils were very dark. I could see the delicate tracings of blood vessels in the whites of his eyes. He was talking in that funny voice I hated, crisp, very icy, very clipped, and I was scared. He was not my father. I didn't know who he was.

"Daddy," my hands were shaking as I spoke, "I hate it when you talk in that funny voice."

He grabbed me by the shirt front of my flannel pajamas and lifted me out of my chair.

"What funny voice?" he roared. "A funny voice? There's nothing funny about my voice. Don't you forget, little girl, this is my house. I can talk in it any way I want."

He thrust me against the back door, my elbow hitting the

latch. The back door opened and I fell through it into the mudroom.

"Get up!" he shouted, and I scrambled to my feet, my leather-soled slipper socks sliding on the cold tile floor.

"This is my house, don't you forget it. What I say goes, and if you don't like it, you can get out. It was one, wasn't it, you lying little bitch. It was one!" He pushed me against the outside door, took me by the shoulders and shook me, my head banging on the door like a drum. "This is my house. Any time you don't like it, you can just get out!" He hit my head so hard against the door that I fell down into the open closet and into the pile of boots on the floor. The coats came down on top of me and a rain of stars fell over my eyes. I couldn't catch my breath, and when I started to cry he picked me up by the shirt front of my pajamas and opened the outside door, shouting, "Get out!" He pushed me onto the stone breezeway. The dutch door was open, so I banged my head again. Reeling, I tried to get up but could not. He slammed the door in my face, I heard the dead bolt lock.

He would let me in any minute, I thought. If I just sat still and didn't make any noise, he would turn on the hall light, open the door, and let me in. I waited and listened, my breath puffing hard in my chest. I could not hear a thing. I stood up, listening some more. I put my hand on the panel of the door, calling, "Daddy?" But there was no answer. "Daddy!" I cried louder, slapping my open palm on the door. "Daddy? Daddy?" With both fists I pounded, then began to sob, pounding with all my might. "Please, let me in." But he did not come.

I ran out onto the shoveled terrace walk. It was snowing gently now. The kitchen light was still on and I could see my father weaving his way through the living room and upstairs. I jumped into the snowbank in my leather-soled slipper socks, the snow over my knees, and then struggled toward the porch, calling and calling. When I got to the porch I banged on the window, the snow falling on my hair and shoulders, my breath billowing in clouds. I rapped and rapped with my bare knuckles, but my father did not come. I banged and banged and banged until I thought I would break the glass. Why didn't he hear me? Why didn't he let me in? I cried, "Daddy, Daddy!" The snow came down on my hair and shoulders, and nothing stirred inside the house. I stood there on the snowbound porch, looking into the warmth of the kitchen light.

It was so cold. I had no coat or hat. I was wet up to my underpants. I stumbled out to the terrace, back through the deep prints I'd made in the snowbank. It was snowing ever so gently, but the air was very still. I had to think. I had to stop shivering and think. The car! I could sleep in the car. I trudged around the woodshed and the gold triangle of light from the kitchen window disappeared. The '51 Chevy was just a shape in the darkness. I crawled into the back seat and shut the door softly, so I wouldn't wear out the hinges. I sat with my arms folded on the front seat the way I did when we were driving somewhere. I had to think. I had to stop shivering and think.

"I wish I could drive," I said out loud, wiping the tears from my face. "I wish I were older and I could drive—I'd drive away from here, right now, tonight, and never come back. I'd go south, to Florida, where it's warm and there are palm trees, and the sand is hot and there's an ocean as big and blue as the sky. I'd never come back, not even if you got old and sick and died!" I pounded my fists on the back of the seat. "I'll never come back, I'll never come back, never, never, never."

I lay my head on my arms and sobbed, because I would miss spring and the field of daffodils and jonquils up to my knees, and the red maples' violent budding, and the clean sheets snapping on the clothesline, and the water, rushing, rushing, rushing down the driveway from the top of the hill, in rivulets, in streams, the mud sunning itself like snakes of sand, and the mild air moving over the bright grass as gently as a newborn baby breathed across its bunting.

The snow was falling outside the window of the '51 Chevy,

covering the windshield, the passenger windows, and the oval
pane in the back. It was quiet, quiet as death, and I was shivering. I heard a muffled thumping somewhere outside. What
was it? I was going to be killed, wasn't I? Something in the
darkness was coming for me and it wanted me dead. I listened
again. No, it wasn't footsteps. It was coming from the carriage
house, a riotous, muffled thumping. Flap's hunting dogs! The
blue-tick coon-hound puppies who were only half-grown but
already as big as I was. They were thumping their tails inside
their house. The dogs! I'd go into their house beside the carriage shed. I'd sleep with the dogs.

I stepped cautiously out of the car, into the snow again. It
was so dark I couldn't see anything. I whistled to them and one
of them whined with happiness. I called to them, and kept
calling, and continued walking forward, listening for their
answering whines and thumping. It seemed like such a long
way in the dark. I climbed up to the door, feeling for the outside latch. The door, wired on its hinges, opened out. I stepped
over the threshold, and both dogs leapt at me joyfully, lapping
my face. I pulled the door closed. Their house was so small I
couldn't stand up straight. I squatted down and held their
freckled bodies in my arms. They squirmed and lapped my
face, accidentally clawing me with their eager paws. I felt
through the sawdust for the grain bags they slept on, where
they had scratched them into a nest. I crawled under the layers
of one hundred-pound burlap feed bags, curled into a little
ball, the dogs yawning, stretching, scratching, until they finally
lay down on top of me and went to sleep.

It was quiet, except for the breathing of the pups and me,
and the wind came up slowly over Barker Hill from the valley.
I heard it howling through the rafters of the carriage house. It
pulled questioningly at the tar paper on the roof and the tar-
paper shingles outside. I tried to imagine the snow roaring up
from the valley, falling and falling until it covered the doghouse and the carriage shed and the tops of the barns, snow

falling and falling all through the night until it drifted over the top of the door. I gradually stopped shivering, and as I sank back into the sawdust I remembered a story I'd heard long ago.

There was a little boy who sat in his classroom at the Highland School and spent most of the day gazing at his beautiful young teacher, Miss Cochran. On one particular day, the pupils had been asked to write a short essay. She'd collected them, marked them with her little red pencil, and stood in front of the blackboard with her handsome smile.

"First, I think," she said with her tantalizing beauty, "we will hear from Richard Green." And the little boy, who was my father once, blushed in his seat, shyly cleared his throat, drew himself up, and wavered down the long aisle in his vest, beige plus-fours, and green argyle socks, his heart beating hard, daring to be a bit proud, trying to smile as he looked down the rows and rows of students. She gave him his paper and it trembled in his hands. He paused. Then Miss Cochran said, pointedly, "Children, this is an example of how you must never write." And she gestured that he should read his essay out loud to the class.

His face fell, and he looked at her in disbelief. He stammered. His plus-fours scratched the backs of his knees, his hand shook, and he slowly read the words that had betrayed him, "I was befallen by a snowstorm."

I thought of his humiliation that day before his beloved Miss Cochran and the entire class, how he had stood as he had earlier on the porch, how he'd appeared out of nowhere, a face without a body, snow icing his cap and mustache, how he'd looked into the kitchen, where Tutu, the marmalade cat, was curled up in the chair by the stove, where it was warm and light, and how he hadn't seen us at all. I thought of how he'd stood there with the snow falling all around him, and how he did seem befallen by something, but whether it was the snow that bewildered him entirely, I could not say.

Now my father was lying in his bed, his face to the wall,

and he was not my father any more, but that little boy who was just my age, and as I lay there in the sawdust under the feed bags, I took him into my arms and held him tightly. We nested like two little spoons in the sawdust together and cried ourselves to sleep while the snow came down around the doghouse, in a room no bigger than a grave. I dreamt that when they found us in the morning we had fallen asleep forever, the blue-tick coon-hound pups regally guarding the doghouse door, the way two lions would protect a pyramid.

The carriage-house loft was a place in a fairy tale where nothing had moved for a hundred years. I would sit perfectly still, and words like "dust" and "dusk" would settle like ash on my shoulders and hair. Here I could smell death, changeless and heavy with old leather and sawdust and hay. Under a mildewed army blanket infested with larvae beneath the curved runners of a long-abandoned sleigh, a rope coiled like a headless snake. I leaned against the back of an old commode and saw where the rafters met the top of the window frame, generations of spiders had left behind them a web so dense and wide that I thought it would hold me like a hammock.

From the loft I could see the ridgepole of the ell and the roof of the cooperage, the weather vane's copper horse frisking in dressage. The outside world was bursting open, fluttering petal by petal, wing by wing, into life, into spring. Inside. Outside. The beauty, the light, the mild transparent air, the fragrance, the bird song—none of them would ever come inside my parent's house. The house was dark and full of burning, as though the smoke of a thousand fires from the wood stove hung over their heads. It was like trying to breathe through burlap. My mother and father never kissed or held hands or embraced. They seemed almost unrelated, people who lived in a house together without having anything in common. I had no notion of marriage as a relationship between two grown-ups; they rarely spoke to each other. There were always so many people around—my brother and sister; Flap; Granny and Boppa, my father's parents, who came to the farm every Saturday; Granny, to rearrange the furniture, Boppa to slide under the belly of his Buick and spend the afternoon tinkering. I had begun to think that marriage was an arrangement that forced people to live together against their will. The house was impenetrable, like a clouded aquarium, its depths sealed at the bottom of the ocean, where the thundering voice of my father boomed out the tides like Poseidon, and we shook mutely as blades of sea grass in reply. There were no membranes, no tissue between us; we were inseparable, intermingling beings. My father's fury passed through my pores, the barb of his trident trapped in my heart, pinning me mercilessly in place. Among the seawrack and mizzenmasts of rage, contempt, despair, I tried to lie quietly and let their sorrows wash over me, soaking up the bitter tincture of failure like a sponge.

And yet, from my perch inside the carriage house, through a spot of glass I'd cleaned with my breath, I could see the sun on the tops of the maples, the wind lifting the ruffled skirts of forsythia, swallows returning again and again to their nests, woven from the remnants of autumn that winter had stored for safekeeping until this day. Outside, there were cycles and seasons and stars. Outside, there was color and movement and tender new leaves.

Inside. Outside. I pressed my hand against the glass but couldn't reconcile the two—that such different worlds could command my complete loyalty, protection, and love. Outside was life and death. Inside nothing died and nothing lived. It was a kind of timeless negation, a purgatory suspended in water, neither life nor death. And into that O—the silent, open mouth of a child raised as though to take a sacrament—poured my family's desperation, confusion, and fear. I understood too late that consecrated on my tongue lay their own mortal fear— of life, of death. My mouth could not sing for the cup of fire it had to swallow again and again.

Outside, it was balanced: life was life because we died, death was death because we lived. Inside, everything merged and was weightless. Each world existed side by side but never met, except in me. I ran like a bright-faced messenger between the territories, longing to make peace between two ancient regimes, to carry tokens of forgiveness, acceptance, and welcome from one to the other. But I couldn't bring the light into the turbulent darkness any more than I could bear the weight of my parents' lives into the sun. To choose one world was to betray the other.

And so, on a perfect spring day sometime after my eighth birthday, I took the heavy coil of towrope from the loft in the carriage shed and dragged it like a sled through the long grass to the foot of the apple tree I loved best. I climbed as high as I dared into the branches and sat with the rope beside me like a companion, swinging my bare legs back and forth to some little song I would sing absent-mindedly on the playground, at a picnic. I wasn't afraid. I was calm. I sat among the blossoms like a statue in a Japanese garden, part child, part capuchin, grateful that the solution had finally come to me. I would give up both worlds rather than be forced to choose between them. The last thing I'd remember would be the smell of apple blossoms, heady and strong, and then there'd be rest and quiet and the end of everything.

For weeks Flap and I had been sitting in the doorway of the toolshed on two overturned nail kegs with the black barn cat kneading a grain sack crumpled in the grass and the sound of sheets snapping like sails on the clothesline in the stiff March air. He'd been teaching me to tie knots. Hour after hour, day after day, Flap showed me the intricate mysteries of rope in his wizard's hands as it became a monkey's tail, a Turk's head, a long-running eye, the sash cord with a life of its own twisting into a toggled bight, a crown-and-star, a cat with seven tails, the rose, the manrope knot. He guided my fingers in, out, under, up, and through each knot, repeating the steps patiently

over and over until I could take the rope ends and make them
perfectly myself. On an oblong piece of plywood, next to a
map of the world on the wall of the tool room, he nailed and
named each finished knot in his barely legible, awkward letters,
spelling out sheepshank, slath knot, the Josephine.

Flap was once a sailor, and in his small dark room under the
eaves he would speak in a secret language on his ham radio
with farmers in Mexico, teachers in Newfoundland, the musical
Morse code traveling along the horizon, star after star, thread-
ing the night sky with voices, with meaning. On the map in
the tool room he had recorded his naval travels, each exotic
port marked with a thumbtack—Halifax, Lisbon, Dakar,
Maputo, Dar es Salaam, Djakarta, Manila, Guam. With an
index finger, he followed each route, spinning his stories from
continent to continent, drawing the shapes of knots around
each port until the world itself was cinched and battened down
because he had tied it securely in place. As I watched his finger
move across the latitudes, I traced the longitudinal line from
his fingertip to his forearm where an anchor tattooed in ink
moved with a tide as he talked. An American eagle scowled
and spread his great wings on Flap's shoulder. As each port was
called, I could see the delicate pinfeathers twitch. On his left
shoulder was an Indian chief with the profile of a buffalo nickel
in an elaborate headdress and cheekpiece that seemed to be
carved out of granite like the Old Man of the Mountain,
fiercely proud, stone-jawed, his nose like a precipice. Beneath
him on the left forearm strutted a bantam cock in wattles and
comb, one talon raised and partly tucked under its wing. I saw
how the needle of the tattoo artist had calligraphed the parchment of his arms, weaving a kind of tapestry of knots in ink.
The knots I'd made in sash cord were the same intricate jour-
neys of weaving—the world, his tattoos, my knots.

A noose was the simplest knot of all, but trying to tie towrope required more strength than sash cord. I sat on the bough
of the apple tree and made a loop, easing it over my hair to

my shoulders. Draped around my throat like a necklace, the
rope was as wide around as my wrist. I wove the end about and
under the bough until it felt tight. Clouds like a flock of lambs
were frisking over the alfalfa into the trees at the edge of the
field. A robin kept questioning his mate. Sunlight brightened
and darkened on the grass. The barn cat was crouched low in
the milkweed, stalking a mouse on its haunches, nibbling a
crumb of prayer. A wave of sadness came over me. It was so
beautiful. It hurt so very much. I laced my fingers together for
a moment, then closed my eyes, kicked off from the bough,
and was falling.

The rope clutched at my throat with the fury of a grown-
up's hand. It held there and shook me hard. I hung from the
branch above a swimming green pond flecked with white clover and could not breathe. And then I was falling, the rope end
was unraveling from the bough, and the noose and I and the
towrope landed together with a thud in the grass. Showering
petals covered me in a sweet blanket of snow. I watched the
clouds pass through the interlacing twigs and blossoms, and
after a while I wound up the rope, took it back to the loft, and
went into the house. No one knew I'd been gone.

Last night I dreamed of her, that child who tried to die in
the arms of an apple tree. I stood knee-deep in alfalfa, grown
as I am now, between the gateposts where two elms, given over
long ago to Dutch elm disease, still rose into the air. Under
the canopy of oval leaves, I saw the farm as I loved it best, in
summer, when the trumpet vine billowed like a wave over the
ship's bell hung at the corner of the ell to call the men in for
supper. Hummingbirds stitched the air and darted like sewing
needles into the orange cornets. The carriage house had black
eaves for epaulettes and crisp white windowsills like a coachman's cuffs. The blue-tick coon-hound pups were tumbling in
their run. The corral looked newly built, parallel lines of cut
saplings roped together into fence posts, and the donkey Rosita ran briskly, flicked her long ears, and kicked up her heels,

braying in mourning for the loss of her son, Pedro. Sun shone off the cucumber frames beside the biggest barn, and Flap was sitting on the stoop in his dungarees, smoking his pipe, his tattoos like bruises at that distance, patiently waiting like Andrew mending his nets.

The child I was at eight stared at me from the doorway of the house. The cooper shop seemed freshly painted, the brass knocker of a ram's head still bright. The Baldwin trees bowed low with fruit, and I could smell peppermint and dill from the old kitchen garden grown wild. The well sweep hung over the well. The grass was long and soft by the garden, an acre of fragrance, sleepiness, and bees. The child stepped forward, shading her eyes.

"Who are you?" she asked with an edge in her voice.

I paused, and when I spoke, my own voice came from somewhere deep, underwater.

"I'm the woman you'll become someday," I said.

"No, you're not! Go away and leave us alone!"

Us? Who did she mean? She stood by herself in overalls and a flannel shirt. She'd probably been weeding. Her hair was damp and curling; there was dirt on her knees from kneeling in earth. Then I knew that she meant the family inside the shuttered house were still turning their faces from the world, from her and from me.

The wind began to thicken. Leaves fell gently like an autumn snow, then roared up the driveway as though someone were vigorously raking them into piles, the bare black branches of November turning to charcoal and burned-out wicks. All at once the carriage house, dog run, corral, and donkey's house had disappeared, long grass growing in place of blackberries. The huge barn we used for the chicken house had collapsed and tar paper flapped angrily somewhere in the grass like a frightened flock of hens. Shingles blew off the roof of the house; a shutter screeched from one hinge. The child, terrified, couldn't move.

I shouted over the howl of the wind. "It's all gone, can't you see? Nobody's home anymore."

The horse, cantering at the ridgepole, was green and fractured at the fetlock. It no longer seemed to know north from south but ran blindly in circles, as if immersed in a panic of smoke.

"Come here!" I called to my younger self.

Her eyes filled with tears, and the trumpet vine tore from its moorings on the eaves.

"Go away," she shouted, crying now. "Go away, go away!"

The din was deafening. Glass shattered in some of the windows; the rooftree gave a great crack and thundered like the mast of a foundering ship.

"Come here!" I yelled, my breath harsh at the breastbone, as though I were speaking to my own child. "I remember a girl even younger than you, hardly three, who tiptoed out of the house one night in a white nightgown and bare feet and ran across the wet grass, her arms outstretched to the moon and the evening star. You wanted to travel toward that beauty. You had no name for it then. Do you remember? It was poetry you loved. Come with me. I'll show you."

She looked at me, her chin thrust in doubt, in disbelief. She picked up her pail and the broken breezeway door slammed shut behind her.

Our house was not haunted, that much was clear, but it groaned and shifted and stirred all winter long like a great white bear turning over in its sleep. Frost expanded and contracted the mortise-and-tenon beams of the shed chamber, the upper room of the farm's original ell, built about the time of the Revolutionary War. The narrow, steep attic stairs creaked as though from tentative footsteps, and the pantry door unlatched itself and swung open on such a regular basis that we invented and named a fourth child as the culprit—a freckled, red-headed invisible boy called Harry, who was responsi-

ble for mischief we dared not own. His favorite trick, and one
we secretly championed, was to sneak into the pantry after
supper for something more to eat. We knew he had a terrible
sweet tooth because each of us did, and when I sat at the
kitchen table doing my homework and the door heaved and
swung open silently, I imagined Harry's ghostly fingers quietly
searching the shelves for cookies, and in my mind the shelves
bulged with boxes of lady fingers, brownies, hermits, Oreos,
impossibly rich confections stuffed with marshmallow and
chocolate, fruit squares and Fig Newtons, almond puffs and
oatmeal raisin bars. With my pencil diligently scratching in my
notebook, I heard Harry's orgy of chewing and fed myself to
bursting on his invisible treats.

   Our house was not haunted, but on Saturdays when I carried
the washing outside in an old wicker basket that had been my
first cradle and stood at the clothesline with wooden pegs in
my mouth, my arms loaded with towels and pillowcases, I felt
the presence of the six generations of my family that had lived
in this house before me. Perhaps it was the way the mid-March
air snapped the crisp sheets so matter-of-factly or the way the
sheets themselves seemed to respond, as if they were flinging
themselves out to dry, or even the sharp sound of linen billowing like sails and the smell of sunlight absorbed by the
sheets like sachet. All of it conspired to make me feel *this has
happened before, many times, there has always been a woman at this line
hanging sheets for her babies, dungarees and work shirts for her father, her
husband, and brothers.* Pegging dish towels, aprons, and socks, I
felt warmed by more than exertion. The sun itself was cherishing the place where I stood. I was taking part in an ancient
ritual, sacred because it was a place where a woman worked
peacefully in her own thoughts, where she let down her guard
and paused to dream. It was beautiful there in the sun, even on
days when the sheets froze solid on the lines. I felt a wrenching
kinship with my mother, Granny, and my great-great-grand-
mother's husband's mother. All around me were a dozen ghosts

in long blowing skirts. The whispering of grass and the heaviness of the wicker basket seemed to carry the urgent bustle and bristling arguments of their lives, the tragedies of summer sickness, infidelity, and madness, and a future of working oneself quietly to death. They had made soap from lye and ashes. They scrubbed out the grime of despair, the film of iniquity on washboards. Their lives had been much more difficult than mine. I wanted to wash clothes without complaining, as they had, but it was very hard.

Gray rinse water poured down the narrow trench to the drain. The wringer squawked when I turned it on. I took the dungarees by their cuffs and fed them through the double rollers, squeezing out the excess water until the basket was full but not too heavy to carry. Once when I forgot to pay attention, I fed my fingers through the wringer and the machine screamed as though I were hurting it. I ran the wringer backward, freeing my hand that looked hoary with frost. These white shirts are gray, I thought. They will never come clean. There are five more loads to wash. It will take all of Saturday, and they still won't be clean.

I was ten years old and no longer flinched when my father called me a dirty little slut. I hung the trousers by their cuffs and the shirts by their shoulders. A warm sheet fluttered around my arms as if it wanted to embrace me. They were standing near me, my women. The leaves of the maples were ruffling their undersides like petticoats. It will rain by four o'clock, I thought, as I walked down the worn steps for another load of dungarees.

The cellar was dark with a mostly dirt floor and two tiny transoms that opened under the porch's trelliswork for light. The washing machine stood at the foot of the stairs like a white potbellied stove, the agitator swishing gray suds back and forth with the soft sound of a cow chewing its cud. The hard well water never made good suds. Minerals dyed the porcelain of the toilet, tub, and sink a permanent sepia, stains that no

cleanser and no amount of scrubbing could remove. I sat on the
bottom step and stared at generations of Mason jars stocked
on the shelves, the pears and peaches and plums of countless
summers that had never been eaten, tomatoes stewed until all
the ripe sunlight had been boiled out of them, jars of one-
hundred-year-old jams and jellies, fruit once sweet and succu-
lent cemented forever in the clouded containers of a family's
unwritten history: *these beans were put up the year Pearlie tumbled off
the cooper-shop roof; these beets, the year the horse chestnut fell on deaf
Uncle Charles who hadn't heard his brothers hollering "timber," the tree
killing the man but leaving the oxen a foot away unharmed.* The old jars
stood next to the butter beans and succotash we'd canned three
years ago: *I had picked the last of the Swiss chard, taken down the vines
from the beanpoles, and on my way into the house bent to pick up a
sumptuous pear that had dropped from the tree to give to Rosita, and the
wasp that was crawling on its sticky underside stung me with supernatural
fury. It hated me and wanted me to die.* The hypnotic rhythm of
the washing machine lulled me half to sleep. I inhaled deeply,
smelling the black loam left on the potatoes we'd dug up in the
fall, the sweet fermenting of Baldwins and Macs we'd gathered
to keep cool all winter gone to rot, the cloying aroma of burst
grapes from an old bottle of homemade wine that had
exploded. I sat on the bottom step, my chin in my hands, and
imagined a different kind of life for myself, where children
could be children instead of having to work to earn their keep.
While the hen-manured work shirts and dungarees convulsed
in the washtub, I watched a long black and gold-flecked snake
slip through the foundation stones beside the bulkhead and
dreamed of another sort of house.

I dreamed of Nanaquaket on a shield-shaped neck of land
on the Sakonnet River in Tiverton, Rhode Island, where beach
rocks dressed the coast in armorial beading and green velvet
rolled back from the cliff's edge like a heraldic field, the late
heat burning off the water. On summer nights I pictured its
colonnade of elms, the boathouse, playhouse, gazebo, stable,

and barn gleaming white, the gabled house bright on the promontory and the sun-silvered steps of the beach pavilion running down to the river. Nanaquaket became my Manderley, my Tara, my Thornfield Hall, and in winter when nor'easters thrashed the coast and the weather alternated between blizzard and fog, I imagined it to be the grange and moors of *Wuthering Heights.* I dreamed of being wed and widowed there. At Nanaquaket I wrestled for my soul.

The white clapboard house with a turret, a round room, and a porch that looked out over the fields to the river on three sides felt as if it were surrounded by the sea. It was built in the 1880s as a summer house by the Church-Humphrey-Chase family, with that combination of grandeur and austerity so admired by the Yankee heart. Yet it had none of the lavish ostentation of the Vanderbilt cottage at Newport fifteen miles away; Nanaquaket had been brought into being in accord with the strict middle-class, albeit modest Protestant virtues of merchants and mill owners, and those who could afford to stay at the nearby Stonebridge Inn. Farm fields of alfalfa and salt-marsh hay stretched for miles. And *rosa rugosa,* the hardy beach roses, grew along the Atlantic where the smell was the sweetest and the Sakonnet turned and bent in upon itself along a bluff.

I was with my mother, my sister, and my brother when I first saw Nanaquaket. We were going there to visit my aunt. Turning off the main road, we crossed a narrow stone bridge and drove through an imposing pair of pillars at the gateway. The main house sat under a canopy of shade between a double row of wine-glass elms in a wash of light, so big and sprawling in the distance, it looked like a castle. We drove past flower gardens in bloom, a trelliswork archway of roses, the gazebo among massive Japanese beech trees with their wrinkled, elephant-gray limbs and aubergine leaves. We turned again at the two-story playhouse with its cupola and porch. At the water's edge the boathouse luffed on its stone foundation. We parked under the porte-cochere, and I stepped out of the old Chevy, pretending it was a victoria or an elegant coach-and-four. Looking back over the lawn to the stable or down to the water's edge, I knew that Nanaquaket was a haunted place.

There was nothing sinister about the house. It stood in bright sunlight, laundry snapping on the line behind the carriage house, and yet it had the distinct feel of a place that had once been lived in quite differently. I imagined a ghostly orchestra playing in the gazebo, the faint notes of horns and violins hovering on the edge of human hearing, the wind blowing in gusts as it carried the smell of food and flowers, the commotion of garden parties, sailboat outings, and the laughter of girls in long white dresses playing tennis on the lawn. I closed my eyes, thinking of the beginning of all magic, and whispered *I wish*, but standing with my foot on the Chevy's running board, I wondered what to wish for. I knew in a minute: *I wish we were rich.* Daydreaming in the shade of the porte-cochere, I imagined how it would change my life: *I will be nine for a long time yet. My name is Nelly, short for Eleanor, which I hate, but it will be a good name when I grow up. I have long fiery ringlets, a sailor suit with a white middy blouse, a straw hat with blue ribbons down my back, a hoop, a bisque china doll, a chestnut gelding named Rothchild's Biscuit, and a golden retriever named Jenny Lind. All my clothes are made by a French seamstress. Nothing is a hand-me-down. I never do chores—we have servants for that. I've watched my older sister and her friends from the gazebo all summer, and they tell me I am their mascot. Now Cathleen is standing in her bridal gown for pictures on the lawn, and I love her more than ever. She has always been kind to me. She cried last night in our big white canopy bed and said, as she buttoned the eyelet lace of my nightie, that she would miss me absolutely to death. Then she gave me a flurry of kisses. In this house I am never cold, there is plenty to eat, and my shoes are never too small. My sister loves me. She is standing with one arm full of roses, the other linked at the elbow of her husband, Bertie, who looks a bit like the Prince of Wales. With them are their friends Wesley, Reggie, Brett, and the girls unfolding in the petals of their dresses*

*like flowers—Hattie, Gwendolyn, and Grace. My brother Dickie, a cadet
at West Point, is so handsome in his uniform as he bends down for a kiss.
He does not torture cats. He never teases me. He lifts me into the air and
laughs. My father, in his handlebar mustache, comes over to squeeze my
hand, to let me know how much of a comfort I will be to him in his old
age. The sun is in my eyes, and I am happier than I have ever been in my
life. I am their most beloved child. A soft deep bell is ringing somewhere
close by, and I can hear my mother's voice:*

"Stop daydreaming and get up these stairs this instant!" my
mother shouted from the front porch. She had already rung
the doorbell and was waiting for someone to answer.

That is as rich as we'll ever be, I thought with a sigh—me
with my foot on the Chevy's running board in the shade of the
porte-cochere. I ran up the stairs to have my bangs brushed
out and my collar impatiently straightened as a pair of heels
clicked on the hardwood floor inside. My brother and sister
stood quietly in their Easter coats. The door to Nanaquaket
opened slowly. A young girl in a black dress with white cuffs
smiled at us.

"Please come in," she said softly, and stood back so we could
pass.

The room was dark and full of light at the same time. Polished and intricately carved wainscoting divided the walls in
half. A gleaming staircase with a shiny balustrade slipped
upstairs. There were bow windows on each end of the room, a
marble fireplace with an oval mirror above the mantel, and a
basket of blue hydrangeas where the fire would be laid in winter. The three of us sat gingerly on the brown velvet sofa. Its
arms curved like snails' shells. My mother paced, trying not to
smoke. Outside the window a dozen old-fashioned shutter-
green rockers were lined up facing the river. In one corner of
the porch was a five-sided room, a sort of glassed-in turret
with a big mahogany table inside. Perfect for afternoon tea, I
thought. *I am here to visit Mrs. Humphrey and Miss Chase. I am wearing a mauve silk-moire dress and a wide hat with an ostrich plume. It's a*

warm day so I take off my gloves and fold them neatly in my lap. A breeze is blowing. A cut-glass bowl of yellow roses fills the turret with the soft fragrance of summer. Mrs. Humphrey is talking about her children. I am nodding politely. Her boys are hellions and the girls aren't a bit pretty, but I smile and say how proud she must be of them. I am waiting for the tea tray. I hope they have scones and blackberry jam. I am partial to blackberry jam.

Someone was clearing her throat. It was my mother, scowling at me. Quickly I said to her, "Imagine what it would have been like to live here in the olden days!"

She snorted. "You would have been a servant, in any case, not upper class. Sit down and be quiet."

I sat tapping my fingers on the antimacassar. Tap, tap, tap, tap. I knelt on the fat brown cushions and peered over the sofa into the dining room. Glass-fronted china cabinets furnished every corner of the room, along with more paneling, two more bow windows, and the well-stocked pantry beyond. It was time to hazard my second wish. So I would have been a servant, would I? *I would come into the room in a black dress and crisp white-bibbed apron with ruffles, and a ruffled, ribboned cap on my hair, carrying an enormous silver tray with the second-best tea service on it. I would set it down on the mahogany table inside the glass room, and I would understand from my employer, Mrs. Humphrey, by the way she rattled the monogrammed teaspoons that our visitor, my mother, is not very important, and I needn't be more than civil to her. I pour the tea and curtsy half-heartedly and return with the tray to the kitchen.*

I have worked my way up from kitchen girl to assistant housekeeper. I am friends with the cook, the coachman, the new kitchen girl, and the groom. They call me Pendleton now. Miss Turnbull, the housekeeper, is very busy, but she trusts me with starching and ironing the table linens until they are crisp, polishing the silver, stocking the larder with flour, sugar, butter, eggs, and herbs so that there is always enough food in the house. I am invaluable to her. I know what goes where on the shelves in every closet in the house. I am surrounded by beautiful things. The towels are sparkling white, without darns, without worn places thin enough to see

*through. I go to the fish market with the cook on Wednesdays. I have every
other Thursday off. I traipse down to the gardens in the afternoon, two
hours before dinner, and fill a woven basket with roses, delphiniums, lilies,
hibiscus. I take care of the kitchen garden at the end of the porch where the
hayfields run down to the edge of the water. There are no worms or mites
or rodent teeth-marks on my vegetables. The kitchen is spotless. My vegetables are bright and sparkling under the pump handle. My apron is pristine.
I have my own room under the eaves and I am left alone when I'm not
working. The family treats me with respect. Mrs. Humphrey shows me
bright swatches of damask for new curtains in the dining room. I choose
the prettiest one with pale blue irises on it. Someday I will take Miss
Turnbull's place. I will never leave this family.*

The young girl in the black dress with white cuffs came into
the room and murmured to my mother. My mother said,
"Thank you, Sister." Then the young girl nodded and disappeared.

Sister? My mouth fell open in astonishment. She was a nun?
But she was pretty! She had long curly hair pulled back with a
barrette. How could she be a nun? Nuns had moles with hair
growing out of them. Nuns wore long black habits with stiff
white bibs and corrugated wimples covering half their faces
like horse blinders. They were ageless. They did not wear lipstick or show their teeth when they smiled. They walked
everywhere in pairs and held their hands together inside their
sleeves like monks. I was never sure if they were men or
women, and for a while I thought they were a third sex altogether. I craned my neck to look out the window into the yard.
The young woman was taking down clothes, revealing the
secrets of the clothesline: plain linen sheets were hanging from
plain wooden pegs; on the hidden, inner lines were towels and
facecloths, and further inside, where they couldn't be inadver-
tently glimpsed, were the cotton chemises and knee-length
snuggies of nuns.

I put my head in my hands. I hated being ten. You didn't
know anything at all.

A tall figure in black came into the room, gliding silently over to my mother. They kissed. It was my aunt, her sister called Peggy. Her name in the convent was Mother Ann Thomas. She was the Provincial of the order. I didn't know what to call her or where to kiss her so I shook hands with her solemnly and sat back down on the sofa. We hadn't seen very much of her because the sisters weren't allowed to travel, they couldn't write letters, and could only have visitors once a year. She couldn't visit us but sometimes she went to Rome to see the Pope. It was all very mysterious.

She had joined the Holy Union sisters, a teaching order, in 1940 when she was just seventeen. The mother house consisted of three mansions side by side on a hill in Fall River called Rock Street. The sisters had acquired Nanaquaket in 1924, turning it into a preparatory school for girls who were planning to enter the order. They had squared up the round front parlor and filled it with pews to make a chapel. The stable had become a dormitory. They'd extended the kitchen toward the river, taken up part of the porch, and made a refectory where pupils and teachers could eat. The upstairs bedrooms had been converted into tiny classrooms. There was a cross on the peaked roof of the porte-cochere and a statue of the Blessed Virgin under the beech trees in the garden. The carriage house was the bishop's summer residence.

My aunt's face was very bright. She offered my brother and sister a glass of ginger ale which she called tonic. She gave me tea with the grown-ups, poured from a teapot into china cups embossed with Birds of Paradise on top of saucers so fragile that they were translucent. I sat up very straight and splashed in milk and five sugars. I worried that I might have used too much, but there seemed to be enough for everyone. Over my teacup's blue-feathered brim, I watched Peggy. She had long white hands. She was wearing a silver band on her wedding finger. A black rosary dangled from her belt. Her face was smooth and she was wearing round wire-rimmed spectacles, speaking as softly as a saint to my mother. She was very beautiful.

Then it really is a convent, I thought. There were ivory candles on the sideboard and heavy black missals with red-trimmed pages and colored ribbons for bookmarkers. The furniture was old-fashioned and smelled of lemon oil. The only servants here were the servants of God. The figure of Jesus was writhing over my head and I indulged in my third and final wish: *This will be my last day in the world as myself. I am wearing my best outfit. My family is in tears because they know I will never be the same after this cup of tea. I will marry God in a long white dress at High Mass. The bishop will welcome me and lay a hand on my brow as he did at my First Communion. He will say that I have been chosen. I am shriven clean, the beloved of God, and must gladly forsake all my worldly possessions and every vestige of earthly life. I am very devout. I go back behind the rail to the private rooms behind the altar. My hair falls in long locks onto the floor. I will put on a black dress with white cuffs and a white veil, and later a black one, and it will be the happiest day of my life. I will live out my years at Nanaquaket serenely, surrounded by my sisters who will forgive me my faults and guide me with infinite love and patience. There will be no more quarreling, no more harangues, no more punishment. Living without luxuries will be easy because we do so by choice. We will eat simple food and not go hungry. We will sleep in simple beds and they will be comfortable because we are sleeping in a house near God. We will sit on the porch in shutter-green rockers and watch the river go by for the rest of our lives: Please,* I close my eyes in a silent prayer, *I want to be good. Let me leave everything, right now, today. It will be the easiest thing I've ever done. And I will be so loved. Mother Ann Thomas rises from her chair. She comes to me with her hands outstretched and I run into her arms. Yes, I will stay with the nuns forever.* Peggy kissed me quickly on the cheek, then my brother and sister, and finally embraced my mother. We were leaving Nanaquaket, down the steps to the old Chevy waiting under the porte-cochere. The sky had clouded over and the river was the color of steel.

Later that summer I got poison ivy from blackberrying. It

began as a ruby bracelet of bug bites on my ankles. On the fifth day when I woke up, my fingers and toes looked like fat decomposing sausages and I couldn't put on my shoes. On the sixth day my body was covered with oozing, fiery sores. On the seventh day the poison was in my ears, my mouth, and under the lids of my eyes which were swollen shut. I lay upstairs on my bed in my underwear, hoping I would die before nightfall. No one came to see if I was still alive. Our family did not believe in doctors. My parents went about their day like sleepwalkers and I was not in their dream. The stair treads sighed with age and weariness but no footsteps, and the organdy at the window shook out its skirts and looked away. Flies were hovering over my corrupted body, buzzing above the bed. Flies were gossiping on my pillow, and the one that was gingerly exploring the length of my leg, the way a bird would walk on a half-decayed carcass in a field, flew to the window in disgust to wash her velvet hands. *It smells of rot in here. It smells of festering. And it is me.*

I could not sleep because my body was on fire.

After a while the fever was so bright, I thought Saint Theresa moved out of her portrait on the wall and spoke to me. *"Go to Nanaquaket,"* the saint said. Yes, I thought in my dream, I must save myself from this plague or I will die. Like Moses set adrift in the bulrushes at the time of the scourge of the pharaoh, I imagined myself in the big wicker basket as if it were a raft, sailing slowly down the Squanicook under the cool trees. The water was clear all the way to the bottom. Birds sang to me as I passed. I was going home to Nanaquaket.

I paddled gently by the farms, the library, the Grist Mill until I was leaving Townsend altogether. My father and mother were on the riverbank. My father was furious. He knew I was going to stay with the nuns and not come back.

You think you're going to find God there, don't you? You won't find God in a henhouse, he roared without moving his mouth.

No, I said. *I will find God like a mountain in their hearts. He will make me cleave unto Him only, and I will be clean.*

My mother was knitting and she did not look up as I floated by.

You're disfigured now, she said. *They won't want you.*

Yes, they will, I screamed silently. *They care for the sick, the poor, the orphaned. Even lepers are loved. Their white hands will bathe my body in cool water and wrap me in linen sheets still smelling of summer sunlight. They will take me into their family, and I will be clean enough for God.*

The Squanicook had turned into the Sakonnet. The gentle current had taken me many miles. Nanaquaket was as white and as beautiful as I remembered. The river was murmuring all around me. The nuns were standing together on the porch of the bishop's house with their hands in their sleeves.

Sisters, I said joyfully at the beach-house steps. *Here I am.*

But they were silent. No one moved to help me moor my boat.

Sisters, I cried. *I've left my old life forever. I have come to find God.*

The nuns were carved of marble. Their bibs and wimples were so white that they were almost transparent. They watched me float past the landing on my raft, and said clearly, without words, *There is no place for you at Nanaquaket.*

Please, I begged them. *Don't send me away. I want to live with you.*

It is not what God wants, they said.

What does He want? There was no answer, and I drifted away from shore, Nanaquaket growing smaller and smaller on the bluff until it disappeared. Suddenly exhausted, I lay down in my wicker-basket cradle and stared up at the empty, God-abandoned sky. It began to rain, and it rained for an eternity.

✥

We stood stock-still in our Sunday clothes on the stone wall under the rain-black elms and shouted over the snow fence across Rossbach's field to St. Cyr's barn, shouted toward the white steeple of the Methodist church in the valley until we heard the ricochet of our voices over the Squanicook River, each of our cries a skipped stone heading south from the railroad trestle to Groton, Littleton, and Boston. We shouted until we heard our cries come back to us, hollow, faint, and for a fleeting moment it seemed that other children were calling back to us, my brother and sister and me.

It was Thanksgiving, and we were crying. We were beside ourselves with happiness. Company was coming and we wouldn't be alone.

Our farm was at the top of Barker Hill, up a long rutted driveway from the gravel of a partly paved road. At this time of year when the woods were quiet and empty of leaves, you could hear a car coming from the four corners at Dudley Road four miles away. It would shift gears at Ben Newton's house and again at the Retina Foundation, coughing up the last slope and curve before our stone wall with its stanchions of elms. Someone had nailed to one of the trees a crudely carved, crooked wooden sign that said Green Acres. If anyone was foolhardy enough to climb to the top of Barker Hill, especially in winter, they were probably coming to see us, because beyond us, straight north, a stone's throw away, was New Hampshire, acres of state forest, and occasionally the foundation of a house, not far from the granite quarry, which had been shut down for a hundred years. Sometimes cars came to our mailbox and turned around, strangers who had found their way to our driveway by accident. The stab of disappointment when they backed out and drove away was intense—we were so alone.

From the window in my bedroom I could watch the road, gray as a river under the elms, and sometimes in the soughing of pines and the ominous shiver of clouds passing over, I felt that our farm was fixed at some terrible extremity, a shabby, surly outpost of civilization before the wilderness began, a way station en route to something inevitable, beyond the broken granite hitching post that marked the boundary between New Hampshire and Massachusetts.

We were at the verge, the edge of something profound. There was a dirt road that ran through woods, but this road and these birch trees conspired to make even the most subtle, benign light full of paradox. The road dwindled to sand and gravel at the state line and may have been a highway once, but that was a long time ago. In the woods were oxen roads, logging tracks, trails that led to the quarry, and cellar holes where only a tall solitary stand of lilacs or a soup plate's few blue and white fragments, dug up from under the fern fronds next to an empty well, marked the threshold of a summer kitchen. There was even a little clearing where the weather had scoured off the names on four headstones that were sinking into the ground. On moonlit nights when the gray road shone clear and the air was still except for the scrabbling of night animals, the road north became a path into the past.

And yet it could only be a road into the future, because our barn had already fallen, the cooper shop's roof line curved like a swayback mare, and every year sumac and bramble crept closer and closer to the house. It was only a matter of time before we, too, would crumble into the past, and there would be no memory of us. But at what point did we leave the land of the living and enter the land of the dead? Perhaps we didn't enter the land of the dead at all, but the land of the dead entered us, like nature overtaking a barn.

The notion of boundaries was extremely comforting to me. There were stone walls to measure each parcel of land, each town's circumference, the width and breadth of a state. Stone-wall walking was like following the railroad tracks: you might not know where you were going, but you knew it would get you somewhere. The walls had been beautifully built. They made a solid, reliable border, from which I inferred with a sense of relief that everything was already divvied up. Two states, so joined, could be equivalent to states of being. I could leap from a granite boulder in Massachusetts and fall into a pile of leaves in New Hampshire. I could jump from a rock in New Hampshire and land on Massachusetts' snow. But the states were not the same, so how could I be the same person within them? Which one was the truer me? Another equally confusing game was to walk on top of the stone wall—the actual border—the way a gymnast negotiated a beam, toe to heel, arms out straight, eyes forward. Clearly, I couldn't be in two states at once, so where was I really?

In the northernmost corner of our land, two stone walls met at right angles and the New Hampshire state forest sloped off in two directions. There, an iron disk was hammered into the ground, a marker from a U.S. Geological Survey done in the 1930s, noting the elevation of that point above sea level. If I stood on top of it I knew I was at the highest point for miles around. It was also the furthest point north in central Massachusetts. But the fact that only a few steps away was New Hampshire tormented me beyond measure. It was thrilling to think that our farm was as far north as possible. To me that meant we were superior to the farms south of us. We were north, I thought, true north, and yet if I took a big leap I'd be on the furthest point south in New Hampshire. So what kind of north were we? North was supposed to be as high as you could go. North was the top of the map of the world in Mrs. Gionet's classroom, the top of the blackboard in Mr. Quimby's, the North Star was up. South was down, below, underneath, my teacher's slip was always "showing down south." South was the playground's term for hell.

My brother and sister and I would go out walking with my father on Sunday afternoons—past the brooder house, the rotting chicken-wire cage nailed between two saplings, the remnants of our treehouse that had, for a summer, been occupied by Nubbin, a wild raccoon, up the well-worn path past the rusting chassis of three abandoned Buicks, sumac growing through their rusting grilles, ivy pushing through the hoods, their windshields riddled with bullet holes made by a stranger who had shot them up for sport. We'd set out, intending to walk the entire parcel of land, but we never got that far. We always ended up clawing our way through tangled undergrowth and found ourselves surrounded by mountain laurel that twisted in upon itself and rose high over my father's head like a grove of women—grapes hung like clusters of beads at their throats and wrists, knotted their waists like sashes with bows. Sometimes the laurel was too dense for even the smallest of us to crawl through, so we would turn back the way we had come. The property itself had became a fragment of myth. We'd claim proudly to ourselves and to everyone else that we owned forty acres when there were actually thirty-eight. A kind of presumption lay in those two imaginary acres, a sense contrary to any documented fact, for if we traced the fields and woods on foot until we had walked from one end of the acreage to the other, there would be forty acres, we were sure of it. A farm with forty acres was more substantial, more worthy of attention, than a farm with thirty-eight.

Still, there was a troubling duality in the notion of boundaries. I liked knowing that what was ours could be circumscribed and separated from what was theirs, but on our white chicken farm at the end of a long rutted road, on top of an almost forgotten hill in a place called Townsend, we felt ourselves to be alone, the way asylums, prisons, and hospitals were once built above the towns that suffered to have them. Infection and stench would waft safely over the rooftops, borne away on breezes; the noises and torments of inmates and madmen would be lost among the rustling of leaves and the rumble of wagons going by. We were alone and apart because we were other than those who lived below us. We were contaminated in some way and dangerous to other people. An undiscovered contagion infected us, and though we were allowed to go to school, to church, to McNabb's drugstore, and Fred Tenney's haberdashery, it was only to visit and never to stay long. In turn, we were never visited except by the bravest, most intrepid travelers who were identified only by their professions, as if having them as friends would have made them too vulnerable, and so they always remained nameless—the mailman, the milkman, the bread man.

The mailman drove up the hill in a sand-colored beach

wagon, the driver's window permanently rolled down, drag-
ging his rackety muffler behind him. Whichever dogs we had
at the time—the collie-retrievers, the setters, the shepherds—
would race from the egg room where they liked to doze, past
the brooder house, the battered '41 Cadillac parked in the
woodshed, the rhododendrons and geraniums in front of the
cooperage to the mailbox by an elm tree at the foot of the
road. Madly barking and flagging their tails in greeting, one of
the dogs would mark his territory at the gatepost and another
would follow suit. I would run down behind them urgently,
wanting to be there in person to take the papers and magazines
directly from his hands.

The mailman always looked the same, winter or summer,
year after year. A few copper wisps of hair were combed over
his vast and densely freckled forehead. A Chesterfield with a
three-inch ash drooped from the corner of his mouth. He was
a red-haired gruff ambassador from town who slouched at the
wheel and spat into the weeds by the side of the road, but who
nonetheless pulled from his leather sack riches from the outside world: greetings, elections, changes in policy, news of
local dynasties falling, accidents, births, suicides, the home-
town scoreboard, the number of tractors in town, how many
dogs were vaccinated, how much money the Couples Club had
raised for the scholarship fund at their bridge party, how many
elms the tree warden saw shawled up in gypsy moths and
marked for death. It was reassuring to read the *Townsend Times*
every week; lives were going on elsewhere, out of our range.
The mailman brought them to us, if only in the pages of *Good
Housekeeping*, the *Ladies Home Journal*, and *Reader's Digest*—happy
families in beautiful houses; children who had adventures and
playmates; hard-working, sober fathers; women in bright, fash-
ionable clothes. It didn't matter that the mailman only grunted
in reply to my good morning; he looked me straight in the
eye. The sound of his tires turning in the gravel and the engine
sputtering down the road thrilled me as much as any applause.

As I walked up to the house with my arms full of advertise-
ments, newsprint, and bills, I felt, for a moment, that I
belonged to the human race.

I would always be in love with Roger St. Cyr, but the milkman was my first taste of a grown-up flirtation. He came on
Saturdays, and when I heard his white Dew More Farms truck
rumbling into the yard, I would fly from the ironing board and
clatter, blushing, out to the terrace in my clogs. The milkman
was a tall, dark, lantern-jawed fellow with Brylcreamed hair
straight from a forties' movie. I was eleven, my hair in a ponytail, and I had just finished reading *Pride and Prejudice, Wuthering
Heights,* and *Gone with the Wind.* It was impossible to imagine the
milkman's broad shoulders rammed into a velvet frock coat. I
couldn't see him doffing a fedora in a courteous bow either, so
I settled for thinking of him as an uncouth but charming
tradesman courting the kitchen maid, who threw insults back
at him with a knowing smile as she flounced to the scullery,
hair tumbling like a fountain from under her cap. I would shyly
take hold of the steel carrier's handle, rattling the six-quart
bottles with the cream on top, and when my knuckles brushed
against the milkman's hands I'd look boldly into his black eyes
until he said, with a lot of breath in his voice, "Tell me those
three little words." I would blush but could never reply. Once,
when he bent over to take the carrier of empties from me in
return for our week's order, he put his hand on my breast, still
sleeping beneath my undershirt, and I jumped like a scalded
cat, a carton of cottage cheese crashing open on the bricks. I
was punished in the kitchen for my clumsiness, but the following Saturday when he purred for those three little words, I said
to him as brazenly as I could, in a kind of triumph, "No—
cream—today!" After that I returned to ironing shirts, renewed,
because I'd feinted at courtship like a grown-up, thrusting a
clever reply. It was true it had taken me a week to think of it,
but everything was bound to get better with practice, even
flirting.

Ironing was the one chore I liked. It did not require lifting, stooping, or kneeling in the dirt, hauling or shoveling hen manure. Sprinkling tap water from a Moxie bottle tenderly onto the sleeves, across the breast pocket to the hip, from the shoulders to the wristbands, I would lovingly baptize each shirt and fold it in half, in half again, and roll it into a ball, even humming while I worked, until the table seemed lined with loaves of damp bread rising. I was happy ironing indoors where it was warm, and I was highly visible. As long as I kept rattling hangers I was safe. A cotton shirt took twenty minutes with the right amount of flourish, so a basket of them could take all afternoon.

As the hot tip of the iron passed over the collar of my Peter Pan blouse, I thought of the milkman with a strange kind of cricket chirring inside me. *Milk. Milk-white.* Starched. Crisp. Pristine. The well-blessed blouse of a good Catholic girl. *Milk. Milk-white.* The color of my soul without sin, no black marks on my clean white slate. *Milk-white teeth, his smile, as he stood on the running board.* I wish I could have touched his wrist. *Milk-white, his uniform and cap and truck.* His fields were heavy with white clover; his cows, black and white. His cows were clean. Their long-lashed eyes were kind; their hocks were white. His barns were white with green trim, clean white milk squirting into tin pails. *Milk-white. Milk-white. The land of milk and honey.* Somewhere there was a place without winter where children were wanted, where honey oozed from day-lilies' hearts and white milk from milkweed was wonderfully sweet. Somewhere there was a blizzard of manna, a soft white falling, a rain of sacred wafers where guardians of tranquility resided, where only sorrow sickened and died. *The milk of human kindness.* Men and women, not angels. A place where the savages were calmed, the dispossessed were taken in, where I would be held safely in someone's arms. There I would lay my head on a milk-white pillow and count the white candles in the Milky Way.

The bread man came on Tuesday in an old wood-paneled

roadster that coughed and heaved its way up the drive. The car braked hard and sputtered when he turned it off. He propped open the door with a sawed-off broom handle and leaned over the bounty in the back of his wagon. It was fragrant with the smells of a warm kitchen, laden like a feast table with bread, bagels, corn muffins, bran muffins, cupcakes, donuts, pies, macaroons, and homemade penuche with walnuts the size of dimes. He was a little man, bowed in one leg with a lift on one of his boots. He brought out the loaves as though each were a book of great value, piled them into my arms, and as I ran into the house to give them to my mother, I'd call over my shoulder, "*Merci, monsieur.*" He would always shut the trunk and cross the lawn with a sandwich wrapped in brown paper, then sit in the old Adirondack chair under the two big elms, take a handkerchief from his pocket, shake it open on his lap, and quietly begin to eat lunch. I would come from the kitchen with a large tumbler full of well water balanced in both hands and put it down on the flat arm of his chair.

"*Au revoir, monsieur,*" I'd say, with a dip I hoped he would think was a curtsy, and fly back into the breezeway where I could watch him from the shadowy screen door. The dogs came to lie at the bread man's feet. The geese gathered, murmuring in dialect. He ate thoughtfully, as if each morsel was a separate delicacy and he needed to consider the perfection in every bite, pausing only to break off a corner of the crust for each of the animals. He chewed slowly, dabbing a handkerchief at the ends of his pencil mustache, and his mind seemed miles away.

I knew he spoke French and very little English. How awful to be in a country where hardly anyone speaks your own language, I thought, how awful never to hear a syllable of the tongue you love. I said thank you and goodbye in French to make him feel more at home. If I were exiled from everything I knew and sent to a place where I never heard a word of English, I would die of loneliness.

Because we could not talk together, the only translator I had was my imagination: the bread man was the banished archduke of Pomerania who had lost his ancestral lands during the war. He'd been a cavalry officer, wounded at Herzegovina, and had a saber scar the length of his thigh. He was a widower. His children were grown. And as I watched from behind the cross-hatchings of the screen door, the banished archduke would fold up the brown paper, wipe his ,ands methodically on his handkerchief, and take out a leather-bound book to read for a while in the shade. What was he reading? Was it in French? Latin? Greek? Perhaps it was the Bible in his native tongue. I'd found a Bible once, in Finnish, among the remains of a house that had burned to the ground. The leather was charred at the edges and some of the pages bore the starry marks of still-smoldering ash that had settled on its pages in the last of the smoke. The pages were still ruffling open when I found it under the skeleton of a kitchen table. It made me cry—people had lost their home, perhaps their lives. Their most cherished possessions were left out in the rain, and the powerful, unknown words would outlive me.

I never saw a man read a book in the middle of the day, not my grandfather, father, or brother. Only my mother read, sequestered in her room, and only after she had finished her chores. I read at night under the covers with a flashlight. If my father caught me reading during the day, he'd slap the book out of my hands in a fury and say as a curse on my disposition, "If you had your way, you'd lie all day on your back in bed with a book eating bonbons!" It was true. Not only did I want to read all the books in the world, I wanted to write them. Seeing the bread man read in the middle of his workday as just another part of his life gave me the infinite if fleeting hope that someday I could read as much as I wanted. *And the archduke will escort me into his library for tea, ask me to sit beside him on the red brocade sofa, and let me choose my own book. He will tell me of Alexander and Caesar and Cleopatra. We will read Shakespeare together all afternoon, I*

will be Titania, Queen of the Fairies, or the beautiful Juliet. He will dab
the corners of his white mustache and the corner of one tearing eye, and he
won't think me lazy, selfish, stupid, or spoiled. And then I will write books.
My family must never discover my transfer of loyalties, I
thought. I'd be adopted by the archduke secretly and become
the bread man's only heir. Because I saw in code that bread was
the stuff of life, and that inside the word *bread* was the verb to
read, I had permission to write books because the word itself
said go and be-read. I knew that bread was the same as *pain* in
French and that *pain* was the same as pain, and in some way I
recognized that a pendulum swung between the life of bread
and water and the life of bread and wine.

It was Thanksgiving, and we were crying. We were beside ourselves with happiness. Company was coming and we wouldn't
be alone.

Sometimes when unexpected company came, I had just
enough time to peer out of the dark dining-room window to
see who it was before I ran upstairs to hide. I wouldn't come
down to say hello to anyone. I couldn't bear to be in a room
with strangers. Sometimes I couldn't even stand to be seen,
even by people I'd known for a long time. I always wanted the
rest of the family to say I was away or dead. I had the eerie
feeling that I had no skin, as if people from the outside who
came into the house and took one look at me could see at once
what was wrong with our family. I imagined their horrified
expressions—I had no skin, my brown-gristled heart was beating hard, there was a sickness in me, the marks of humiliation,
the scar tissue of despair. If I stayed out of sight, my family
would be spared disgrace. So when anyone came, I'd lie flat on
my stomach in my brother's room above the kitchen, where an
iron grate festooned with spider webs could be opened in the
floor, and the disembodied voices would rise with the smell of
beer and cigarettes and coffee and wool socks steaming on the
stove. I could hear their conversations and their arguments but

I was safely out of rifle-range. Occasionally, when someone asked about me, I was grateful that they'd remembered me at all and blushed to the roots of my hair, but I was thankful that I wasn't with them and didn't have to stammer a silly reply.

Thanksgiving, however, brought another kind of company, guests I cherished and whose visits sustained me throughout the year. Granny and Boppa arrived first, of course. Howard and Bunny—Aunt Maggie's dead husband's brother and his wife—usually came. Howard was also our dentist, whose hands shook badly when he worked and who had never heard of Novocaine, but he was soft-spoken, and his face smelled wonderfully of shaving soap and tobacco. His wife Bunny was the homeliest woman I'd ever seen. She was just my height and as wide as she was tall. She had one terrifying eyebrow like a scar across her forehead. Her face reminded me of a mushroom, but I loved her because she seemed to be the only truly happy person there. My brother's godparents, Rommie and John Nolan, and their children, Joycie and Bruce, came sometimes. Rommie was glamorous, usually dressed in sweeping red and black, drenched in Intimate perfume, wearing a fascinating scarab bracelet with necklace and earrings to match. John tickled and teased us unmercifully, and was given to loud, boisterous laughter at his own jokes. Joycie and Bruce were close to me in age, but curiously set apart and envied because they were adopted. Marge Sower and her spinster sister Kate often had Thanksgiving with us. They were potters who lived just over the line in Mason, New Hampshire, and had no family of their own. Sometimes one or both of Mama's white-haired widower uncles came up from Fall River—red-cheeked, jolly Uncle Mike who looked like a Christmas leprechaun, and crabby, opinionated Uncle Frank, who could stuff his entire earlobe inside his ear and make it pop out magically when we clapped our hands. Once in a while a guest would bring an unexpected cousin or neighbor or maiden aunt I'd never met. But I would not let myself be afraid, because it was Thanksgiving.

All week at school we made construction-paper Pilgrims and horns of plenty with pumpkins, apples, and grapes spilling out until everything tasted like paste. We brought home brass-colored paper buckles fastened over our shoes with rubber bands and turkeys whose elaborate tails looked like an Indian headdress. All the feathers seemed cut from sheets of autumn, from leaves that turned gold and red, leaves that had blown down from the trees all fall until someone raked them up from the schoolyard and stacked them in Mrs. O'Donnell's art closet. At home we hung our decorations from the kitchen mantel over the chimney bricks with Scotch tape. All over America, children were hanging up their Thanksgiving Day greetings, and so were we.

Every year, like a play, I divided Thanksgiving Day into three beautiful acts: setting the table and waiting excitedly for the first cars to arrive; the dinner itself, as complex and stirring as Mass; and washing the dishes before we said goodbye. On Thanksgiving we opened the doors to the dining room to let in the warmth that came from the kitchen's wood stove. We only used the dining room on Thanksgiving and Christmas. It was closed up the rest of the year because it had no heat. In a shallow wooden bowl on the trestle table, I'd arrange all the things I'd been gathering for the centerpiece: two gourds, an acorn squash, three big pine cones, walnuts, filberts, sprigs of princess pine, and stems of bittersweet I'd found growing near the old Chevy parked behind the brooder house. I put out the brass candlesticks with two new candles the color of beeswax. I counted the number of guests we were expecting and added one place for someone who might wander in at the last minute. I laid down place mats and napkins at each Windsor chair and down the length of the spindled bench under the windows where the children always ate that some relative had stolen from a stagecoach waiting room. Beside every plate was a dinner fork, a dessert fork, a knife, and two spoons. Above each knife-point stood a water or wine glass. On Thanksgiving and

Christmas, my brother and sister and I drank from the hand-made clay mugs with our names drawn on them made by the potters, Marge and Kate, whom Granny called the Gish girls, after the silent-movie stars.

In the kitchen we laid out more pottery dishes for green and black olives, pickles, raw carrots, and celery stuffed with cream cheese. There were toffees, dates stuffed with peanut butter and rolled in powdered sugar, figs, tangerines, grapes and red apples, walnuts in the shell, and the Revolutionary War soldier nutcracker. I dusted off the cut-glass in the shape of a leaf for the cranberry sauce. I found the gravy boat and silver ladle. I fanned out the serving things by my mother's place, then filled the little glass saltcellars, each with their own ivory spoon. I cut butter into pats and stamped each of them with a wooden mallet that had a single star cut out beside a quarter-moon. I folded some index cards in half and trimmed them with the pinking shears, writing out name cards in my most elaborate and perfect handwriting for everyone at their usual places. Light flooded the snowy fields and filtered into the room through the organdy curtains and the original violet-tinted panes, the sunlight reflecting off the snowbanks, shining through the golds and blues of old whiskey flasks and elixir bottles set on the sills for color. Every year the dining room looked more beautiful to me. Our house was a palace for the day and everyone in it was a royal guest.

When the intoxicating moment arrived, I ran out leaping into the yard with my brother and sister and all of the dogs. We came up to each car, tears pouring down our faces, and flung open the doors. We were crying with relief, with happiness, because it wasn't an ordinary day; we were so glad to see people. If only for a little while, our family would be different than it was, and we would not be alone. On Thanksgiving we would be fed and fussed over, and when we gathered together for the Lord's blessing, we even believed we could be saved. The back door opened, and the clean cold air rushed in and all the windows steamed up with happiness. Husbands slipped wives out of coats—men with glasses and suspenders that held up their big gray pants—women trilling with laughter, clouds of perfume, and rustling petticoats, their faces bright with lipstick and rouge, hugging and kissing us, leaving prints of their bright red lips on our cheeks. We trundled off armloads of coats to the hall closet, where I would stand on a step stool so I could reach, one by one, the coats as they were handed up to me, some too heavy to lift as high as the rod. I buried my face in fur collars and scarves, and drank in the smells of toilet soap, cigars, of D'jer Kiss dusting powder, and Halo shampoo. I heard ice cubes tumbling into the ice bucket, the clatter of glasses, and my father making his famous Old-Fashioneds. The sweet aroma of oranges and angostura bitters drifted over the kitchen, weaving an invisible wreath around the basting turkey, biscuits, mince pie, and chatter, wafting us finally into the dining room. My father would carry in the turkey and begin carving. Each of the guests brought in a serving dish. My mother lit the candles, the charms on her heavy silver bracelet tinkling toward and away from the flame. Everyone talked at once as they found their seats.

The plates were passed around the table to the person on the left, and soon all the guests were sitting before turkey and dressing, mashed potatoes and gravy, cranberry and biscuits. Onto every plate I scooped green peas and baby onions, as if each were a serving of emeralds and pearls. There was a peaceful moment when the plates were filled, throats were cleared, and the candles flickered as we bowed our heads to pray. Then my brother stood up to say grace. *Bless us, O Lord, and these Thy gifts which we are about to receive from Thy bounty and thank You for letting us all be here today.* My eyes stung and a tear slid down my cheek. *And let us all be together again next year.* The knife blade of the blessing cut as deeply as the knife into the turkey, to the bone. *Please, God,* I clenched my hands together, *we are a family today, like other families. Please keep us this way forever.* In unison we sighed a deep *amen* and picked up our forks to eat. Across the table my grandfather spoke kindly to Flap, my two grandmothers chatted like old friends, and at the head and the foot of the table my father and mother raised their glasses and drank, contentment and truce settling into the silent pleasure of eating. The three of us children ate quietly, with perfect manners. We basked in the warmth of their laughter, our squabbling ceased, and the grown-ups in their party clothes traded stories like baseball cards. Who were these people who seemed so at home here, women with golden smiles, men with waxed mustaches, their shirts fastened with collar buttons and ties? They were like figures in a mirage, shimmering in the candlelight like palm trees gently beckoning. If I suddenly clapped my hands, I half-expected them to disappear or fly into my face like Alice's pack of cards. But the meal went on without interruption. People genially offered one another seconds, some politely accepting, others refusing. I was so happy my heart was racing.

When my mother nodded to me, I scraped back my chair and began to clear the table, piling all the plates, silver, and serving dishes on the kitchen counter. I went into the pantry and reached up to the nail where an apron was hanging and tied it around my neck like a surgeon about to operate. My brother and sister and I walked back and forth between the dining-room table and the kitchen sink, bringing in more dishes, while my father poured his jewel-colored liqueurs into tiny goblets. My mother cut the apple, mince, and pumpkin chiffon pies and poured coffee from the big silver coffeepot into the best cups, nesting in their matching saucers on the pine blanket chest that we used instead of a sideboard. My sister crawled onto my mother's lap, my brother crept into the empty chair beside Aunt Rommie with her beautiful scarlet fingernails, and I coughed down a bit of liqueur that tasted like licorice when no one was watching. While everyone laughed and the talking grew louder, I picked over the plates in the kitchen, dividing the scraps of meat, skin, and fat for the dogs, making sure to remove all the bones. I filled a bowl with vegetable peelings, squash seeds, apple skins, and scrapings for Rosita and put coffee grounds, bones, and eggshells into a coffee can for the compost heap in the barn cellar. I filled up the sink with hot soapy water and started washing the dishes, wanting the meal to go on and on, begging the day to never end. I rinsed the plates and silverware, listening to a grown-up joke I didn't understand, and when the laughter came, I felt deceived by being too young and too old at the same time. I wanted to know why it was so funny, I wanted them to explain it to me, but I knew the day would come when I'd understand the joke, and all this would seem so far away. I wanted that day to be now and I wanted that day to be never.

Soon the Windsor chairs scraped back from the table. I heard the hall closet open and the sounds of coats being shaken and put on. I dried my hands on the dish towel and became engulfed in hugs of goodbye. But their departure was more than I could bear. I put on my boots, jacket, scarf, and mittens and followed the guests outside. It was almost dusk, we could see our breath, and the white fields were already sleeping. We stood by the cars, waving our hands and crying because the wonderful day was nearly over and we were waving them down the road. We ran and climbed the stone wall to listen to their tires creaking on the frozen pavement by the mailbox. We stood stock-still in our Sunday clothes on the stone wall under the rain-black elms and shouted goodbye to the company, goodbye to the disappearing brake lights, our shouted goodbyes wafting over the snow fence across Rossbach's field to St. Cyr's barn, toward the white steeple of the Methodist church in the valley until we heard the ricochet of our voices over the Squanicook River, goodbye, until each of our cries came back to us, hollow, faint, and for a fleeting moment it seemed that other children were calling back to us. A few flakes salted the air, the sky turned to tungsten, and we lay down to make angels in the snow. I thought of Squanto, the Pawtuxet, who taught the Pilgrims how to sow the best crops. He'd lay three silver herrings onto each turned hillock to help the seed corn sprinkled over them to grow, and the little fish, nose to nose with their tails fanning out, would stay there all winter under the snow. As I lay there making my wings, I thought, *What a long, long time we have to wait.*

"Shirt-sleeves to shirt-sleeves in three generations, that's what always happens," my mother said with conviction, handing me the colander. "The bush beans must be ready by now. Bring me a dozen ears of corn and a couple of tomatoes and a cuke, if there are any."

Mama had made that shirt-sleeve remark before. I guessed that she meant old Mr. Green, Boppa's father, had come from Ireland with only the clothes on his back and made a fortune which his seven children had squandered, bickered over, wasted, and now my father, the third generation, was working with his hands again as a farmer because the money was gone.

Mama opened the Spam with its little key, the silver cover rolling back in a tube revealing the congealed block of pink marble larded with white. She shook it out of the can, scraping off the jelly with the only sharp knife we had in the house, a thin paring dagger with a black wooden handle that one of the dogs had taken and chewed on under the porch. I stared at the Spam as she sliced it. It would feed all eight of us if she cut it sparingly and fried it with onions and peppers. It was disgusting, anyway you looked at it. I wasn't going to touch it with a four-hundred-eighty-foot pole.

"What are you standing there for? Go, go, your father will be in any minute." Sunday dinner always had to be served at one o'clock or there was hell to pay.

The screen door slammed behind me, and I ran for the garden, ducking under the clothesline as I went. Thank God we could grow real food, I thought, tearing off the yellow beans

GLASS   *109*

and tossing them into the colander. Most of them were young
enough that I didn't have to string them. The dirt was hot and
dry under my bare feet as I squatted, batting away horseflies
that spun around my head. Beets and beet greens were my
favorite, followed by Swiss chard and brussels sprouts. No,
peas were the best, but they were gone by. No, I decided,
sitting between the rows to shuck the corn, the best things
were the Kentucky Wonders: sweet, green, raw, juicy pole
beans hung among the vines twining like ivy up the sumac
saplings that Flap had pounded weeks ago into the muddy
spring ground. Every summer I ate my weight's worth of Kentucky Wonders while I picked other things for supper. I'd
crunch into one while I pulled the silken hair from the corn,
chewing the bean thoughtfully like a cigar. The golden corn
silk was smooth and full of light—the hair of a fairy princess
that I used to leave overnight on the window sill of the breezeway, intending to sew it into a shining wig for my doll. But the
next day, still wet with dew, it would be shriveled and brown
and I'd throw it away, crying because it had turned into garbage. It made me furious that everything had to rot.

I rested the full colander on my hip and set down the pail
of corn under the pear tree. The syrupy late summer air was
full of bees. Rosita stood under the apple tree, flicking off flies
with her tail. I toed one of the fat ripe pears, looking for wasps
drowning in ecstasy on the juicy underside just waiting to sting
me, then brought it over to her. Her tired half-bray was pitiful.
Her graying velvet lips took the fruit gratefully, and I cleaned
the flies away from her eyes as she chewed. In the driveway I
could see my grandfather, father, and brother, standing around
the Buick and the Chevy with the hoods up, doing what they
did every weekend—argue, holler, swear, and try to fix whatever was wrong with the cars.

Richard Winthrop Green, my grandfather, was called Dick.
Richard Winthrop Green, Jr., my father, was called Richie.
Richard Winthrop Green III, my brother, was called Rick. It

wasn't confusing to us, only to strangers who occasionally rang the phone at the farm and seemed bewildered to find out that there was more than one Richard Green, casting doubt onto their certainty about which Richard they wanted and even their reason for calling.

It seemed perfectly reasonable to us that there should be three of them. They worked in tandem, like men on a chain gang, each one tied so closely to the other that a sudden movement in one would cause pain in another somewhere down the line. They always spent Saturdays tinkering with the cars, tools thrown down when they weren't being used, oil-stained rags hanging out of their work pants, the three of them discussing the problem like greasy surgeons about to perform a tonsillectomy. My grandfather, the foreman of the crew, was the tallest with white hair, spectacles, and a plaid flannel shirt, the elbows always out, and khakis with holes in the knees. He was never wrong. My father, who was never right, was dressed in the same kind of shabby uniform, though shorter, dark-haired, slender, constantly smoking a cigarillo, and nervously pacing toward and away from my grandfather's voice. My brother, a tow-headed, curly-haired boy, shirtless, in madras shorts and sneakers, stood silently scratching himself, listening to their diagnoses and disagreements, seeming to be thinking through the problem on his own.

Today was no different. Boppa let go with a string of curses and pointed his finger into the bowels of the engine. Daddy bellowed at Boppa, tossed down a wrench, and kicked the grille in a fury, then turned his back on his father and cuffed my brother on the ear, just because he was there. My brother quietly moved away to the old wooden stairs that led to the shed chamber over the woodshed and sat in the shade of the trumpet vine, waiting for the fire to die down. After more volleys of hollering, my father slammed into the house in a huff, opened a beer, and was gone for the rest of the afternoon.

But I knew from having watched before that Boppa and

Ricky would continue to work on the cars and fix whatever
was gasping or grinding or creaking. Boppa was very patient
with my brother, in a way he could not be with his own son.
He explained things like an engineer, let Rick try things himself, but when the boy did something awkward or backward,
Boppa never criticized him or raised his voice. He simply
explained it all again, showing him how to fix the problem
with his own large white hands. Then my grandfather would
reach out with affection and ruffle the boy's yellow hair.

Boppa was very kind to my sister too. He cuddled her, called
her Katie, which no one else did, and in his own blunt, blus-
tering way, tried to make up for Granny's rigid, irrational
hatred of my sister. Granny, my mother, my sister, and I were
also in tandem, but there was never an unexpected reprieve
from the hidden fury. Granny would arrive at the farm and
smother me with kisses and hugs, sneaking me two forbidden
rolls of Necco wafers and two packs of gum, and then would
walk past my sister into the house as if she were one of the
dogs wagging hopefully at the door. I thought that Granny
and my mother despised each other, that maybe they were
fighting over my father but couldn't bring themselves to yell
out loud about it. So Granny took possession of me and Mama
took possession of Kathy, and they pitted us against each other
in their stead. Later, as we got ready for bed, my sister would
attack me like a savage and I would fight back in kind—
scratching, kicking, biting, screaming, pulling her hair—until
we were broken apart by my father, walloped, and all our
strength and madness was spent. *It's not my fault I'm Granny's pet,*
I would plead silently in my bed. *I didn't ask to be her favorite.* But
I felt guilty, guilty, guilty. I could never make up for Granny's
meanness. In the end, my sister rolled over on her side, and I
felt her turn her back to me for the rest of our lives. I pictured
a huge chasm with Granny and me on one side and my mother
and sister on the other, the grown-ups flinging us, white-
limbed, across the canyon like a couple of alley cats who clung

and scratched and bit for their very existence. We were plummeting through space, half-clinging to and tearing at flesh to
get away from the falling, torn body of the other. I thanked
Almighty Christ that it was time for sleep. In sleep I could
pretend that I was not a pariah. I could forget that Mama and
Kathy blamed me for Granny's cruelty. I could pretend that I
didn't hate my sister for hating me.

Dinner was ready. Boppa always took Daddy's place at the
head of the table, Granny was in Mama's place, and the three
kids on the bench under the window with Daddy, Mama, and
Flap across from us on chairs that were brought in from the
dining room. We passed the food in silence. In vain I looked
for the smallest piece of Spam, slathered with green peppers
and onions, but they were exactly the same size. It didn't matter, because I would slip it to my brother when no one was
looking. We weren't allowed to have a drink with any meal.
Daddy thought that we'd "swig" our milk first and not eat our
food. Meals went down like sawdust with nothing to wash it
down, but it was the way we did things. Milk was rationed out
in little jelly glasses as we stood at the sink after we finished
eating.

There were only two subjects of conversation at the table.
No one talked about books, because only Mama and I read.
No one talked about politics, because no one gave a damn. No
one talked about religion, because we didn't believe in anything but the Greens and the rest of the bastardly world
existing solely to cheat us. The only two subjects of impor-
tance were money and cars. I ground my teeth loudly in disgust, sick of hearing about carburetors, gaskets, universal
joints, and chokes. I slammed down my shredded ear of corn,
laughing to myself because I'd chewed it from end to end, row
by row, and silently "dinged" at the end of each row, as though
it were a typewriter. I was still going to be a writer, if I ever
got out of here alive.

Granny always started on money, how much things cost at

the market these days, how she'd "jewed" somebody down for
some old piece of furniture, how she'd saved thirty cents here
and a dollar and a half there, and what a virtuous thing it was
to buy day-old bread and donuts. The Greens never invested
money or spent it, they squirreled away every nickel. They
hoarded it, getting more pleasure from seeing the pennies turn
into dollars than they ever had from buying something they
needed. So they did without rather than spend a dime, used
duct tape and baling wire to fix things rather than go to a
hardware store and replace a worn part. Everything looked
ugly—bolted and hammered and jerry-rigged—but became a
masterpiece of ingenuity because it hadn't cost a cent to repair.
Granny hoarded food the same way. She got more satisfaction
from seeing fifteen cans of tomato soup and corned-beef hash
stacked frugally on the pantry shelf than she ever would by
eating any of it. Cans would bulge and sometimes burst
because she had saved them too long. I knew about the
Depression, that people were still afraid, but what was the
point of saving something so long it spoiled?

There was one other subject at the table, but it was discussed
without words—a complex conversation of superior sniffs,
hard looks, and a hierarchy of rudeness. It reminded me of
chickens quarreling in the dooryard of the henhouse—one hen
would peck the tail feathers of the one next to it, then that hen
would turn and fiercely attack another, and so on. There was a
rigid and mysterious system to their viciousness that I never
understood and always one wretched, exhausted hen at the
bottom of the ranks, the bloodiest, who'd been torn apart by
the rest of the flock because it was weaker or smaller or crip-
pled. It was a conversation about drinking, though the word
was never spoken.

Granny didn't touch alcohol, so she considered herself
beyond reproach in that and all other things. Boppa used to
drink, had once been violent and abusive, and gave it up only
when the doctors said that another drink would kill him. Mama

drank quietly in her room at night, convinced that no one knew, yet sniffed her silent, martyred criticism at my father, who drank every day after work in plain sight and was a dangerous, frightening drunk. Meanwhile, Daddy bitched constantly about Flap, who hitched rides downtown, got shit-faced in public, was forever being robbed by his so-called drinking buddies, and then would weave his way home in the morning, still drunk, to sleep it off for the rest of the day.

Granny never believed that my father drank, only that he was sensitive and nervous and had to be treated with kid gloves. Mama believed that her secret was safe and would have been mortified to know that from the time I could walk, when Saturday morning moved toward noon and she hadn't appeared, my father, reeling from the night before, would bark at me, "For Chrissake, go see if your mother's still breathing." My heart in my mouth, I would lift the latch quietly, say a quick panicked prayer at the threshold, and go into the room, my blood thumping with the fear that she really might be dead. I'd stand over her crumpled body, listening, begging God to let her breathe. After minutes of waiting, not daring to believe that she could be dead, I'd be in tears. Finally, she'd open her rosebud mouth and emit a long staircase of loud crude snores. And so denial and self-delusion propagated the myth that the only drunk in our family was Flap. He made a spectacle of himself, he lost all his money, he drank in taverns and even went to jail once. He was a disgrace. The rest of them were pure as the driven snow. I loved Flap. They were all wrong, about everything.

Boppa's chair scraped back, signaling that the meal was over.

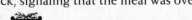

I had not thought of Albert Ferry or the field mouse or the well on the farm in thirty years until one night I saw them all in a dream. The well was just as I remembered it, abandoned under the pine trees at the top of the hill between the oxen road and a breach in the stone wall where there once was a barway

between pastures. My great-great-grandfather and his brothers
had built the wall, dug the well, and cleared the road with oxen
one hundred years earlier. Then in the decade after the Second
World War, the well ran dry and was boarded over in the
brambles and long cool grass. When my father took my
brother, my sister, and me walking through the woods, we
passed by it on our way to the fields where the flowers grew
wild—tall velvet shafts of pussy willow in spring, black-eyed
Susans, Queen Anne's lace, summer daisies, and purple star
asters in the fall—and we would pick a bouquet for my mother
who loved flowers but would never walk with us. Our arms
full, we retraced our steps the long way back along the curving
path, spattered with afternoon sun and shade like the green
and gold marbleized paper inside of old books, until we could
see the tin and red tar-paper roof of the brooder house and
knew we were almost home.

An old man named Albert Ferry who had a white beard that
hung to his belt buckle got me thinking about wells in the first
place. Albert lived in one room of an unpainted farmhouse
on the other side of Bayberry Hill, where he kept stacks of
newspapers, a fire going all summer, and hadn't washed or
opened a window in fifty years. Granny and I visited there
during my childhood, often enough for me to remember one
leprous scrap of masthead stuffed between the window frame
and the unpainted sill overlooking a sugar orchard. I couldn't
read it at first, but I always tested myself, hoping by some
miracle that someday the letters would become words I could
understand. It was years before I could spell out in triumph
Ashby, Massachusetts, April 12, 1904. And each time we returned,
I saw with delight that it said the same thing, as if Albert were
Father Time himself and the same sunlight would be blazing
on his window sill for eternity.

One drowsy afternoon I was stretched out on the bare floor
next to Albert's white-whiskered dog who couldn't bark but
who hadn't stopped snoring the whole time we'd been there.

I'd been leaning on my elbows for hours, my tongue between
my lips, drawing a picture of Albert in his soot-stained winter
underwear and suspenders, listening to him talk to Granny
about old man Fessenden and the Fessenden Mill, the Stewart
sisters, Bessie and Sadie, the hospitality of the Finns, and the
way the town was going to hell in a hand-basket, things that
had happened long before I was born. I listened intently
because it was all so interesting. I drew dark lines in Albert's
cheeks. He had a face like a mountain, chiseled out of granite,
but his beard was as soft and shining as a young girl's hair. I
drew in the checks of his flannel shirt and imagined teams of
horses with gleaming harnesses jauntily pulling carriages or
lumbering with wagonloads of feed down Main Street under
the elm trees and women in long dresses and large plumed hats
walking up the steps of the Congregational church. I had just
figured out how to turn my pencil on its side and sketch the
pipe smoke that was wreathing Albert's head in gentle circles
and was concentrating on drawing the toe of his boot when I
realized that Granny had been calling me for some time. I
looked up guiltily. Granny gathered up her carpetbag and
petal-soft cardigan and said it was time for us to go.

Albert rarely addressed me and never by name—even
Albert's dog didn't have a name—but once in a great while he
would call me *my girl.* That day, he motioned me over to the
armrest of his chair and made me bend down so he could whisper something in my ear. I smelled his tobacco and the
cooped-up-all-winter odor of his body, and bent close enough
to see the curly white hairs growing out of his ears and feel his
soft beard-end brushing my cheek. His voice was like gravel.

"You know where to find fairies, don't you?" he whispered,
and my mouth fell open in astonishment. In shock, I shook my
head.

"They go where it's cool and wet, y'know, especially near
old wells." He winked at me and I knew he was speaking the
truth. As we drove out of the yard, I looked back at Albert

through the Chevy's lozenge-shaped window. He was sitting on the granite step scratching the dog's ears, and the white-whiskered dog yawned as if to say, *All that stuff about fairies is pretty commonplace, if you ask me.* I don't remember if Albert ever said a word to me again.

The next Sunday my father took my brother and sister and me walking to the top of the hill. I dragged my feet and let the others go ahead, pretending to be inspecting some fungus that grew on the underside of an elm that had fallen over during the winter. How would I know if I found fairy tracks? It was cool and shady near the stone wall as I sat on the old boards covering the well. A few leaves had fallen across them. The wind lifted in a percussive symphony and rained pine-tree needles over my head. The day was very bright; the voices of my father and brother and sister were growing fainter as they rounded the curve. I sat very still, waiting for fairies.

Then I peeked through the cracks of the old boards—nothing but darkness and a cool clean smell. I pushed them apart and they moved away easily until there was room enough for me to put my whole head through the gap and look down. Bright green moss grew on the rocks at the lip of the well, softer than velvet. My eyes followed the curve of the black rocks around the well's circumference like a circular staircase that I had to step down carefully so I wouldn't miss my footing and fall. At the bottom where it was darkest I saw a glint of light—there must be water in the well after all. I saw a shadow of myself staring back at me with clouds passing swiftly overhead. I leaned forward for a closer look and heard a silvery tinkle of something, metal on stone, and under my left hand I found the end of a rusty chain pinned to the lip of the well with a kind of hasp. I picked up one of the links, heard an answering jingle and a splash echo from far away. There was something attached to the chain, something a bit heavy. I pulled hand over hand, the weight moved into the light, and I saw it was a pail, a pail of tin, with water in it. I drew it up within an arm's length and saw a field mouse, bloated and half-submerged, floating on the surface of the greenish water. I knew field mice always pulled the fairies' tiniest coaches. I felt sad for the mouse and reached into the bucket to take him out and bury him in dry ground when the pail went sailing out of my hand and I was taken by the shoulders, slapped, and shaken hard.

My father stood above me in a white fury. His head seemed to be in the branches of the pine tree. Out of the corner of my eye, I saw his huge hand moving toward me in slow motion like a scythe. I flinched as the force of his wrath landed on my face, then curled up like a comma in the grass.

"Don't you ever," he huffed, "let me catch you," kicking me on my back, "near this well again!" kicking me twice.

I didn't make a sound. Crying only made him madder.

"You could fall in there and drown and no one would ever know what happened to you," he snapped. He took me roughly by the arm and dragged me to my feet, shaking me all the while. "Stay away from the goddamned well, all of you," he said, turning to my brother and sister who stood behind him on the path, wide-eyed, their arms full of goldenrod.

I swallowed hard and stood up straight, clearing my throat, and hoping to mollify him, offered him the word of another adult.

"But Albert says there's . . ." I began. My father slapped me again.

"That goddamned old fool is crazy!" he roared, and the little kids dropped their flowers and ran down the path away from us. "Come on! We're going home."

As we walked past the brooder house in punishing silence, I thought about the well. The well was a dangerous place. I could have fallen in and drowned and never be found by anyone. The well was magic, but there was no magic. A field mouse had drowned and field mice always pulled the fairies' carriages. But there must be fairies, I thought. My father never spoke about the well again.

I had not thought about Albert or the field mouse or the well until one night I saw them all in a dream. It was summer, the crickets were conversing at a fever pitch, and I was walking barefoot in a long skirt up the turning of the path, thinking of the warm sun as I neared the barway between the stone walls and the well. A field mouse darted through the grass. A man stepped out from behind some hedge-high blueberry bushes: it was Albert Ferry in a flannel shirt and dungarees, the cuffs of his long underwear showing above his boots. He seemed to know I was coming. He motioned me closer, and in his voice like gravel, he said, as a kind of gentle command, "Look into the well, my girl."

I had to move the boards so I could see. Nothing smelled damp now, no hint of mildew or moldering leaves. The well was warm and dry. I lifted the boards, and a white light shone up from the bottom, where every shade of color in the world lay in a kaleidoscope, fractured, mirrored, and protean, glimmering just beneath the water's surface, and the walls of the well were not made of black stones but of brilliantly cut, infinitely faceted diamonds. Under my right hand was a rope of gold braided with silver. I drew on the rope, hand over hand, and the pulling was effortless. The weight at the end of the rope came easily into my arms—a crystal bucket full of rubies.

Albert's voice was clear water running through a culvert.

"What do you see there, my girl?" he asked.

I reached into the pail and the jewels sifted through my fingers like sand. "Rubies big as cherries," I said, "round as satin Christmas balls, red as an August watermelon, red the color of . . ."

Albert waited for me to go on.

"Red the color of . . . blood."

Suddenly I saw the farm, and myself at two sitting in the sun in my jump chair at the end of the porch. Geraniums were all around me—in wicker baskets, in stone pots—and my mother was standing in a strawberry-colored sun dress, pressing the dirt around the flowers she was planting in the window box by the back door. She pulled up a bouquet of wilted blossoms out of the dirt and tossed it onto the bricks. It was Decoration Day. We were going to see the parade, to watch the soldiers march to the old stone bridge in West Townsend and shoot off their guns. One of them would play a trumpet over the Squanicook. A man and a woman sitting in a white rowboat would drop petals over the side into the water. Then we would plant geraniums at some of the graves.

I squinted up at the sun through the red maple's leaves and heard my father come outside, his voice angry and dark. He stumbled toward my mother in a rage, but she, answering quietly, kept planting geraniums. He yelled again and he hit her. She made a mewing sound and fell onto the porch, a trefoil of blood splashing from her nose onto my white baby shoes. I cried out in pain, pointing to the dead geranium blossoms, the color of rubies, reflecting the light at his feet like blood.

I looked at Albert and he nodded. I poured the bucket of rubies into a running fire over the ground. Leaping into the culvert, ropes of flame sped through the undergrowth, racing downhill toward the farm. And then the little fires began to flicker and each flame darkened to an ember, each red coal cooled becoming a stone flecked with mica, a stone with a heart of quartz.

Albert nodded again. I lowered the crystal bucket into the well once more and drew up a pail of sapphires—bright April blue lapis lazuli, teal, and turquoise, sapphires the color of clouds, the color of smoke, of iris, of starlight, of madonna-blue delphiniums, cornflowers, and the violet-blue wisteria that used to hang from the porch.

I remember a white letter carved on a blue block and the fragment of a sing-song rhyme: *B is for blue, B is for block, B is for Bridget gone for a walk.* I was two and a half in a navy pinafore with white smocking, sitting in my playpen in the living room, peeping between the bars. I was playing with blocks, singing an alphabet song. There was sunlight on my dress. White curtains were blowing at the window. Outside the trees were gold. My father came into the room and sat heavily in his chair. I tried to play peek-a-boo with him, but he coughed and wheezed and would not play with me. He'd been stung by a bee. His wheezing grew loud, and he began to cry. I dropped my block. His face was turning blue. His face was swelling, even the tongue in his mouth was turning blue. And the blue man slid slowly out of his chair.

The room was filled with shouting. Men were calling his name, men were lifting him from the floor and carrying the blue man out to the kitchen. They laid him on the table. He did not move. My mother held my little brother in her arms. She'd been roasting pork. It was Sunday, and the firemen were in the kitchen shouting. The blue man would not answer. One of his feet was bare. He'd been stung by a bee. He was dying. They were putting a mask over his face, trying to make him breathe. He would not breathe. He would not breathe. Then he began breathing.

I was standing upstairs in the doorway of my father's room. He was lying on his side with his face to the wall. The shades in his room had been drawn, the window closed. The gray-blue light of twilight shrouded the room. Tears were rolling down his cheeks but he did not make a sound. He did not know I was there. There were dust motes dancing in his water glass. He wouldn't get up. He did not answer me when I called his name.

I took a deep breath and sapphires rushed from the pail like a blue waterfall flung from the top of a gorge. They crashed together like rocks in a tidal pool, each bit of blue twittering, growing the wings of indigo buntings, singing and flying into the trees.

Albert and I nodded together, and I drew a pail of yellow diamonds from the well—yellow with lion-colored light and sulphur medallions on a green field, the honey-colored air of afternoons in late summer, pale like pond lilies, the bright gold

of buttercups, jonquils, sunflowers. The diamonds sifted
through my hands like corn, like sand, like petals falling from
forsythia.

I remember wearing a yellow apron, gold like the sun. I was
so small that I could still walk under the kitchen table without
ducking my head, and laughing I peered out at my mother
from under the green-and-white-checked oilcloth. She wore
quilted potholders like mittens on each of her hands as she
bent down to pull an unheard-of treat from the belly of the
cast-iron wood stove. The aroma steamed up the windows of
the butter-yellow kitchen and filled the room with cinnamon,
allspice, and clove—my first baked apple. It smelled so good.
I sat at the table and there on my plate was a shriveled lump,
a wrinkled oozing. Steam drifted into my nostrils and a cry of
disappointment rose to my mouth. Where was Snow White's
apple, so perfectly red, so sweet and cold and crisp inside?
Where had my beautiful apple gone?

I wailed and stormed and would not touch it. I hated it. It
was ugly. It had changed beyond recognition. I sat at the window, sobbing, holding Sycamore, my yellow stuffed dog. The
sky was dark; it was snowing, flakes turning gold as they fell
through the light. I was sobbing because Daddy had been
stung by a bee. He lay on his bed and would not get up. Someone had called me honey and said it was because my name
meant bee. Bees made honey but they stung. And now it was
winter and Daddy wasn't coming back. He had gone to Florida,
and I was to blame. Frost flowers were growing on the windowpanes, curling like ferns, yellow in the glow of the little Christmas candle that we'd put in the window, a light so he could
find his way home through the snow.

The dream-snow dissolved. I held the bucket of diamonds
high in the air and flung them in a bright arc above my head.
The flakes of diamonds rose, quiet as snowfall, turning and
turning past the tops of the trees until they reached the sky,
each one like a candle flame finding its place in the constella-

tions, flickering petal by petal into the stars that would always light my way.

I dropped down the crystal bucket and drew up a pail of amethysts—purple and violet and mauve, the color of laven-der, lilac, azaleas, the deeper shades of gloxinia, petunias, some as big around as grapes, dark as plums. One was a bright magenta-blue, a color I always loved. It was the shade of Mama's best dress, a matching skirt and sweater that she often wore to parties with a twinkling charm bracelet and my favor-ite silver pin on one side of her purple chest in the shape of a horse's head, his carved mane like a helmet. *Purple, purple, purple,* the way the coffee sounded in the percolator as she dressed, *purple, purple,* like the flecks in her opal birthstone. She sprayed perfume on her throat, some on mine, and powdered my nose with a laugh. She was always happy when she was going out. I liked to see her so happy but I wished she would stay. I looked in the mirror at us. I was wearing her opal like a cross on a chain, I smelled of Bond Street and for a moment I believed I was beautiful, too.

I remember it was after supper. Mama had gone out and left us. Daddy was snoring, asleep in his chair in front of the TV, and I was coloring at the kitchen table. I hadn't learned to stay within the lines yet, but I knew all my crayons by heart. I had picked out my favorite colors for the day, and they were all in the family called Purple. It seemed funny that purple could be so close to red in one crayon, and so much like blue in another. Some purples were dark, others so light you might mistake them for gray. I drew a purple horse with purple reins and a bright pink saddle. I had looked at so much purple, my eyes were playing tricks, and I thought that even the color of the light coming across the fields and into the kitchen was purple. It was getting dark. I saw a star through the window and heard someone crying from far away. I listened. The small crying noise would not stop. I listened harder, then opened the kitchen door and closed it carefully behind me. I went outside.

The grass was a little bit wet. The crying grew louder and louder as I walked under the trumpet vine, and even louder as I ran toward the barn. It was my sister crying *Mama, Mama.* I couldn't see her but I could hear her. I called out her name and she called out mine. I ran toward a dark shape on the grass— the rabbit hutch that used to sit on two oil barrels near the barn cellar away from the foxes. My sister had opened the door and crawled inside to be with our bunnies. The hutch had tipped over and now the door was on the bottom, and I could not get her out. The cage was too heavy to lift. The bunnies had soft velvet fur, but my sister was afraid because they were nibbling her hair. The rabbits were piled on top of her, nibbling her face, and I couldn't budge the hutch at all. I could not get to the door, and my sister was crying so hard.

I ran back to the house saying the magic word *purple, purple* to get Daddy's help, but when I ran inside he was still snoring, louder then, and he wouldn't wake up. I kept calling and calling, but he wouldn't move. I patted him on the arm but he would not wake up. I patted him harder, and his throat made a funny noise that sounded like purple, but he did not wake up. I stepped closer and was about to pull the end of his mustache, but I discovered that my feet were wet. I had tipped over his can of beer and now everybody would be mad at me. I was crying, too, but he did not hear me; he snored and waved me away as if I were a fly. My sister was in the rabbit hutch, I couldn't move it because it was too heavy, and Daddy wouldn't help me. I could not wake him up, and I kept crying. I was helpless until my mother came home to rescue her. It was dark, and I could do nothing but sit at the table, drawing circles and circles and circles, crying and saying the magic word purple over and over again. *Purple, purple, purple.*

Now I had all the time in the world. I took the pail of amethysts and turned slowly on my heel like a skater, spinning faster and faster until all the amethysts flew from the pail. The purple unfurled into a skein of silk and covered the grass as gently as gauze, soft as twilight. The purple turned itself quietly inside out, each amethyst choosing its place, blossoming in the field, free as clover.

I drew a pail of topaz from the well—topaz like Christmas tangerines, pale as nasturtiums in my first garden when I was four, like the heads of marigolds that my father planted every year by the back door, the color of orange-blossom honey and the bells of the trumpet vine billowing like a wave over the ship's bell that hung at the corner of the ell to call the men in for supper.

I remember standing in the doorway of the front room during a terrible summer storm when the trees bent over in near-hurricane winds and rain slashed at the windows like arrows. A wild bolt of lightning arched across the field, over the hay, half-cut, and Rossbach's tractor stopped mid-row because of the hail. A spear of lightning split the sky and the heavens opened, sundering the earth, and a bright spark rang the telephone in the corner of the kitchen, and a knife-bright bolt of lightning sped in front of my face on its way to the sink. I saw it, and a ball of fire as big as a grapefruit flew through the living room's open window and dove for a floor socket where it burst into flames, spent like a kamikaze comet. A fire was running up the rabbit ears of the old Zenith, leapt at the curtains, and my father thrashed the flames with his old army coat as if he were trying to smother an acre of blazes. His coat flew down, flew down, flew down until the fire went out.

It was another day later that year, and the three of us were sitting at the kitchen table with three different-sized pumpkins on spread-out newspapers, sketching a face with magic marker on our jack-o'-lanterns. My father was carving out the stem. It was my job to stand at the sink on a stool and scoop out the meat and seeds with a big wooden spoon. Daddy carefully followed the marks we had made on the pumpkin rind, slicing out the triangle noses, the horrible eyes, the grinning, vicious mouths. It was not like snow, where a broom and an apron could create a snow woman. All jack-o'-lantern faces looked like men, the killers and monsters of my dreams. I stood at the sink, rinsing and rinsing the seeds, pulling off the strings and meaty raw flesh, piling the clean white seeds on a cookie sheet, patting them dry with a dishrag and salting them down before they went into the oven to roast.

My brother was wearing a pumpkin-colored shirt. He wanted to wear the jack-o'-lantern on his head and be the Pumpkin Man, but my father said no. My brother clowned at the table, balancing the stem-end on his head and scaring my sister. My father told him to stop. My brother picked up my sister's pumpkin, the smallest, and pretended to wear it like a helmet. My father reached over to backhand my brother, but he ducked out of harm's way, and suddenly my brother was dashing out the door, and my father was chasing after him, the giant carving knife still in his hand. I heard my brother scream-ing, my father swearing, and we saw them go by the front window like figures in a Saturday-morning cartoon, my father with the carving knife over his head, my brother's legs pump-ing fast but not fast enough. My sister and I ran outside; my brother flew past us with his shirttails torn, one of his sneakers had come off and he was crying, my father bellowing behind him like a rogue elephant with a silver tusk in his hand. My sister and I stood there crying as they flew around the house again, my father getting closer and closer, my brother so little in his crewcut and patched shorts. My father tossed the carving knife into the bushes and went after my brother with his hands. I wanted to pick up the glistening knife and kill my father but I could not move. I was paralyzed as my father grabbed my brother at the cooper shop and beat him and beat him and beat him, while my sister and I held each other in the driveway, crying outside the kitchen that was filling with smoke because the pumpkin seeds were burning.

It happened long ago and will not happen again. I scattered the topaz from the pail like pumpkin seeds, like amber beads from a broken necklace, the jewels tumbling like handfuls of feed, cracking open like grain, growing wings and soaring from their chrysalis as monarch butterflies in a cyclone of gold.

I drew up the crystal bucket once more, and it was full of emeralds—the size of snap peas, the color of ivy, the shape of turtle shells, the greens of willow, malachite, jade, the bright spring green of fiddleheads, an emerald summer shower, the deep shade of June. Everything in the world seemed green to me—the grass, the trees, the unknown destiny of my name. What did it mean to be a Green? We sat around the dinner table for years at a green-and-white-checked cloth, squabbling, trembling, cherishing the oft-recounted antics of an ancestor or two, but most of the time we ate as if we were playing checkers. My father would criticize. My mother would answer. He would raise his voice. She would be still. Mother Nature was green, beautifully rich and growing. Inside, green was envy, rot, ruin. In summer the green food was bountiful: green beans, Swiss chard, brussels sprouts, beet greens, Kentucky Wonders, bright green peppers as big as baseballs, and green beefsteak tomatoes. I'd sit beside my father while he ate stonily, afraid of what would happen next. Most nights we were on constant alert because his mood could turn stormy in a flash. But in warm weather he seemed easier to understand and forgive. I looked at the forceps marks on his forehead, and it hurt me to imagine how he had come into the world. Something cruel had clawed him into life, he was too little, unprepared, he was hurt on the day he was born, and that's why he was cruel to us. When my brother talked back to him at the other end of the table and he backhanded me because I was closest, I refused to cry. He hadn't really intended to hit me so hard, I thought. It was the hurt that was driving him.

The house closed in around us in winter. The vegetables were gone, our bread was often moldy, my father would drink more. The quarrels were darker and every argument was about the Greens versus the rest of the world. Every sentence began with the goddamned shanty Irish or the goddamned niggers, and the words were so ugly that I couldn't stand to hear them, but I made myself listen, made myself repeat the ugliness (*kike, guinea, wop*) so that sometime in my life I could atone for such hatred. It couldn't be this ugly, out there in the world, away from us.

After supper, the family tumbled from the table like chess pieces thrown down in a fit of pique. My mother fled to read in her room, my brother and sister hid behind closed doors, Flap signaled on his short-wave radio under the eaves, my father fell asleep in a stupor in front of the television, and I sat doing my homework at the kitchen table, night after night, running from room to room like a Red Cross volunteer with cups of tea and books in lieu of bandages, even though the family was fragmented beyond repair. I kissed my father good-night, told him I loved him, turned down his bed, put on his electric blanket, and cried myself to sleep without making a sound.

Albert's face was very bright. He was smiling. We watched together as emeralds rolled down the field from my crystal bucket, and wherever they came to rest—a wall, a stone, a stream—they broke open and an apple tree appeared. There was no more envy. I had remade everything. Albert turned to go but stopped to gaze back at me, and for a moment he was my father, grown older since his death, with a long white beard, soft and shining as a young girl's hair.

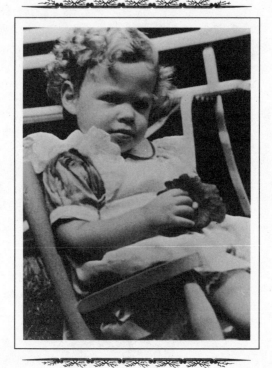

MIRROR

In essence, I was Granny's child. My father's mother took me home with her whenever she wanted, away from school, the farm, my brother and sister, even my parents, and after a week or a month or two she would send me back. These seemingly random visits began when I was six months old. I grew up not knowing to whom I belonged.

When it was time for me to go to Granny's, my mother, in a white fury, would pack my brown plaid suitcase with the mouse-gnawed straps, muttering crossly under her breath, while I timidly stuffed my red vinyl ballet case, thinking she was glad to see me leave, and I must have done something terrible to deserve being sent away. I'd put my paper dolls and coloring books where a sequined dance costume should have been; pencils, crayons, scissors, a ruler, and glue where there should have been toe slippers; and—in case I never returned— I brought my fragile white rosary, a gift from my aunt and blessed for me by the Pope. Then, with my loden coat buttoned up tight around my throat and a rabbit-fur hat over my hair, I would crawl onto my father's knee and beg him to let me stay. But he would look at me with sad, dark eyes and say nothing, explaining everything as clearly as if he had said: *You are saving my life. You have to go. I know how hard it is, but I will always love you the best because you are doing this for me.*

My brother and sister, their eyes burning, would watch in

silence from the doorway. I would never know them, I thought. As Granny's favorite, I was severed from them as surely as if she had chopped off my hands. Whenever I came home from Winthrop and ran out happily to see them, they would stand suspicious, open-mouthed, as if I were a stranger, then go back to their playing without a word. Once one of them picked up half a brick and hurled it, hitting me hard above the eye. They were little wild animals with a language all their own.

For a long time I thought my life was a fairy tale. Sometimes I dreamed I was the Little Match Girl, shivering unwanted in the cold, my eyes fixed on a golden feast through the window of a house where I would never be welcome—candles flickering in their long fluted silver candelabras on top of snow-white cloths, roast meat and Yorkshire pudding, potatoes, onions, and trifle, red wine in crystal goblets. I lit my matches, one by one, to keep warm long enough to see the glorious food steaming on gilt-edged plates, but when I lit the last match, I saw Granny beckoning from the darkness and I followed her, leaving a foggy handprint on the window glass, my body frozen in a bank of snow, an empty box of matches clutched in my other gloveless hand.

Sometimes I was the Little Mermaid who lived with her grandmother at the bottom of a tourmaline sea. When I sang, my voice was so beautiful that oysters opened their hearts to give me their lustrous pearls and all the bright sea anemones bloomed and waltzed, leaving their scent on the shining emerald sequins of my tail. As I sat on the shoreward rocks toward evening, brushing my golden, sea-green hair, I crooned a lullaby so sweet that pink and violet clouds gathered drowsily on the horizon until I sang the sun to sleep. The moon slipped into the sky like the most beautiful pearl of all, and I welcomed her as she drenched my silver seaweed shawl with light. I sang such ancient melodies, even the oldest stars came out to listen. But this was a dream within a dream that could never be real, for in my heart of hearts I knew I was Rapunzel.

I imagined my mother, great with child, craving rampion which grew over the stone wall past the cooper shop at the edge of the orchard, and my meek, soft-spoken father, bowing his head to her demands, walking out under the wine-glass elms by the old kitchen garden, shyly stepping through the briars and ivy that ran like a garland along the wall. Jumping down into the field where the rampion grew wild, he bent to pick the sweet young leaves, green and perfect as spring's first fiddleheads.

Then, turning to cross the wall once more, a witch appeared in a cloud of fire and said, "You married against my will. I gave you the farm for a wedding present and now you are picking rampion in my fields without my permission."

"But my wife must have it," my father stammered, shielding his eyes from her bright gaze.

"You will pay dearly for that handful of rampion," the witch smiled, sparking her blood-red nails against each other like flints. "You will give me your first-born child."

"Yes, Mama," he replied humbly. And then I knew: the witch was Granny. These had been her green fields, her white farm. She never forgave my father for marrying and leaving her, and because he had disobeyed then, he would have to obey her now. She would take me from the farm and lock me away in her big black castle until my hair, long and golden, was billowing about my knees.

In my mind, all the parts fit perfectly and the layers of each story lay down over my life like pieces of acetate on an overhead projector. Granny was all-powerful, mysterious, full of fury and fire. She had an uncanny ability, like magic, to get what she wanted from the world, and from the minute I was born she wanted me. Unlike my mother, she had stood at the hospital glass, tapping at my hooded ivory bassinet, assuring me later and often that I had looked at her as if to say, *Yes, Granny, I will live, I will live for you.*

At home my father would sit in his black leather chair by

the fireplace like a beautiful prince under some deep enchantment, my mother on one side, Granny on the other—between
the woman he married and the woman who bore him—each
of them wheedling, cajoling, and demanding his love, his
devotion, his undivided loyalty. He seemed to hear their cries
like a sleepwalker who had blundered into someone else's
dream, the cost of shaking off sleep too great to risk being
awakened, until finally he surrende.ed to his mother's wishes:
he gave me away.

And so when Granny, Boppa, and I would drive off in the
big Buick, I'd wave frantically out the back window, watching
my mother wipe her fingers on her apron as if she were washing her hands of me, and my father in his shirt-sleeves wave
back and forth in a sleepy gesture of farewell. Only the dogs
would cheer us raucously down the driveway. Down the hill,
past the Retina Foundation, the four corners, over the storming
Squanicook's little white bridge, and then out of Townsend
altogether, I'd change into a different child. The yellow curls
that my mother had scraped angrily into a ponytail would
spring free. I was prettier, smarter as the miles fled by, shed-
ding the ugly names I was called at home—*spoiled, rotten, lazy,
selfish, brat*. At every bend of the road I became my grandparents' prized possession: beautiful, intelligent, precious, loved. I
was as pretty as any of the bisque dolls with real hair that
Granny kept locked in her doll collection closet, lying in their
shoebox coffins, their glass eyes closed, smothered in moth
crystals and tissue paper. We sped past sugared cornfields with
shocks broken and bowed by the cold, past willows with icicles
in their hair veiled like ladies-in-waiting, past hitching posts in
front of post offices, smoke purling from shuttered houses over
silver barns, and horses huddling beside a snow fence, their
coats shaggy with hoarfrost. The road to Boston curved
through hills and meadows where shining ponds were set like
mirrors in the fields. White steeples pointed skyward among
the evergreens. The Buick was warm and I'd get sleepy under

my Hudson Bay blanket. Then we'd come to the crest of Belmont Hill, and below I could see all the lights in the buildings and houses of the city like a shimmering Christmas crèche, and Granny would say, "Look, Melissa, there's Boston!" Suddenly panicked that they'd abandon me there, I'd shout, "But I don't want to go to Boston! I want to go to Winthrop." And my grandparents would laugh as if I'd said something uproariously funny.

We'd arrive at the black house in Winthrop at dusk, when the sun was a soft rose peony unfolding over the town, and as soon as I stepped out of the car I could smell the rich, salty, dark ocean clamoring at the seawall two blocks away. When I looked carefully past the lantern lights on the stone pillars of the Cliff House, I could see the edge of the surf like the hem of my cotton nightie, gulls circling and circling the tide, and a chill of delight would go through me. I was near the ocean, the beautiful, terrible sea, my cheeks flushed with happiness. The locks opened, lights came on, soft and golden, and we'd carry our bundles down the long warm hallway on a runner of rose and black flowers knotted with green.

Granny would put on the kettle before she'd even taken off her coat. My grandfather would stow the groceries into the fat whirring Norge, and the three of us would stand outside the walk-in hall closet that smelled of mothballs and cedar, where blankets were piled softly in nests, and hang up our coats. In the red-and-white kitchen, I'd stand on a step stool and measure the tea leaves into the heavy silver teapot, then Granny would pour in the boiling water. I'd set out the bright Fiesta ware at each of our places, and we'd eat liverwurst sandwiches or bologna and cheese or toast and honey and drink our tea in silence. I always smiled to myself when my grandfather tipped his cup into his saucer, blew on the tea to cool it, and picked it up with both pinkies crooked out delicately, bending it toward his silvery mustache and slurping noisily from the saucer. Afterward I'd dry the dishes Granny washed, in my blue apron with the red and black rickrack. Then I'd snuggle on my grandfather's lap to watch *Mitch Miller* in his old leather chair. Wreathed in sweet-smelling pipe smoke, my cheek pressed against his suspenders, being close to my grandfather was as much happiness as I could bear. Before I knew it, Granny would announce it was time for bed.

My grandfather snored loudly and contentedly at the front of the house in a huge mahogany four-poster bed, his room patterned with plaid pale-brown paper, next to a radio that crackled all night long with shouting and static. Granny's large high-ceilinged room, at the opposite end of the hall, was the color of rain-washed brick. Under a wall-sized mirror festooned with a yellow chintz valance and drapes, between two brass vine-shaped sconces with red-ruffled silk shades, was an old-fashioned sleigh bed. Painted roses peeled from its headboard and footboard and a crisp horsehair mattress crunched when I knelt on it. I had my own cot under the window, but Granny made me sleep in the sleigh bed with her. It was so high that I needed a boost to get up onto the snowy sheets. I would turn on my side so I could look out the window; Granny would crawl in next to me and wrap her arms around my body as if I might try to escape. As the soft pink light went out of the room, she would lift up my nightie to scratch my back, her scarlet nails moving gently over my shoulders, my wingbones and spine, scratching out the twitches of the day, tenderly erasing the sadness, the guilt, the homesickness. She smelled of cold cream and powder and Halo shampoo. She smooched little kisses on my neck, saying she was looking for sugar. She breathed softly into my ear, her pillowy bosoms pushed against my back, one hand clasping me toward her, the other between my legs, her hard thumb pushing deep into my body's dark mouth. I did not move. I did not cry out. My heart withered in upon itself like a leaf, and I stared out the window at the stars.

Once I had seen a man lifting a pancake of cement by the curbstone and climb up a metal ladder from beneath the street.

In the same way, I would leave my body then and walk toward the sky, away from her smell, her scalding breath, her suffocating hold on me, away from her arms and her bed where I could not breathe. I was far away in the midnight-blue and white Milky Way, my nightie soft and light as a cloud.

Later, after she was asleep, I would crawl into my own little cot and curl up under the covers like a woolly caterpillar poked with a stick. There, I would think of the farm; Tutu, my marmalade cat; my own dark bed; and my brother and sister, who were lost to me forever. I cried because I remembered my sister when we were both very small, her sitting in my arms in the old wicker chair on the porch at the farm. It was summer and we were dressed in madras sunsuits. My mother had just bathed us, and I could smell lily-of-the-valley and sunlight on my sister's hair. I was so happy to have her cuddled up on my shoulder, one fat arm lovingly around my neck, but when a cloud came over the sun, she squirmed away, slid down from my lap, toddled off into the shadows, and somehow I knew she was gone for good. Another night when frost flowers had coated the window above the bench where we sat for supper, my brother with his blond curls was singing a song under the kitchen table. He was too shy to sing in front of us, but his tiny tenor voice came trembling up my legs:

> *In Dublin's fair city*
> *Where the girls are so pretty*
> *There I first met my sweet Molly Malone.*
> *She pushed her wheelbarrow*
> *Through streets broad and narrow,*
> *Singing, cockles and mussels, alive, alive-o.*

I cried into my pillow without making a sound. My brother and sister were lost to me. I fell asleep, dreaming of the people who had lived and loved and died so that I could be born and lie alone at night in Granny's room, the color of rain-washed brick, two blocks from the sea.

The next morning I'd find myself wrapped like a mummy in

the cot's clammy sheets. Pale yellow light would shine through the sunporch window, and still half-asleep, I'd imagine the sound of surf on sand, the rushing of a thousand white bulls through walls of water, dying at the cliff's edge. I was surrounded by Granny's things—five large mirrors, a photograph of Lake Geneva, two bronze masks she'd made of herself and my father in 1936, and a charcoal portrait of herself in profile, framed in gold leaf. On her night table was the sad photo of her first and only sweetheart, Winslow Gates, the boy closest to her heart, the one she should have married, she would always say, instead of my grandfather.

The largest mirror, hung with heavy yellow chintz, was on the wall behind the bed and looked to me like a theater. I'd stretch out my leg on the bed's headboard as if it were a dancer's barre and do pirouettes and arabesques in my eyelet nightie, pointing my toes and posing like Gisele in front of the footlights. Someday I'll be a prima ballerina, I'd think, and wear a costume of silver swan feathers, flutter my delicate wings above my breast, and pretend to bend a long swanlike neck upward like a peony toward the sun, then let it fall forward ever so gracefully as I died.

Above the rose-stenciled bureau was an oval mirror as big as a platter, and there I would pose like the Madonna in its silver face, Granny's blue silk robe draped over my hair, my chin dropped down, my eyes deep and wide with sorrow, holding Maggie, my Negro doll, in my arms as though she were my own dead child. I'd make tears come to my eyes, brim for a moment on my lashes and fall, each one weighted like a diamond down my cheek.

On the little blanket chest, painted with flowers and grapes and grapevines, stood a cut-glass hair-receiver full of safety pins, a snowy white puff inside a cut-glass jar with only the faintest scent of powder, an ivory sachet holder carved with cherubs and fleur-de-lys, and a sterling-silver ring box encrusted with sapphires and rubies on four delicate legs that ended in tiny griffin's claws. When I lifted the dazzling cover

and looked into the velvet-lined interior, I always caught my
breath: three monogrammed silver signet rings, four gold wedding bands, a silver circlet with a row of miniature star-shaped
diamonds, a glistening silver-pronged ring with a dark blue
stone, the same color as my eyes, and three dime-sized sparkling diamonds. I'd try on each of them, one after the other,
on and off each finger and thumb, hoping that someday one
of them would magically fit, and I could take it to the farm and
hide it under my pillow for safekeeping.

Over the blanket chest hung two bronzed faces, one above
the other—Granny's crosshatched skin, high forehead, deep
lids over closed eyes, square jaw, large mouth, and the place
between her nose and upper lip that looked like an angel's
thumbprint. *A death mask*, she had said. I shivered. And under
her mask was the one she had made of my father when he was
only sixteen. They looked so much alike that they could have
been twins, though my father's lashes were longer and his face
was smooth. She told me she'd sat him down at the kitchen
table and had plucked out all the young hairs in his beard with
a pair of tweezers, so his face would be as perfect as her own.
It gave me a creepy feeling to think of it.

I put my feet into my bunny slippers and padded into the
kitchen for breakfast. My grandfather had already gone to
work at the Boston Naval Shipyard so Granny and I would be
alone until suppertime, doing the same things we did practically every day. She would put down a dish of stewed prunes
at my place, saying, "I was always bunged up, all my life. I was
always taking a physic. Nothing ever worked—I was always
bunged up. I don't want you to suffer the way I did." She always
talked about her bowels. I'd look at her, trying to understand,
then manage to choke down five wrinkled, hot prunes. Afterward, as a kind of reward, she would give me a glass bowl of
peaches, cut up and dusted with powdered sugar, and a little
ivory two-pronged fork to eat them with. Then I would have
tea, very light and sweet, in my own china cup.

She squeezed orange juice for me every morning, stirring in

a teaspoon of baking soda, so I could drink it without causing my canker sores pain. The juice would foam and turn white, soft, and sherbert-colored. Canker sores had plagued me ever since I could remember. Every day Granny would pack them with alum, and my mouth would pucker in fierce pain, tears squeezing through my lashes as the alum stung and parched each sore, the ache running down to my heart. Once when the sores were as big as dimes, she took me to the doctor, and he pushed an enormous needle deeply into each of them, over and over, but it was Granny who wept and wrung her hands, pacing the dark office as if he were hurting her. I didn't make a sound.

After I drank my juice, Granny would smile her secret smile and turn to me with a bakery box in her hand. Triumphantly, she would pull out a dark pecan roll, sticky with syrup and the faint smell of burnt dough, and put it down on my plate, treating it as if it were a holy thing. My stomach would turn because the roll was so sweet and gluey and hard to swallow, but she would stroke my hair and say in a voice just as syrupy, "You love pecan rolls, don't you? We both love pecan rolls." It was useless to say, *Granny, I hate them.* She would croon, "Eat this— if you love me," and I would bring the sweet roll to my lips, bite down into the sticky mess, and swallow the greasy pecans to prove to her that my love was real. Then she would take me by the hand, open the cupboard beside the sink, and bring out a large bottle of Fletcher's Castoria, the Children's Laxative, and give me two heaping tablespoonsful. I'd choke it down, along with more of her love.

When the breakfast ritual was over, she would take me by the hand into her bedroom, sit me high against the pillows under the mirror and yellow chintz drapes, and rummage in her closet for her camera. She'd decorate me with earrings and many strings of pearls. She'd dot my lips with Coral Sunset, put spit curls on my cheeks, and make me pose with my legs apart, my nightie falling softly on my thighs, my fat dimpled elbow and fingers provocatively on my chin. She took lots and lots of pictures. She wanted me to put my chin up in the air and look superior like Gloria Swanson. Then she'd order me to put my chin down and look into the lens with big eyes. She told me to pretend I had a secret, to flutter my lashes and flirt. The flashbulbs hurt my eyes. Then she would put away the camera, take off the jewelry and my nightgown, and march me into the kitchen for an enema. I was six years old.

The kitchen had a big double sink with a corrugated porcelain shelf that fit over the deeper sink on the left. I would stand on the step stool, take off my panties, and lie stomach-down on the cold porcelain, which felt like a block of ice. I did not want to hear the water running until it was the right temperature, I did not want to see the enema bag and the long red hose like a poisonous snake. I'd look up through the velvety leaves of the African violets on the window sill and try to count the blossoms—blue, pink, lilac—but when I could feel the end of the hose in my body I'd go farther away, up into the green and silver birch tree outside and watch the leaves rippling like a shiny stream in the wind, and when the water began coursing through my bowels, I'd find the sun through the branches where it was warm and bright, where it was always warm and bright.

I loved it that Granny's black house was so close to the sea. We'd go down to the water sometimes, her iron grip on my hand like a god's, past the waving beach roses and the rustle of tall feathery fragmites. We'd stand and look at the sea. It was always a different color—opaque green, the color of smooth, smoky beach glass, deep midnight blue, or the steely gray of a battleship. The surf never stopped moving; it seemed to have a will of its own, sweeping in as softly as the hem of my petticoat, or crashing against the seawall as if it wanted to shatter anything in its path.

But our walks were never frequent enough. Most of the time we stayed inside with the wooden venetian blinds closed, the curtains drawn, the front door locked and bolted until we seemed to be swimming in amber. I spent my days drawing reams of pictures with colored crayons on letterhead pilfered from the Boston Naval Shipyard. Reading the stern black logo made me think of rows of sailors in short blue brass-buttoned coats and white Popeye hats. I saw admirals with golden-tasseled antimacassars on their shoulders, shaking slightly from their brisk salutes. Mostly I imagined a place where ships were born, a vague forest of boards, pulleys, and cranes, with a halfbuilt schooner cradled out of the water and the sounds of men shouting and hammering. I wanted to be on the docks with the smell of sawdust, the sea, and the hard noise of work.

Granny's house was not meant to entertain children. I carried my doll Maggie until her arms fell off, her sunflower-yellow bonnet was the color of old parchment, and one of her eyes wouldn't close. I spent hours in front of the button basket, describing to her the beautiful ballgowns each button had come from, inventing stories of how they'd been cut from the cuffs of soldiers' coats and pirates' capes. But the most wonderful game was to sit in the parlor at Granny's cherry secretary and explore the contents of the delicate, doll-house-sized drawers. In one drawer were hundreds of stamps steamed from old letters, where all the countries of the world slept side by side, torn like the remnants of treaties and decrees, and where I imagined all the kingdoms and cities and princes and czars had finally agreed to rest. In another drawer were packets of foreign money, creased from being carried in the pockets of strangers long ago. How had they come to be in Granny's desk, etched with the color of lilac, the color of pond lilies, the color of hummingbird wings? Who were these men with white walrus whiskers? Where were these houses, large as palaces, that were inked brick by brick behind them?

But the drawer I came to with fear and longing was full of tiny envelopes and tissue-paper packets—some tied with crumbling ribbon, some wrapped with frayed crochet yarn and lace, as though each stood for a single year of the century, older than my father, older than Granny, older, maybe, than Jesus. In one was a lock of hair belonging to Granny's mother, whose portrait in a gold-leaf frame stood near me on the desk blotter. I knew her name was Alice, that she had died of consumption two weeks after the portrait was taken, at the age of twenty-nine. She had a sad and delicate face. The broach at her throat was gold. The dark lock of hair I held in my hand had been cut from her head as she lay in her funeral clothes. The hair, curled in upon itself from being pressed in lavender so long, was all we had left of her, all that could describe what she had been like. I knew nothing, only a deep astonishment that hair could last longer than life; that when this lock was cut, I had not been born—neither had my father. Even Granny had been a little girl in braids.

The next envelope was marked with my father's name. From it spilled two baby teeth, the first ones he had lost as a little boy in this house, like two ancient bone chips dug up at a grave, yellowed from lack of exposure to the air. I felt my own teeth with my tongue. They didn't move. Someday I knew I would lose them, and I was afraid.

There were many envelopes with my name on them, one after the other. The smallest held pale amber threads from my first haircut. The next held strands from when I was one—a deeper yellow, the color of dandelions. The next strands, at two, were different yet—hair the color of a halo, shining as though it had just been brushed. My hair would get darker when I was eight and nine and ten. I looked at the picture of Alice, her sad face, and thought of her long brown hair. Would mine become that color? Would it stay that way after I died?

Sometime during the year I turned seven, Granny called me into the kitchen. She was wearing a smock and sweating over the sink. Paste the color of dumplings was smeared all over her hands.

"Come here," she said. "I'm going to make a mask of your face."

I stopped short, dropping Maggie on her head on the black and white linoleum.

"Get up here and lie down," Granny said, pulling a chair from the edge of the table. I climbed up. Newspapers had been spread out and a bedsheet was hanging over the back of the chair. Why did she want to make a mask of my face when she saw me all the time?

She took off my sweater, tied a red bandanna over my hair, and made me lie down on the newspapers. She lay my arms down by my sides. I could feel the ribbing of my undershirt as she pulled the white sheet up to my chin and tucked it in under my shoulder blades.

"There," she said. "Now don't move."

She unscrewed a jar of Vaseline and covered my forehead, my nose, my cheeks, my lips, and when she came to my eyes, she said, "I want to make a mask of your face, so that when you die I'll have it to remember you by. Now close your eyes."

My eyelids slammed shut like the lid of a box. When I died? Was it to be so soon? I felt a tear creep out from the corner of my eye but I called it, frantically, back. I mustn't move a muscle. She would be so angry if I did.

Through the two straws in my nose, I could smell wallpaper paste; I felt a coldness on my skin from the plaster of paris. It was so dark, so heavy on my face. I was shivering. I scolded my body then, ordered it to stop trembling. Like a bossy older sister, I told myself, *Granny is making a mask of your face. So she'll remember you. So when you die. Feel how cold it is. You can't move your feet, they are so cold. You mustn't move. You are dying now.*

And my body obeyed. Under the sheet my arms and legs grew stiff. My heart in its cage stopped fluttering like a bird, lay over on one wing and slept. The plaster of paris hardened on my jaw. It was too late. This was death, and as the mask hardened I heard the mantel clock ticking. My body turned to marble, my hair was white above my wings, and sometime after that I fell asleep.

On winter mornings in Winthrop, the fog rolled in like wind-borne sheets of smoke, drifting thickly through the houses and trees, softening the salt-blackened slate roofs and smothering the bare maple limbs until the whole world seemed wrapped in yards of out'n flannel. Snow lay on the lawns and skirted the crisp hedges like muslin. The streets were still. Only the deep mournful boom of the foghorn moved through the gray air, a ghost calling for a long-lost companion, shipwrecked on the shingle of Yirrell Beach.

In the kitchen it was quiet, except for the gentle plup-plup of eggs in a saucepan. I was standing on the step stool in my underwear and a white flannel petticoat with polka dots like gouts of blood. Granny had her mouth full of common pins and was steadily tucking up the soft folds of material into a hem. She could not talk with her mouth full of pins. I watched the skeins of fog slipping through the tines of a picket fence, through telephone wires stretching from street corner to street corner, taut as a Chinese jump rope. The fog sped over the grass lightly as pipe smoke and threaded itself into the tangled hair of a sleeping forsythia at the edge of the field. The windows turned white, and soon I couldn't see Doig's house or Aunt Emeline's or the fan-shaped ancient maple in front of Murphy's porch that clutched and crumpled the pavement, its roots like the misshapen, fierce claws of some giant amphibian that had crawled up out of the sea.

The house was wrapped in bandages of fog. Granny stood up then, her blue hair illuminated by the ceiling light. Her hands on my shoulders were eagle's claws; I was a field mouse caught in their grip. Her face was granite, a mountain carved against the red-and-white kitchen sky, her ice-blue eyes were wide and deep as two gorges thrashing with run-off, her mouth the blackish-red of a canyon forest fire. She was the firmament.

"Get dressed," she said, her voice a silver plane breaking the sound barrier.

I scurried into my clothes. Granny sat down at the sewing machine, the cogs and wheels catching when she pressed the foot pedal, the needle piercing the white skin of the petticoat in a rapid scar, and then she began to talk.

Granny was always talking. From the minute I opened my eyes in the morning until I closed them wearily at night, her voice wove over our meals, our errands, our chores, and afternoon tea. It was an endless recital of her life, starting with her birth in an old stagecoach tavern in New Ipswich, New Hampshire, and including all the characters and incidents that had marked her unhappy and desperate childhood—John Kimball, her sadistic father; the tragic death of Alice, her young mother, from consumption; the steady influence of Anna Watkins Reed, her English immigrant grandmother, called Gram. I loved hearing about the old days when ladies wore white lawn dresses down to the tops of shiny black boots done up with button hooks, and rode in rickety pony carts, carrying parasols, before there were Buicks; how they had closed the indian shutters at night to light kerosene lamps because there was no electricity; how they pumped water from the well and carried buckets down to Bessie and Maud, the Guernsey cows, and made johnny cake in cast-iron pans in the old wood stove. I could see the men as they drove spikes hard every winter into the maple trees and hung them with pails in the sugar orchard, boiling down sap in a silvered sugarhouse to make maple syrup that the children ate on snow. I laughed each time Granny and her sister Madeline fed whiskey out of a teaspoon to the cantankerous white rooster that ruled the barnyard and imagined him indignantly falling on one wing, furiously shaking himself upright, only to fall down on the other. I knew how cows calved without ever having seen them do it. I knew the sound of a snowy owl high in the fanlight above the haymow that Bull Bartlett had shot and killed, just for laughs. I trembled with Granny and Madeline as little girls huddling in bed, hearing their father down the hall flinging things in a fury from the dresser, smashing their mother's pretty things, snatching up a silver-backed hand mirror, one that matched her brush and comb, and beating their mother with it, over and over, his lips curling in its reflection. It seemed such a long time ago, but in Granny's mouth it was all true again.

I didn't get tired of listening, really, just tired of listening so hard. It seemed as though, if I paid close attention, something terrible might be changed for her, some deep wound would not be inflicted. I might be able to warn her to stay away this time from her father's belt or from falling off the stern of his boat, the *Madge-Ellen*, into the murky depths of Lake Champlain. Or maybe beautiful Alice would not die, the horse would not bolt, the tree would not fall, and the lightning would not burn the barn to the ground. Sometimes I listened so hard that it hurt, and I would withdraw from the constant barrage of her talking, but even then her voice seemed to reverberate from the hills and valleys of New Hampshire with the soft, faraway sound of a machine gun. I felt like the place on the front stairs where the eaves' constant dripping had worn down the tread in one spot to become the firm, unmistakable shape of a thumbprint.

What was it like when you were little? was the question I asked everyone in the family, but only Granny seemed able or willing to tell the stories I so badly wanted to hear. My father could not talk to me about his growing up. It was as if he had forgotten everything about his life except for the last five minutes, or that whatever had happened so many years ago was not worth remembering. Flap would tell silly, incomprehensible stories when he was drunk, dancing with a bowl of popcorn on his head. My grandfather hardly spoke at all; he grunted gently, chewed on his pipe, and turned up the ballgame. When I asked my mother, she always put on her stage-actress smile, her eyes shone with a faraway look, and she said the same thing over

and over as if she had memorized a part and needed to keep
the words identical so she would not forget it. She was smart,
she was beautiful, her golden ringlets were much prettier than
mine, and the nuns at Sacred Heart Academy had never gradu-
ated a more brilliant student. She went to school when she was
four and skipped a grade. But when my teachers wanted to put
me ahead a grade, my mother smilingly refused, because of
course I wasn't as smart as she was. In junior high, after she'd
finished an exam with time to spare, she tossed off a sonnet in
Latin. And when I would race home from school in a flurry of
excitement over a new book I had discovered, hoping to talk
with her about it, she would look down over the corner of her
newspaper and sniff, "Are you just reading that now? I read
that book when I was six, and all his other books too." It was
hopeless. I would never catch up. My mother was born knowing everything.

Granny, on the other hand, told wonderful, crazy stories—
some sad, some hilarious, some hard to believe except that the
glitter in her eye meant that they were true. She had a special
language, full of curses and hexes she would put on people she
despised. "Shit a cat's ass!" she would bellow when she dropped
something. "You can tell him he can stick his right eye in a rat
hole!" she would curse at a workman she thought had over-
charged her. And when the man came to the door to be paid,
she would snap, "You can kiss my fat arse on both cheeks!" and
slam the door in his face. Sometimes, when she came to a
particularly dramatic scene in her breathless monologues, she
would stop to fan herself and say, "Christly Jesus, I thought I'd
have a shit hemorrhage!" She was constantly feuding with the
neighbors, and one time she announced over breakfast, "I'd like
to dig out that woman's eyes with a grapefruit spoon, fry them
in pepper and garlic, and feed them to her cocker spaniel!" She
never had an education. She went to school sporadically until
the fifth grade, and I could already read better than she could.
But her mind was just as curious as mine. She invented words

if she didn't know the proper one. A marvelous idea was a
"stormbrain." She never said, "I hope so," but always, "Well, I
should hope to kiss a pig!" When she went out, dressed in her
Sunday clothes, she would say, "I guess I'm all gussied up like
Mrs. Astor's horse." She didn't say things by rote like we did
in school. From some fiery, fluid part of her, the words tumbled
out, jumbled, strange, silly, and completely her own. Who else
but Granny would say, lapping her chops, "I could eat whipped
cream on a horse bun"? She was not like anyone else in the
world and the people in her stories became more real to me
than the people in my life.

Granny told me stories of her childhood so often, I could
picture everything as if I had been there myself, as though
I'd actually lived in the changing and unchangeable landscape,
heard and seen the sleigh bells' silvery jangle on the great bay
horse as he trotted through birches under the Advent moon,
the rustle of waist-high blueberry bushes on a baking August
afternoon as berries plunk-plunked in the milk pails, holly-
hocks shivering in the shade of the yellow stagecoach tavern
with green shutters and a wide piazza where tenants paid three
dollars a week for room and board. I saw the dark room on the
second floor at the back of the house where Granny slept as a
little girl, and watched her creep through the unlit ballroom in
bare feet, her heart in her mouth, crossing before the high
white windows where a branch was always tapping like a finger. I saw spider webs festooning the unlit sconces, the ceiling
fanning out its marble garlands toward the corners of the room,
the eerie murals of houses and barns and iridescent trees
painted by the itinerant artist, Rufus Porter, in exchange for
his meals. I heard the house creaking around her as she sat on
the blue-and-white chamber pot, her nightgown drawn over
her knees because the room was so cold, saw the candle leap
and flicker in its brass holder by the bedside table as the wind
blew down from the hills and howled at the indian shutters.
One of her family's boarders had fallen drunk into the well and

drowned, and at night Granny would hear him pacing the next room where no one slept. The ghost would stomp down the stairs from the attic in his boots and rap hard on the door of the parlor, but when her grandfather in his long white beard stood up from his chair by the fireplace to open the door, no one was there. An icy draft flew into the room instead, and all the candles on the mantelpiece wavered as it went by.

Granny kept a box of old photographs, faded fragile pictures threatening to crumble under her hands, which we looked at so often that when I dragged the box out of the closet and trundled it into the kitchen, I felt as though I were carrying my own childhood in my arms. When Granny pointed out Aunt Edith, Uncle Ned, Bull Bartlett, Ford Reed, and Pearlie, her father's brother, I had the strangest feeling that I knew them— not just their names, but that I actually recognized them, knew them for who they were, as if I and not Granny had heard their voices, watched them eat, and seen them grow old.

We sat before the box of pictures the day Granny made me a flannel petticoat, and the fog wrapped around the house like a mother embracing a child. I looked at Alice in her striped shirtwaist and long dark skirt with the plackets, standing in front of the barn with a croquet mallet in her hands, the wickets marching off into the shade. I saw John Kimball sitting on the end of a hay wagon, wearing a bowler hat and a walrus mustache, a brindled dog panting at his feet and a rifle propped up against the spokes of the wheel. I studied Gram as she stood in her black taffeta dress, her big bosom glistening with beads of jet, one hand on the back of a rocker where she seemed to pin her husband in place with her glittering black eyes. The grandfather, Ford Reed, wore work pants and suspenders, his white hair and beard very bright under the scalloped awnings.

I felt like a spy. The camera had caught them in the middle of a smile, in the middle of the day, in the middle of their lives. They were looking into the lens for each other and themselves. Could they have imagined that a girl like me, hungry and feverish, would drink in the details of their privacy, so many years after they were gone? I knew how it had ended for them. But I wanted not to know because they didn't know it themselves. It made the pictures so sad. I felt like some dwarfed and fallen god who could create nothing and change nothing, but could predict their fate with cruel certainty. I could point to each of them and say, *You will die of consumption in your twenty-ninth year. You will marry a man you do not love and never have children. You will drink yourself insane. You will live well into your nineties and neither of your daughters will forgive you—you will die alone.* The sorrows that were set to happen to them had already happened. I knew what was coming, and like a train wreck that couldn't be stopped, I wanted to cover my eyes so I wouldn't see the smoke and the burning.

I looked at Granny and saw that we were turning into a photograph too, in her red-and-white kitchen with the sewing machine open on the table, a half-hemmed flannel petticoat with blood polka dots and fog at the windows. I would remember this moment for the rest of my life, and someday the image would be discovered in a cardboard box. A girl about my age might look at the picture and think: she knew how it had ended for us. And she would see on my face that I did not.

A funny thing happened then as I sat beside Granny, gazing at a photograph of a picnic I'd seen a thousand times. Granny's voice began to fade—like the bellows of an infinite and inaudible concertina, time folded in upon itself, caught the silent note of the photograph, and seemed to stop. I was standing with the picnickers by the stone wall beside the orchard, and they were innocently at rest. The bellows of time were expanding, and the concertina was breathing the sound of the stories I had heard. Summer was fading, my lungs began to ache, and I saw that Alice, shading her eyes, would get up from her knees, brush off the back of her skirt, and take the picnic basket into the kitchen. Softly, she would go upstairs, so as not to wake the children, undo the small pearl buttons of her shirtwaist, unlace her whalebone corset, and lie on the bed in her slip, the back of her wrist against her forehead.

The pleats of the concertina opened and closed, and I watched the picnickers in their straw hats entering the orchard, hours earlier, the bow of a fiddle sawing back and forth. There was a soundless singing, a game of tag, and then only the dog's feathery, freckled tail crashing through the hip-high Queen Anne's lace. The people were motionless on the sleigh's flocked blanket, the sandwiches half-eaten, the sun at the heaven's mid-point. Gram, Grandpa, Alice, John Kimball, Pearlie, Bull Bartlett, Aunt Edith, and Ned—they would forget this day, and the days afterward; they would race through their lives into the arms of death. They would never be as innocent again, but in this one note of time's concertina, something of them was saved—pure, untouched, untroubled—and could never die. In the breath of the universe, a summer day would always be dawning, hot and bright. Picnic hampers would be full, a flocked rug would be pulled from the seat of a sleigh. My flesh and blood would walk down a crooked path through the pasture to the orchard at the top of the hill and lie contentedly in their shirt-sleeves in the shade, and it would always be a day in which there were no clouds, no coffins, no crying, a day of perfect peace on the summer grass.

My grandfather loved to play cards. He'd slap down variations of solitaire by the hour at the kitchen table, with the grease-blackened, bent-cornered blue Bicycle cards that he wouldn't give up on a bet. Every year at Christmas someone in the family would give him a new set, but he wouldn't even crack the seal. "I'm just getting my old ones warmed up," he'd say with a wink. He'd rope me into a couple of games of five-hundred rummy whenever Granny would let me loose for an entire afternoon. Boppa made me keep score to improve my feeble math skills, but basically he wanted me to learn how to cheat.

Boppa first taught me rummy when I was seven years old.

He cheated outrageously and won every game we played, until I caught on. He wanted me to learn to outwit him, to be quicker and cagier than he was. I was fresh from the Baltimore Catechism. I thought cheating was a sin, that people won by virtue, goodness, and love. I wanted to win fair and square, because of Jesus and because of my cleverness.

But I understood very early that there were different ways to think about card-playing. My grandfather thought winning was the only important thing. He tried to teach me to count cards, to remember every discard and pickup, to keep track of which diamonds had been played, how many trumps were out, and to know at all times what remained in your opponent's hand. Maybe because it seemed so much like math, counting cards took all the fun out of the game. I couldn't seem to remember anything, which wouldn't have mattered to me one bit, except that it mattered so much to Boppa. It was a game, after all. But drawing cards from the face-down deck seemed to mimic life somehow: it was dangerous, exciting, mysterious, it made you think by the seat of your pants.

After a while I began to beat him all the time. It was unnerving at first, and I watched for signs that he was making it easy for me. But I was winning legitimately. He would sit, rubbing his eyes under his spectacles, coughing deep in his chest from pipe smoke, and have me deal more and more of the hands because his knuckles were stiff with arthritis. I felt guilty. Here was a man who needed to win so badly that he would cheat like hell to beat a seven-year-old child. Over time, I had wised up to his dealing from the bottom of the deck and I felt stricken. He was an old man. Winning at cards had been a great pleasure for him. And now he couldn't even beat me. I felt so sad that I began to lose on purpose—intermittently, so he wouldn't catch on. I didn't have the killer instinct. And I didn't want it.

My grandfather was also a ferocious and unstoppable bridge player. He might have cheated at poker down at the yacht club, but when he and Granny played bridge with friends, he'd play fiercely by the rules. In fact, Boppa would holler at Granny continuously—she could never do anything right. She didn't bid high enough, she over-bid, she forgot to count trumps—but Granny just laughed. She said you had to have the skin of an armadillo to be partners with him, and only my mother, who was also a superior bridge player, was smart enough to play with Dick.

Granny had a bridge club, a group of ladies she played with every week, and sometimes she would take me with her, where I'd be paraded before them like a trained monkey and then sent off into a corner to amuse myself for the rest of the afternoon. One day in particular, Granny seemed frantic to get us there. She struggled into her girdle, fastening her stockings with a snap, and stepped into her black-and-white spectator pumps. She put a lacy slip on over her camisole, powdered her armpits and back, smeared a slick stain of Coral Sunset on her lips, and sprayed perfume from her atomizer on her throat and wrists. She opened her compact and ran a beige puff over her nose and cheeks. She brushed her pale blue curls, put on a blue-and-white-flowered poplin dress with a rustling full skirt, filled her white handbag with cigarettes, two hankies, her billfold, and lipstick, rummaged through her drawers for her white cotton gloves, found her blue velvet hat with the navy braid, then bent down to dress me.

"I want them to look at you," she said.

Her eyes were impatient and cross, as though she had something else on her mind besides bridge.

"I want them to look at you," she said again, pulling on my white anklets and turning over the lace tops. "I want them to look at you," she repeated once more, buckling my red sandals, pulling my arms through the sleeves of my red velveteen dress, yanking it down over my stiff petticoat, straightening the yoke of the organdy pinafore, buttoning the small pearls in the back.

"You are my treasure, my precious, and I want them all to be jealous." She brushed my hair, tied a white satin ribbon on one curl over my ear, and pinched my cheeks until they looked like apples.

"Now bite your lips," she said, "until they look like cherries." I bit down hard, holding my stomach, still roiling with cramps from the morning's enema.

We drove down the quiet, shady streets of Winthrop in the old Buick, past the porches full of wicker furniture and pots of geraniums, down the short streets off the boulevard with names like Trident, Sea Foam, Wave Way, and Crystal Cove. The houses were silvered from the sun and the sea, the beach roses blew along the yards. It was as silent as a tomb. We stopped at one house or another, indistinguishable to me, and walked up the steps through doors with leaded or stained glass windows. In the sunroom or dining room, ladies with blue hair like Granny's sat in colorful print dresses and flowered hats, pulling off their coats and white gloves. The foyer was cool and large pots of Boston ferns feathered the light onto the shiny wood floors. I stood still, holding my coloring book and crayons, hoping no one would notice me, that no one would fuss with my hair or kiss me. I wanted to disappear into the flowered sofas and overstuffed armchairs, but Granny always had to show me off.

That day she stood me up on a piano bench, the room grew quiet, and she said to her friends, "Now, look at this child. Have you ever seen anything so beautiful in your life? Those yellow curls, those big blue eyes—have you ever seen such a beautiful child in your life? And she's mine, aren't you, my precious face? All mine! Couldn't you just eat her up? She looks like me, doesn't she? Everyone says so. Just look at her!"

There was a rustling noise as the ladies turned to stare, and the room filled with cooing sounds, like dozens of pigeons roosting, and I saw each one gazing at me as if I were a doll, an exotic animal, a strange and unusual antique. They were looking at me, but they weren't seeing me at all. My eyes filled with tears under their scrutiny, and I hated them for staring, for knowing this was false and not objecting. I was ugly and fat and stupid, and I knew the ladies were secretly laughing at Granny. Water from the enema was trickling into my panties, I squeezed my legs together hard and prayed for it to be over.

Someone sat me down in a corner at a little table by myself and brought me a glass of ginger ale with a maraschino cherry in it. I laid out my coloring books and crayons and did not look up. The ladies were laughing, shuffling cards, clinking ice, eating bonbons from cut-glass dishes. They were drinking Rusty Nails, Old-Fashioneds, and Rob Roys. I listened to their voices, but *trump, no-trump, rubber, dummy, double, and redouble* were words in a foreign language. Their laughter grew louder, and some of them began to hoot, then quarrel, and I thought of peacocks and parrots and intricately feathered tropical birds with strange calls, their noses turning into red beaks before my eyes, their ruby nails growing into talons, and I was afraid to look into their glassy eyes because they might think I was good enough to eat. The smell of their perfume and cigarette smoke rose in a cloud above the bridge tables as they cackled and gossiped in curious shrieks. I lay my head on my arm and colored in a picture of a little girl on a swing. Her hair was yellow, her dress and shoes were red. Then I gripped the black crayon and scrubbed over the silly picture, turning everything black, until her feet, her velveteen dress, her face and yellow hair had disappeared.

When we got home, I went into the bathroom to change out of my dress and pinafore. I stood in my undershirt and panties, saw myself in the mirror and began to cry. I found the fingernail scissors and hacked off each curl close to my head and dropped them into the toilet bowl. I snagged the scissors through my bangs until they were ragged. I shredded the hem of my undershirt. I sat on the edge of the clawfoot tub and stabbed at my thighs with the sharp pointed scissors until they

looked as though they'd been clawed by the talons of some
terrible tropical bird.

Granny burst into tears when she saw my hair. I had hidden
the torn clothing and put on trousers so she never saw my
bleeding legs. She kept fingering the ragged ends of my hair,
crying heartbrokenly, "How could you do this to me?" Then
she wouldn't speak to me at all for two weeks.

It was much better when Boppa and Granny played bridge
together at someone's house. There were just four grown-ups
then and me, instead of flocks and flocks of women fluttering
their charm bracelets and scaring me. Sometimes the three of
us would walk down the hill to the yellow house at 56 Floyd
Street to play bridge with Cap Bergman, a retired ferry-boat
captain, and his lady friend, Abbie Anderson, who lived in the
apartment next door. They were my grandparent's age, which
I knew to be about seventy.

Cap's real name was Joseph, but he'd been called Cap ever
since he ran the ferry from Winthrop to Rowe's Wharf in Boston, which used to cost a penny. Cap was the most immaculate
man I'd ever seen. His shoes always shone brightly, the tips of
his fingernails were white and smooth like half-moons. In all
the years we visited, I never saw a piece of lint, a thread, or a
stray hair on his suit jacket. The crease in his trousers could
have cut cake. He was jolly, forever making "chokes" in his
thick accent—I never knew whether it was Swedish, Danish,
or Norwegian—and teasing Abbie until she giggled and
blushed like a schoolgirl.

I didn't know much about Abbie, except that she was Cap's
girlfriend, that they weren't married even though they lived in
apartments side by side, and that they loved each other devot-
edly. She was pretty and round, and she, too, was always carefully dressed, with pristine collars and cuffs, stocking seams
straight, her hair carefully marcelled and combed. She wore
Chanel No. 5 and thought everything that Cap said was hilarious. She was almost as good at bridge as my grandfather,

though she usually looked flustered and unsure of herself. I guess that was her secret.

Granny would primp for the occasion, too—perfumed, girdled, wearing gloves, a hat, and her best coat to see friends only three blocks away. She and Cap were fond of each other, and she thought of Abbie as one of her best pals. My grandfather always wore the same plaid shirt with worn elbows, the cuffs rolled up, a pair of grease-covered work pants, and an old golf sweater if he wanted to be a bit more formal. Granny fussed and fumed and tried to get him to wear some of the beautiful clothes that he had hanging in his closet, or at least mend the ones he wanted to wear, but he was stubborn and paid no attention.

"Ma, Ma, nobody cares what I look like. It's not important," he'd say. And so he would go to Cap Bergman's house dressed like a mechanic, even though he hadn't worked at the Highland Garage for thirty-five years. He didn't give a good goddamn and I was proud of him.

Boppa smoked Chesterfields, Abbie smoked Camels, Granny smoked Pall Malls, and Cap smoked a sweet, spicy pipe that made me drowsy. I would lie on the lumpy, flowered couch in the shadows of the lamplight, watching smoke spiral up toward the chandelier, while they laughed and told stories about the world before I was born.

I learned that my grandfather's birthday was the same day as Harry Houdini's, the Emperor Caracalla's, and the day America declared war in 1918. I learned that Granny bought Richie the first Betty Boop watch ever made in the thirties, and it cost two dollars and ninety-five cents. Granny talked about a terrible day in December when it rained as if the world was coming to an end and King Edward VIII gave up his throne for the woman he loved—how Granny had sat in the front room listening to the radio with the lights off and cried all through the broadcast and for the rest of the afternoon. Cap could always get meat coupons during the war because he knew so many

people. Glenn Miller was only forty in 1944 when his plane
went down. M-I-C-K-E-Y M-O-U-S-E was used as the pass-
word when the Allies landed on D day. Ernie Kovacks was a
genius and only Imogen Coca was funnier than Uncle Miltie.
At Cap's I tasted my first lox and cream cheese on a toasted
sesame bagel and thought I'd gone to heaven. I had caviar on
thin crackers, which made me pucker and sneeze, and drank
from tiny glasses of banana or crème de menthe liqueur. I
tasted my first sardines and loved them, though they thor-
oughly disgusted Granny. After that, when Boppa made lunch
for just the two of us, he would take big round Crown Pilot
crackers, layer them with dark mustard, horseradish, cheddar
cheese, tomato, and cucumber, then lay down sardines on
top—and we'd go into spasms of happiness, made all the more
delightful by knowing how revolted Granny would be.

Usually I brought a book to Cap's with me, but I never actually got around to reading it. His house was too interesting,
especially the sunroom of mahogany and brass. You entered it
by a low door, as though you were on board a ship, and there
in every window were ships-in-bottles—squat, fat-mouthed,
pale green, light blue, bottles with crimped outsides, and inside
each one was a beautifully constructed ship, sails flying in the
wind, in the middle of storms, or beached on dunes. There
were nautical charts hung on the walls, a cherrywood-and-
brass telescope, enormous black binoculars, a brass wheel that
looked as if it might have been at the helm of the *Titanic,* sail-
boats on mantelpieces, and iron candleholders shaped like
anchors. I'd sit at Cap's long worktable—my hands in my lap
so I wouldn't be tempted to touch any of his lovely tools, laid
out as carefully as a surgeon's—and look at the sunlight pouring through the bottles, illuminating the furled sails and hulls
of the ships inside.

One late afternoon when the hooting and howling was in
full swing at the bridge table—Cap had been declared dummy
and Abbie was about to play five no-trump—Cap came into

the sunroom and stood behind me, his hands clasped behind his back, rocking gently on his heels.

"It's magic, isn't it?" he asked, suddenly resting both hands on my shoulders.

"How do you do it?" I asked.

"I told you," he winked. "It's magic."

I said, "Will you show me?"

For several days afterward, when ver Granny would let me out of her sight, I would sail down to Floyd Street and fly up the brick stairs to the mahogany-and-brass-fitted sunroom to sit quietly beside Cap Bergman while he built a replica of the *Star of India*—a steel-hulled, three-masted, square-rigged bark—gnawing on my fingernail, speechless with happiness.

First he showed me his equipment: bottles of every shape, size, and color filled one corner of the table. Some were square and squat with large open mouths. Some were narrow-necked and delicate in length. *We have to measure the bottle,* he said, *then build the ship to match it.* Spars, masts, yards, booms, and gaffs were made from wooden dowels. Sails were made from parchment paper, broadcloth (really an old bedsheet), cotton batiste, or Irish linen. To create realistic ropes, Cap used cotton thread rubbed with candle wax or beeswax to keep it from getting "hairy," or sometimes a fishing line. Colored modeling clay was molded to become the water inside the bottle on which the boat rested or was tossed about. He'd insert the clay lump by lump into the bottle, then flatten it out with a long tongue depressor. Sometimes he'd use sash putty, which was a grayish color when it came from the can. He would have to paint it, but that way he had a far better chance of getting a color he liked. He gave me a lump of sash putty on a pane of glass and told me to mix in paint with a butter knife until I got the right color for the sea. I colored the putty carefully, adding cobalt, viridian, and white, until I made an Atlantic green I swore I'd seen by Boston Light in the harbor islands. Cap was very pleased. He pushed the putty into the bottle's mouth,

pleating the waves with the round end of a long nail file on
the bottle's glass bottom, pushing and lifting the putty until it
actually looked like rough water.

Cap used a jeweler's saw for cutting delicate and intricate
soft metals, tweezers—short and very long—clamps, pliers, a
French curve for drawing, brushes for painting, a coping saw,
clothespins, sandpaper, hatpins, an epoxy made of resin, and
several different-sized corks. He showed me the wood he used
for making the hulls and decks: pine, Douglas fir, spruce, balsa,
maple, birch, mahogany, and oak. *First, we draw, cut, paint, and
glue the hull,* he said. I traced his drawing onto the wood and
painted it after it was cut and before he glued it carefully
together. *Draw, measure, cut, and varnish the masts.* I varnished. *Lash
all mast parts together with waxed thread.* I watched. Then we cut
the sails, soaked them in a little starch, and let them partly dry
on the radiator so they would be smooth and full-breasted, as
though they were full of air. *Sew or glue sails to mast.* I glued the
corners of each sail. *Make the deck structures, the cabins, and capstans.*
Abbie brought me tea and I sipped it, completely enraptured
by Cap's nimble hands. *Fold up the boat and pull gently on the lines
to make sure the sails will rise.* I'm testing it for flexibility, he said.
Insert ship into the bottle, rest hull on epoxied sea. He gave me a long
tongue depressor and I dabbed glue on the waves where we
thought the *Star* would look best—tossed to one side in a
heavy wind. Cap pushed the folded-up *Star of India* through the
mouth of the bottle and let the hull rest on my lovely heaved-
up, Atlantic-green waves. When we both agreed it was dry, I
pulled the strings to raise the mast and sails. I was afraid to
breathe. Gently, the bowsprit moved, the masts rose, and the
sails filled with wind. The spars, booms, and gaffs lifted. The
ropes and halyards pulled taut into place. She rode the waves
like a champion. Everything held. And there, painted on the
starboard side in my best penmanship, it said the *Star of India.*

One day when we were both bent over a row of wooden
matchstick-sized masts, brushing them evenly with varnish,

Cap asked me if I knew where Winthrop was on the map. I was in third grade and we hadn't had geography yet, but I was pretty sure I could find it. It was near Boston, I knew that much. He took a map down from the wall and propped it against a chair back so he could show me.

Winthrop was practically an island, no more than a mile and a half square, with the sea on three sides—Broad Sound on the north and east, Boston Harbor on the south and west. One narrow causeway led to East Boston and one to Revere. I saw how many islands there were in the harbor and put their names in my mouth like sweets: Castle Island, Spectacle Island, Gallop's, Lovell's, George's, Rainsford, the Brewsters; and further in, Moon, Hangman, Nut, Sheep, Grape, Raccoon, Slate, Bumpkin, and Peddocks.

"I want to show you something," Cap said, and I followed him around a corner in the L-shaped sunroom. He opened a venetian blind. Light came streaming in and spilled over a hip-high table, twice as big as the table at the farm, and I saw with astonishment that on it was a little town with roads, schools, banks, parks, houses, trees, and water on three sides. There were railroad tracks and Model-T Fords stopped at the crossings, storefronts with painted signboards hanging out front, and down the length of the boulevard were white wide-porched hotels. Cap Bergman had made a perfect, miniature replica of Winthrop!

I couldn't believe my eyes. I ran around the table, pointing at landmarks I recognized, finding the library, the pharmacy, the Highlands, our house, Emeline's across the street, and 56 Floyd and the Cliff House. All the trees were delicately feathered and there was marsh grass and tall fragmites running beside Lewis Lake. Then the Narrow Gauge train came rumbling down its track.

I had only heard tales of the little train that had actually run through Winthrop—for the summer people at first, then for everyone when the town became a year-round community in

the late 1880s—and I'd never really understood where its route
had been, because the stations were long gone and the track
beds had been pulled up right after World War II. But now,
as the miniature train with Pegasus, the steaming locomotive,
chugged toward Morton Street along the edge of the salt
marsh, I saw that all the stations were in place as if by magic.
Cap had reconstructed them and I was enchanted.

The train ran from Cherry Street Station, curved through
the Highlands toward Crest Avenue, along the little streets of
cottages near the beach, past Lewis Lake and across Crystal
Cove toward Thornton Park, through to Winthrop Center,
Ingalls, and back to the marsh. I had to peer under the tree
limbs and between the lampposts to find the stations—Grover's Cliff, Rocky Beach, Ocean Spray, Sea Foam, Playstead,
St. Leonard's, Great Head, Cottage Hill, Short Beach, Point
Shirley, Thornton, Winthrop Beach, Battery. It was thrilling.
The train moved and whistled and stopped at every station,
just as it had fifty years earlier. And at the end of the line was
the dock where Cap Bergman had run the penny ferry across
to Rowe's Wharf in Boston.

It was perfect, more perfect than any real town could have
been. I could smell the sea and hear the great maples rustling,
sense the excitement and anticipation as the train rounded a
corner and pulled into view. It was so beautiful and complete
that I wanted to cry. I never wanted to leave it.

"You see this?" Cap said, pointing to a building on Point
Shirley. "That is the Saltworks built by a man named Sturgis in
1812. It's not there any more, but it's still a part of our history.
And these barns that belonged to the Revere Copper Company
were pulled down after the Civil War. This white house here—
see?—was the vacation home one summer for the great Italian
statesman Garibaldi. Winthrop was the first seaside resort in
America, except for Newport. The train tracks and even the
town itself were laid out on old Indian trails. When they finally
tore down the Center station, they found an ancient Indian

burial ground, and scientists from Harvard came over to take it away. But in my Winthrop, everything is still here—the fields, the apple trees, the Indian bones."

And so Cap Bergman had made a model of Winthrop, his own version, with devotion, care, and imagination. Everything was there—what we could see and what was gone forever. I crept shyly around the table and put my arms around him. He had given me a way of seeing, something that was truer than true.

"Cap," I said. "I love you!"

He laughed in great delight, and we went into the kitchen to see what Abbie was making for supper.

It took my mother a long time to get well after her operation. She went about her ordinary chores, but she was distracted and irritable, as if she were looking at us through the small end of a telescope, and we seemed very far away. I listened at the door when my parents were arguing. The chicken business was going downhill. My father's heart had never really been in it. After the war, my grandfather had sent him and Flap to the farm, because the egg business was supposed to boom, but when the other small farms in the neighboring countryside expanded, bought new equipment and more hens, my father did not. My mother, who had kept the accounts, knew we were in trouble. She wanted to go to work, to get a job outside the house that would bring in a salary. My father was wild. He wouldn't hear of it. But when he sat in his old leather chair by the fire for a year, with arthritis so excruciating that he couldn't walk, my mother became a substitute teacher at Spaulding Memorial School. She even taught in my fourth grade class when I was nine. She also began taking courses at night toward her master's degree at Fitchburg State Teacher's College, so she was gone all day. She'd go to school in the morning and straight to the college after her teaching was over. The house was empty when we got home. Fitchburg State became her

life, and soon she was a full-fledged teacher at Edgerly, a gram-
mar school affiliated with the Teacher's College. She had no
more time to knit us beautiful sweaters in bright colors, with
cables and stripes of special stitches at the collars and cuffs.
The sewing machine was closed and now that she had her own
salary, she took me shopping for clothes.

I hated it. I hated the crowded stores, slouching behind my
mother, scuffing my loafers and scowling, watching her waltz
down the aisles, humming as she slowly inspected the racks,
supremely confident, serenely choosing clothes for herself—
teal and magenta wool suits, creamy rose and jade silk blouses,
lacy slips and satin panties, plum, black, and bone suede
pumps, butter-soft leather purses and handbags, a navy coat
with white trim and exquisite buttons, tapered at the waist with
a graceful, curving skirt. She knew that she would look beautiful in anything she wore.

I cringed when she picked out clothes for me. I was in love
with every shade of red—scarlet, rose, maroon, apple—the
redder the better. I longed for azure and peach dresses, dripping with old-fashioned lace. I wanted to wear the short skirts
I saw in *Seventeen* with patterned stockings—fishnets and polka
dots, some with daisies or horizontal stripes. I wanted to wear
mascara and lipstick and blush. But my mother blithely chose
everything brown, beige, tan, and tweed, big sweaters in khaki
and taupe. I could only wear knee socks and brown oxfords.
The skirts and jumpers were huge and hung down to my
ankles. Why did I have to wear the ugliest colors in the world
when she could wear the most beautiful? I whined and pouted
and swished my fanny in disgust, insisting on being allowed to
try on one or two pretty dresses with flounces and peplums
and leg-of-mutton sleeves, stubbornly stealing them into the
dressing room, though my mother would laugh and say I
looked ridiculous in them. I dreaded the moment I'd have to
stand in front of the triptych of mirrors in my snuggies and
cotton undershirt and have to look at my ugly body, the cur-

tain wide open with salesladies in the doorway, glasses hanging
on cords around their necks, clucking and making remarks. I
was too broad in the shoulders, too wide in the waist, too small
in the chest. Jumpers, blouses, and skirts that seemed decent
on hangers looked like grain sacks on me. Fancy dresses made
me look like a clown. Nothing fit. The colors were wrong. I'd
tear them off in a huff and fling them on the dressing-room
floor. I'd stand in a fury and glare at myself in my ragged cotton
underclothes, pull out handfuls of hair in a rage, and sob until
snot ran out of my nose, wiping my blotched face on the sleeve
of my undershirt. It wasn't fair. I was so ugly. How could anyone be so ugly?

"Stand up straight. Don't slouch. Suck in your stomach," my
mother would snap at me, ashamed, as I tried on the dowdy
brown jumpers, the gray tweed skirts halfway down my calves,
the sweaters that limped over my wrists and fanny. I was as
lumpy as a bag of potatoes.

"We'll take these outfits for my daughter," she would say to
the saleslady, holding them out as if she could hardly bear to
touch them. I stood next to her, hating her perfect skin, her
slender legs, her girlish figure, wishing with all my heart that I
could run away and never have to be humiliated like this again.

Then my mother would try on her beautiful clothes, still
laughing at how silly I had looked in those flouncy party
dresses. One by one, the rich garments would slip over her
head. I'd watch her fasten the tiny buttons and hooks-and-eyes,
and everything would fit as if it had been fashioned for her.
The bright colors reflected a flush in her cheeks and made her
curly hair more golden. She wore a size six and never stopped
reminding me that she had the same twenty-four-inch waist
she'd had in college before she'd given birth to three children.
I didn't have a waist. My father said I was built like a brick
shithouse. My mother looked like a model.

All she saw in the mirror was herself, her perfect carriage,
her long hands, a still photo in new clothes. Next to her I was

a shadow, disappearing before my eyes, in hers. The mirror wavered like the one in the Fun House—it made my mother tall and slender with a swanlike neck, and me a pinhead with no breasts, billowing at the hips and knees. My body had absorbed all her imperfections. I had been branded with her shortcomings so that she could beam flawlessly before me.

"Stop pouting," she'd say furiously. "I'm ashamed to be seen with you. You're acting like a child." *But I am a child,* I raged silently. *Why do you hate me so much? I love you!* Yes, I did love my beautiful mother. And hated her, or myself, so deeply I wanted to smash all the mirrors in the store with my fists.

"You're behaving like a spoiled brat!" she'd say in disgust. Then, as if to confirm her assessment of me, I would whine and stomp out of the store, sit in the car, and sulk for all I was worth.

One day, after coming home from a particularly grueling shopping expedition, and after Mama had finished her speech about how spoiled I was, how impossible I had been, I sat down on her bed with the bags of clothes crackling all around me, drew my knees up to my chest, put my head on my arms, and cried.

"Why can't I look like you?" I sobbed, digging my nails into my arms until they drew blood. "Why do I have to be so ugly? I'm a freak, I'm a horrible freak!"

"You're not a freak. Everyone can't be pretty," my mother said, powdering her nose. "You're just going through an ugly-duckling stage. I never did, but you are, and there's nothing you can do about it." She traced her lips with scarlet, and smugly patted her hair. "You'll probably never look like me. You have your grandmother's genes."

I was doomed—to be a sack of potatoes all of my life with pimples on my face and lank, oily, no-color hair. Oh, God, I would look like this forever! My mother sat down abruptly on one end of the bed, lit a cigarette, and tried to talk to me seriously.

"You'll be getting taller soon." She paused and cleared her throat uncomfortably.

Taller? That was good. I was sick of being a shrimp.

"Your body will . . . well, you'll . . . hair will start growing on your body . . . in places . . . well, where there hasn't been any before." She coughed and took a ladylike drag on her cigarette.

Hair? On me? That's silly, where would it grow? Puzzled, I touched my face. "Will I have to start shaving like Daddy?"

"No," she said, slapping my hand away. "Not on your face. Hair will grow under your arms and . . ." She shut her eyes and gestured, "down there."

Hair? Down there? What was she talking about?

"Pretty soon, you won't be a little girl any more. Your body will . . . change. You'll grow breasts. You'll . . ." She stopped and crushed out her cigarette, then gazed out the window as if she couldn't bear to look at me. "You'll start . . . start to . . . bleed every month until you are old." She stopped again.

The silence in the room was deafening. I shifted on the bed and the shopping bags crunched in protest. What was she trying to tell me? I would bleed once a month? Nosebleeds? I touched my nose.

"No, no," she snapped, annoyed. "You won't bleed from your nose. You'll bleed . . . down there." My mouth fell open in surprise. My mother stood up impatiently and began pacing the room.

"It happens to every young girl. That's how you become a woman. No one told me anything about it and one day at school I found blood in my underwear. I thought I was dying. No one had told me anything. I thought I was bleeding to death. That's why I wanted to have this little talk with you, so you'd be prepared."

She reached into her desk and handed me a pink pamphlet entitled *What Every Young Girl Should Know.* "Read this. It will help you understand."

I was feeling queasy. I was going to bleed every month for the rest of my life—but why? I didn't understand any of this.

"Mom?" She didn't seem to be listening. "Mama?" She turned to look at me and her eyes were burning with embarrassment. "I don't understand. What do you mean?"

She clicked her teeth impatiently. "You'll bleed every month down there, and then you'll get married and have babies," she said, as if that settled everything.

Babies? Me have a baby? The room swam around me and I put my head on my knees. I wasn't going to have a baby, I would never have a baby, I didn't want a baby. Oh, God, this was awful. I started to cry.

Granny had been telling me for years about my father's birth, and it gave me the heebie-jeebies to hear her talk about it. Each time she told me, she wiped her eyes and moaned, she contorted her face and spoke about her agony, her three days of labor, pacing back and forth in unbearable pain in front of the window at the West Roxbury hospital, trying to jump out and kill herself. The baby inside her was turned the wrong way and wouldn't be born. The doctor finally pulled the baby from her bleeding body with forceps. She never forgot the pain, and she never forgave my father for it either—it was as if it had all happened to her the day before.

That was going to happen to me? I cried even harder. I didn't want a baby inside me, tearing open my body to get out. I didn't want to see the blood or feel the terrible pain of it.

"I don't want to have a baby!" I shrieked, punching the shopping bags with both fists.

"Oh, it's not so bad," my mother said, lighting another cigarette. "The doctors will be there and they'll put you to sleep. I almost miscarried with you. The doctor wanted me to stay in bed, but I didn't, and you were born just the same."

"Miscarried?" I asked fearfully.

"Miscarried means the mother's body rejects the baby, or the baby is sick and would be better off dead."

The mother's body rejects the baby? Granny told me that my parents had never stayed home when Mama was pregnant. They went to parties all the time, they were always "helling around," dancing and smoking and drinking bourbon. Granny said that's why I was born early and almost died. She said it was almost as if they didn't want me to live. The baby is sick and would be better off dead?

"You were so tiny when you were born," my mother continued, "they thought you were going to die. They put you in an incubator for six weeks. It was like a little glass coffin, and you were blue, and everybody thought you were going to die." She laughed, a raw, glittery sound out of her red mouth. "In the old days, they would have taken a sickly baby girl like you to a mountaintop and left you to die in the wind and rain. Eagles would have come down and plucked out your eyes."

"Here," she said, thrusting a brown paper bag in my lap. "You'll need these."

I was afraid to look. Gingerly I peeked into the bag and saw a box marked sanitary napkins and an elastic sanitary belt. I stuffed the pink pamphlet into it, ran out of the room and upstairs where I threw myself face-down on my bed and cried. This was the worst thing that had ever happened to me.

At supper that night, I couldn't stop thinking about babies. Having one would be awful. It would kill me. Children weren't wanted. Children died. Horrible things had already happened in this house. I made crosshatches with my fork in the mashed potatoes and thought of Granny's stories.

Her grandmother, Anna Watkins, had come over from England at age sixteen to work at our farm as a housekeeper for relatives of her relatives—Ford Reed and his two brothers, Leonard and Charles. She was also a nurse to their old blind mother. I'd seen pictures of Anna. She was a stocky girl, black-eyed, black-haired with coarse skin and frowzy hair. I wondered idly which room of our house she had slept in, and imagined her feeling homesick for the thatched cottage in Barford not far from Windsor Castle, and crying herself to sleep under prickly gray blankets. Soon she married Ford Reed who was much older than herself, and they had a baby named Joseph. I knew that Joseph had slept in my father's room and pictured a ruffled white bassinet with a muslin curtain draped over the white wicker hood to keep the flies away in summer. There were no screens on the windows then. I imagined Anna Watkins Reed cradling him, crooning an old English lullaby as he fell asleep, the baby in some way bridging the loneliness of her life on the farm and her family across the sea. But one winter night, when Joseph was only a few months old, in the bedroom where my father now slept, the baby had frozen to death.

Granny had told me the story so many times that I knew it had to be true, but each time I gasped in disbelief. How could this have happened? He must have cried, beating his little fists against the blanket. He must have cried all night until he was exhausted, his hands growing colder until his breathing slowed, and his blue eyes, no longer begging for help, had stopped moving. How could his parents, sleeping downstairs near the fireplace, not have heard him? How could they have slept through his anguished sobs and let him die?

I could hardly eat. I pushed around the peas on my plate in despair. Later, Anna Watkins gave birth to two little girls. I looked at the marks of the forceps on my father's temples. Once I had asked Granny why she didn't have any more children, and she'd slapped me.

"Don't you understand?" she raged. "I couldn't stand the pain of your father's birth. I was in labor for three days. I wanted to die. Gram gave me five abortions on the kitchen table at the farm because I refused to bear that kind of pain again. Do you know what abortion means? It means she reached up inside me with something long and sharp and scraped the babies out of my womb."

I covered my ears, screaming inside. Abortions. Five of them. Anna Watkins Reed had killed five babies on the kitchen table, the table where we now sat eating. I saw blood every-where, white petticoats soaked in blood, and something, a buttonhook, and a black-and-beady-eyed Anna Watkins, per-spiring, leaning over Granny's young body to tear out the babies before they caused her any more agony. I looked around at my family silently eating and wondered how they could bear to put food in their mouths. Didn't they know what had hap-pened here? I could see blood spilling across the green-and-white-checkered cloth—like gravy running between the salt and pepper—and pooling under my plate. Children died. Chil-dren were killed. I threw down my fork, ran to my room, and curled up like a fetus on my bed.

That night I had a crazy dream, like the story of Hansel and Gretel. I heard my mother whispering to my father, *There is not enough food for all of us and we only have one blanket between us. Tomor-row we must take our daughter into the woods, far, far away, and leave her there.* Under the moonlight, I filled my apron pocket with white pebbles so I could leave a trail to find my way home. My father carried me deep into the woods, and I dropped pebbles quietly behind me. But he didn't leave me in the woods; he left me on the porch of a licorice-black house with white rock-candy trim, two blocks from the sea. My father wandered through the woods, an ax over his shoulder, and I turned to face the door. Granny came out, her arms flung wide for a suffocating embrace, her voice high-pitched and urgent. "I love you more than the earth. No one will love you like I do. If anything ever happens to you, I will kill myself. If you leave me, I will die."

These were the things she always said, but in my dream I paid no attention. I ran back into the woods away from her, free as a deer. The trees were beautiful, and I wanted to live among them, but I followed the stones back to the farm. My mother sat before the mirror at her dressing table, her face as dark as the Wicked Queen's. She flew into a rage when she saw me.

"How did you find your way home? Your father is so weak—
he didn't take you far enough. It's his fault. Don't you understand—we don't want you here."

The next day I was sent into the woods alone, but again I
dropped the stones of my longing, my grief, my despair. This
time, when I arrived at the licorice-black house with the white
rock-candy trim, two blocks from the sea, the door was flung
open by a witch.

"Ha!" she cackled, holding out a plate of steaming pecan
rolls. "I'm going to fatten you up, then kill you, cook you, and
eat you!"

I turned and ran back through the woods, following the
white stones until I couldn't run any longer. I lay down on the
grass in the shade. I wanted to live beside the brook where the
animals came down from the hills to drink water from my
hand. Bobwhites were cooing in the underbrush. I heard a
phoebe grieve, a pair of cardinals, and a family of quail. Leaves
fluttered gently to the ground. I stared at the stones I had
dropped like beads from a broken necklace and they turned
into crumbs of bread. But the bread was too hard for even the
birds to eat.

I took a piece of the pebbly stone-bread and cracked it open
like a fortune cookie. Inside, like a vein of ore, was a word,
amaranth. I dropped it in surprise and cracked open another
one. Another word was written there—*coracle*. I gathered all
the bread-stones into my lap and found my favorite words
inside each one—beautiful, mysterious words that I remembered from books. They were so strange and lovely; I had
looked them up in the dictionary and memorized their mean-
ings. Now they were mine, my secrets, my special words, and
I fingered each of them like an amulet. *Amaranth:* an imaginary
flower that never fades or withers. *Coracle:* a boat of hoops and
wicker used by the ancient Celts. *Collet:* a flange in which a
gem is set. *Firkin:* a wooden tub for butter. *Glissade:* skillful
descending over snow. *Girasol:* an opal with a luminous glow.

Ignescent: giving off sparks. *Jeremiad:* long lamentation or mourning. *Lacustrine:* like a lake. *Merle:* bluish gray marked with black.
Nacre: mother-of-pearl. *Vade mecum:* come with me. *Welkin:* the
firmament; celestial home of the gods.

In my dream I cried because I knew that as long as I carried
the beautiful words in my pocket, pretending they were stones,
I would never be lost. When I woke up, there were tears on
my cheek.

Granny had mirrors in every room of her house, and when I
grew too old for her to show me off in public to her friends,
she would stand me beside her, gaze lovingly at the glass and
say, "You look just like me." But I didn't. Anyone could see
that. And I had the funny feeling that I wasn't there at all, that
she was seeing two reflections of herself. She would look at me
sadly sometimes, at my darkened hair and lengthened limbs—
the source of deep disappointment—and say, "You were perfect when you were five years old. You were such a beautiful
child. You put your little hand in mine and we would walk to
the beach together. Everyone admired us, and I was the happiest woman in the world. Now look at you." Somehow I had
betrayed her by not staying five years old forever, and I felt
ashamed for growing up to be so ugly. Once, she decided to
bleach my hair so I'd have blond Shirley Temple curls and be
pretty again, but the bleach ran into my eyes and stung them,
and I cried furiously. When it was over, my hair was white and
crisp as straw, the curls were gone, and I was hideous.

There was no place to get away in Granny's house. She hovered over me from room to room. If I tried to draw or read
quietly in a corner, she would come and interrupt me. She
insisted we eat the same things, mouthful by mouthful, and
she wanted us to think the same thoughts. Her voice was a
continuous battering, pushing through the cracks and crevices
of my mind like a windstorm through a rickety house. I'd have
to stop what I was doing, look at her and listen.

One afternoon in the year I turned twelve, I was sitting at
the dining-room table, my heels hooked over the rungs of the
Windsor chair, reading open-mouthed through an old book I'd
taken out of the library, the Winthrop Town Report from
1897. I read with fascination a letter written by the Commis-
sioner for Milk and Vinegar. I scanned the titles of books
which the Frost Public Library had purchased that year. I
traced the route of the Narrow Gauge railroad, imagining
Cap's little clapboard station houses crowded with summer
people—women in plumed hats and bustles and leg-of-mutton
sleeves, men in white seersucker suits and panama hats, children in shorts and straw hats with ribbons down their backs.
The smell of the ocean seemed to drift right out of the pages.
But I especially took note of the births, marriages, and deaths.
I stood with the justice of the peace and witnessed the marriage
of Letitia Louise Adams, age sixteen, to Horace Tewksbury,
age sixty-nine, and imagined a life for them. I wept at the
funeral of Ethel Belcher Floyd, age thirty-one, who died of
Bright's disease; I cried for the unknown woman who had killed
herself by jumping off the cliff near Cottage Hill and left a
note, saying, *Please rite my husband, Patrick Kelly, Bergen, New Jersey.*

When I heard Granny come in, words tumbling out of her
mouth, I did not look up. I was reading, month by month, the
name of each baby, the day it was born, and the names of the
parents. Everything would seem normal, then I would come to
a date, followed by the word, *stillborn.* I knew that stillborn
meant the baby had been born dead, but there were so many:
January 3, *stillborn;* March 14, *stillborn;* April 29, *stillborn.* All the
way down the column, there was a stillborn baby practically
every month. The hair on the back of my neck stood up. The
dead babies had not been given names. The parents weren't
listed. And after the blank places, on the far right-hand side of
the page, it sometimes said, *Washed up on the beach.* My finger
traveled furiously down the column and across to the edge of
the page. *Stillborn. Washed up on the beach. Stillborn. Washed up on*

the beach. Stillborn. Washed up on the beach. I choked and spilled my tea all over Granny's best tablecloth.

While we were mopping up and Granny was scolding me shrilly for being so careless, I though about what I'd just read. Babies. Born dead. Thrown into the ocean like garbage. Children not wanted. Babies thrown into the sea to wash up on the beach like flotsam and jetsam from a shipwreck. Dead infants rolling out of the waves, the surf like the hems of christening gowns, their hands like little starfish clutching at sand.

And then something hit me hard. What if the babies hadn't been born dead? What if they were alive, and the parents didn't want them, so they just threw them into the waves? What if the mother was alone and too poor to have a baby, and she didn't want anyone to know that she had no husband? What kind of mother could stand at the edge of a cliff with a gurgling child in her arms wrapped tight in a blanket, and throw it into the waves, watch it bob there gently, the blanket floating open like a flower, until the baby and the blanket sank out of sight? How could a woman go back to her life after that?

"Granny," I whispered. "Did you know that a lot of babies born in this town died . . . and their mothers . . ." I couldn't finish.

"Oh," she said. "In those days, lots of babies died. Old Mrs. Green, your grandfather's mother"—I looked across the street at the big white house with the stone foundation and curved glass entranceway—"had a pair of twins who died of cholera when they were only a few months old. Then she had seven healthy children, and the last one, little Howard, died of gastritis at five months."

My mouth dropped open in shock. Old Mrs. Green was my great-grandmother, related to me like Anna Watkins, and she'd lost three babies, not one.

"But Granny," I stammered, pointing to the Town Report. "You don't understand. The babies were born, and they . . . they washed up later on the beach. How could that happen?" I wanted comfort, some kind of explanation.

"I don't know," she shrugged. "Some people are crazy. Come on, let's take a tour of the house." She marched into the front hall and called for me to come to her, as though I were a dog. I sighed. She'd already forgotten about the babies who'd died.

I shook my head and numbly padded into the hall. Another tour. I chafed, partly from boredom, partly from despair. Granny's house was stuffed with things—furniture, whatnots, knick-knacks, mirrors, paintings, hassocks, lamps, candelabra, platters, bowls, trivets, and oriental rugs. Everything was covered with gold leaf, flowers, vines, or fruit. There was too much to look at, and you had to walk carefully so you didn't bump into anything or knock some precious ornament from a shelf or the mantel or the top of all the radiators. To take a tour of the house meant that Granny would pull down every object from its niche, a cabinet, a hook on the wall, and make me hold it while she told me where it had come from, how much she had paid for it, and the hundreds of dollars it would be worth if she were to sell it now, which, of course, she would not—for any price. I'd heard it all a thousand times. Each box and saucer was invaluable, as precious as her own blood. I gnawed at my lip for a minute, and understood. She had surrounded herself with this many things so she could exist as a person. Because of them, she had value and purpose and a sense of self-worth.

Of course, everything was not valuable, except to her. Once she and her sister Madeline were in Harvard Square attending the opening of a new Valentino picture when his long black limousine pulled up in front of the theater. Granny elbowed her way through the crowd, opened the door, and flung herself inside. Granny, the flapper in a black-beaded dress, sat beside Rudolph Valentino in his tux and tails, batting her long lashes, and asked him for a cigarette. He raised an eyebrow, slowly exhaled a cloud of smoke, and put the cigarette he'd been smoking between her lips. When she got out, he drove off in a cloud of blue exhaust, and she'd kept his cigarette for forty-five years—oval with violet-colored paper around the tobacco and a gold paper tip, wrapped in tissue paper tied with a lavender ribbon. If she ever sold it, she said, it would be worth millions. I was amazed.

She had never thrown anything away in her life. Beside a blue Delft plate—with a crack in it as wide as a river—was a Toby jug, dating from the Revolutionary War. It too was damaged, and she didn't seem to notice how badly she'd patched the lip of the pitcher. Each of them were worth a fortune, she said. She had a drawer full of Irish linens and would unfold them as if they were the chasubles and albs worn by the Pope himself—except that she hated the Pope and all the Catholics in the world. These'll fetch a lot of money someday, she said, even though the tablecloths and napkins were stained and torn and dotted with cigarette burns. In the pantry was a shoebox full of teacup handles—no cups to match, just the handles— wrapped up and tied with string like a treasure. She could remember to the penny what she'd paid for a facecloth at Jordan Marsh in 1928, and when we checked the original ticket still attached, she would be right. She kept dozens of tin pie plates in a paper bag. She saved coffee cans, newspapers, and string. What she thought she could do with burned-out light bulbs I never knew, but there was also a box of them, bulbs so old they were made of clear glass and I could see the charred filaments inside.

My father's paintings along the wall of the hallway, hung in elaborately scrolled gold-leaf frames, were her pride and joy. He had painted them over the years because Granny had insisted that her son was an artist, had talent and must not waste it. It was embarrassing to look at them. They were awful. I could draw better at eight than he could as an adult. He had no sense of color, perspective, or composition. He never really looked at what he was painting, or if he had looked, he hadn't seen. The still-lifes were flat—his apples had no cheeks, his pitchers had no curves, nothing cast a shadow, nothing shone with light; there was no light in any of his pictures. There was no light in the house. The venetian blinds were always closed, the drapes were drawn. It was like living in a cave.

Before we went into her bedroom, Granny would turn to me and say triumphantly, like the monarch of a great kingdom, "I've saved all of this for you! Just think, all of this will be yours someday when I die! But you must never sell anything. You must save it for your grandchildren. Think how much it will all be worth then!"

I sat down, defeated, on the sleigh bed, feeling completely trapped. I could see the future she had planned for me, and it was more terrible than anything I could imagine. I hated things. I had no patience with knickknacks and doodads. I hated dusting and housekeeping of any kind. I hated Granny's black house—whoever heard of painting a house black? There wasn't a single book in it, just a lot of stuff. All I wanted was to read in peace and be able to write books. But here was my future—a black house full of things. And she hadn't saved any of it for me; she'd saved it for herself, before I'd even been thought of, but she and I were the same, weren't we?

Granny flung open her closet and began yanking out dresses and handbags and hats with little veils and crushed silk roses, talking, talking, her knifelike voice, muffled by coat sleeves, still cutting into my heart. She turned from the closet, her arms full of sky blue and navy dresses, blue sweaters, blue blouses, blue smocks. Every single article of clothing she owned was blue. She wouldn't wear any other color.

"And," she said, her face flushed with some kind of weird and creepy happiness, "after I die, you'll never have to buy any clothes. You can wear everything of mine!" I slumped down on the bedspread, holding my stomach, wishing I knew how to poison myself.

"Here," she said, flinging her clothes at me. "Put these on."

I staggered to my feet, feeling like a sleepwalker in a nightmare. I pulled her blue-flowered smock over my shoulders and buttoned it tight at the throat.

"Now this," she said, thrusting into my hands a curly, bluish-gray wig. *God, Granny, no!* I tried to protest, but my lips wouldn't move. She wrenched the wig over my head, frantically tucking in the strands of my real hair so none of it showed. She stood me in front of the dressing table so I could watch. She darkened my eyebrows with her eyebrow pencil, then put rouge on my cheeks. She traced my mouth hard with lipstick. She clipped her favorite silver flower earrings onto my ears. She was talking, talking, talking, then rummaging again in the closet and pulling out bags. She came back with a hatbox full of musty tissue paper folded around a broad-brimmed white felt hat with a white ribbon circling the crown. She stationed it over the wig and pulled the brim down over one eye—the one eye I could see with.

"There!" she said, rubbing her hands together in delight, turning into the closet once more.

I knew what was coming. We had done this lots of times. She was going to snap my picture—and in it I would look just like her. With the camera in one hand and my elbow in the other, she steered me into the dining room and stopped me in front of the buffet. She opened the white wooden venetian blinds for more light. I was bleaching out, color was draining from my face, dissolving into white film.

"Turn your head and tip up your chin so I can see your pretty profile. Just like Gloria Swanson's. People always told me that I looked like Gloria Swanson."

I glared away from the window. The shutter clicked. I was disappearing altogether.

"Now, face me, and look out from under the hat, the way Veronica Lake peeked out from under her hair."

The shutter clicked. I was buried in Granny. There was no Melissa. Melissa lay still, inside a glass coffin, inside a glass heart. She was dressed in a white christening gown, encased in ice on a linen snowbank, opaque and infinitely quiet.

But suddenly, far away, down the long tunnel to the tiny

pulse that beat like a baby chick's, came a tinkling sound. The prisms on the candelabras were clinking together, the faintest bar of music, as beautiful as rhyme. I opened my eyes. Sunlight was streaming in through the blinds, dust motes dancing like chips of gold leaf in each beam. The light was soft, insistent, passing like a draft through the prisms of the candelabra. A rainbow shimmered on the hardwood floor and the prisms clinked gently. The light was steady. It burned. It pierced the prism, the spectrum shattered, and all the colors were spilling on the floor like living paint.

I had to let that light pierce me. I had to turn my eyes toward the penumbra, between the perfect shadow on all sides and the fullest light, for only then could knowledge permeate my glass heart like a shaft of gold, splintering the spectrum inside me, so all the colors in the world could become my palette.

And then the glass coffin became a room filled with brightness, radiating poetry and light, a dazzling, luminous refraction of everything I knew and everything I would come to know, and in the shining noonday of that moment, crystalline as a prism, I saw all the tints and chromatics and chiaroscuro in the world begin and end with the same language. Poetry gave everything its color and music, the beautiful tinkling of rhyme. In my glass room, inside my glass heart, I would want for nothing. I would have color and music and rhyme, all the brightness between dawn and Hesperus at the end of my pen. In my glass room, inside my glass heart.

I loved school. Our teachers were older women with soft freckled hands, spectacles, and quiet voices, and I felt they cared for us as if we were their own children. It was wonderful being called by the bells. The schedule was vastly comforting. There was a time and place for everything. There were no surprises, no outbursts. I was not afraid of being hit, except at recess. School was like a cocoon on those days when I felt frail and battered, my skin transparent as a butterfly's. I sat in the same

seat all year and felt safe, knowing that my desk was my own.
I was smart, obedient, well-behaved, well-groomed. I didn't
whisper in class. I didn't daydream. I got good marks. Then
Mrs. Chase, my first-grade teacher, called in my mother one
day when I was not there because she thought that something
was terribly wrong—with me.

Mrs. Chase was very concerned. I was too perfect, she said.
Were things all right at home? My mother, of course, said everything was fine. *Let me show you something,* my teacher said, and
brought my mother to my desk, next to the windows, third
from the front. *This is why I'm so worried,* she said, and opened
the lid. Lunch bags, wadded-up Kleenexes, one mitten, half a
tuna-fish sandwich, crayons, workbooks, spelling tests, a bank-
book, issues of *My Weekly Reader,* pencils, old apple cores, all
had run riot inside. The desk lid barely closed over the chaos.

Melissa is so quiet, Mrs. Chase said. *She doesn't play with other
children. She stands by herself on the playground or with the teachers. She
never fusses. She does her work beautifully. But sometimes when a child is
upset, it shows up in other ways—like this.* My mother said I was shy
and more comfortable in the company of adults, but I was fine.
Mrs. Chase hesitated. *I think Melissa—well, there's no easy way to
say this—I think she needs help. Would you consider . . . taking her to see
. . . a psychiatrist?* My mother stood up, deeply offended, and
thanked Mrs. Chase for her time. It was 1960. No one in
Townsend had ever heard of such a thing. *My daughter is fine,*
my mother repeated, and that was the end of it.

I struggled to make friends. I rejoiced in the reading, the
homework, the learning. In third grade I got to be in the flu-
tophone band. I was chosen to play the Virgin Mary in the
Christmas pageant. I won a science award. I was the best artist
in the class. My teachers were full of praise. I was happy in
school until I got to the sixth grade.

Our teacher that year was every parents' nightmare, every
pupil's bad dream. She was spiteful, punitive, erratic, eccentric,
and downright mean. The faculty, the principal, the School

Board all thought she should retire—but we knew she was just plain crazy. We called her Biddy. She had blue hair and cheeks like windfalls. She wore wire-rimmed glasses, stockings with black seams and black lace-up Enna Jetticks with a square black heel, and the same mauve-flowered dress or its sister every day, with a belt cinching the waist near her armpits, her pendulous breasts hanging in front of her cast-iron belly like two misshapen squashes. She never taught the subject she was assigned to teach. She harangued us about politics, religion, rock 'n' roll, Vietnam, drugs, sex, flower children, nigger-lovers, and the evil minds that possessed children at eleven years of age. There didn't seem to be anyone in the world whom she didn't hate. Hours spent in her classroom were a waste of time. Every morning she showed us the proper way to wash our bodies, so that we wasted neither soap nor motion. She dragged an old tennis racket with unraveling catgut out of the closet and spent days giving us lessons in the backhand and forehand. Biddy was so obsessed with our being dirty little children, she occasionally searched our heads for lice. We didn't learn the subjects we were supposed to be studying. We couldn't catch up on homework. We were marooned with a lunatic.

Fourth period that year, just before lunch, we found ourselves in reading class with Biddy presiding. We'd been given independent work as an experiment, to test our maturity, our initiative, our stick-to-it-iveness, and since it was the first time the school had attempted such a thing, there didn't seem to be any rules. In September we were each handed a reading textbook and accompanying workbook, which we were supposed to work on every day during that hour. The previous summer I had read *Emma*, *The Three Musketeers*, *The Count of Monte Cristo*, *Pride and Prejudice*, *Sense and Sensibility*, and half of Dickens. The sixth-grade reader was incredibly dull and stupefyingly easy. I read the text and completed the workbook by the middle of October, even though it was intended to last throughout the year. On the morning I had finished answering the last question, I cleared my throat, gathered up my materials, and stood meekly in front of Biddy's desk.

"What do you want?" she snapped. "Go back to your seat and do your work."

I hesitated. The pointer was sitting at her elbow.

"Well, girlie, what is it? Speak up!"

"I'm . . . I'm finished." I stuttered.

"Finished? Finished what?" Her eyes shrank under her spectacles until they looked like the eyes of a large rat.

"I've finished my reading—and workbook."

"Impossible. I don't believe you. Do you know what happens to little girls who lie? They grow up to become prostitutes and criminals. Do you want to spend the rest of your life in jail? Lies, lies, that's where it all begins, girlie. Return to your seat."

She turned back to her attendance book.

"But . . ." I choked, my heart in my throat. I opened the workbook to the last few pages and fanned them before her so she could see the penciled handwriting filling in each line, down to the very end.

She stopped, her red pen in mid-air, momentarily at a loss for words. I could see her trying to argue me out of it. She took off her glasses and rubbed them several times on a lace hankie with pansies on it. I watched her cleaning and cleaning her glasses. The clock ticked on the classroom wall. There wasn't another sound in the room.

"Well, girlie, anything done that quickly is bound to be full of mistakes. Go back to your seat. Open your book to page one and start all over again."

I stood there stupidly with my mouth open.

"I said, go back to your seat and start over. And not one mistake this time."

I slunk into my seat, flushed to the roots of my burning hair. How dare Biddy imply that I hadn't done the work, or hadn't done it properly. I should have cracked her on the skull with my book when I'd had the chance. I couldn't go through this

tedious book again, I just couldn't. I looked around the classroom. The boys were making spitballs. It was the fashion that
year for girls to weave long chevroned chains out of gum wrappers until the chains had reached the height of a boy they
liked. Some of the girls had their desks propped up with a
history book and were quietly folding gum papers out of Biddy's line of vision. Nobody else was finished with their work.
No one was even close. Maybe I had made mistakes. Maybe I
had read and written too fast. I sighed and opened my book to
page one.

After two weeks of rereading, I knew that everything was
correct. What was I supposed to do for the rest of sixth grade?
I couldn't sit there and twiddle my thumbs, and I refused to
make gum-wrapper chains. Then I had it! I would find Mrs.
Foresman, the reading teacher, and ask for another project. I
raised my hand for a drink of water, shut the classroom door
quietly behind me, and ran down the stairs and the long corridor to the reading teacher's office. She was in the library,
restacking books on the shelves from a gray metal tray table,
the room, with the shades half-drawn, smelling sweetly of
paste and dust. Mrs. Foresman was a pretty woman, a friend of
my mother's, with big brown eyes and short salt-and-pepper
hair. She sat very still as I told her that I'd finished all of my
work, and she seemed to be wincing when I repeated Biddy's
remarks. She opened her mouth to speak, but thought better
of it, got up from her chair and told me I could choose a book
to read on my own. There were shelves of novels lined side by
side, in beautiful alphabetical order. I knew I had to hurry,
because Biddy would be clocking me, so I grabbed *The Scarlet
Letter* by Nathaniel Hawthorne, sighing with contentment as
the book was checked out to me. I slipped it into the pocket
of my jumper and ran back to class. I propped open my reader,
The Scarlet Letter safely tucked inside it, and happily began.

I read in peace for three days until Biddy went on patrol for
comic books. She swore they were the work of the devil, that

any boy who read comic books was bound to be indulging in masturbation and, later, pornography. I always wanted to cover my ears when she started in on the subject of masturbation. It unnerved me. I didn't know what it meant and didn't want to know, ever. But I was so engrossed in the plight of Little Pearl that I was caught unawares—a great shadow fell across my book. I looked up distractedly and Biddy was standing over me with the pointer angrily beating time on her palm like a metronome. She snatched the book, slammed it shut, and tossed it across the room. She ordered me to lay my hands flat on my desk, palms up, and the pointer stung like fire ants as she whipped and whipped my hands. It was days before I had the courage to sneak back into the library to ask for another book. I couldn't tell Mrs. Foresman that Biddy had beaten me. I told her I needed another book. I chose *The Robe*, and promised myself this time that I wouldn't get caught. Besides, the book was about sacred things and I didn't want Christ to be thrown across the room in a fit of Biddy's temper.

I was reading the chapter where the beautiful Diana is cursing the emperor as unfit to be a Caesar and insisting that she be put to death with her beloved Christian husband Marcellus when Biddy suddenly clapped her hands—desk inspection! There was a tremendous commotion of desk lids being raised. Oh, God! My desk was absolute chaos! Biddy grabbed a wastebasket in one hand, her pointer in the other, and began poking through the contents of a student's desk, wrinkling her nose as if she was expecting to smell something bad.

"Slovenly, slovenly, slovenly," she said under her breath as she passed from desk to desk. "Children are spoiled, all of them. A neat desk indicates a pure heart, a clean mind. A neat desk hides no secrets, no evils, the devil can't find a foothold!"

She used the pointer to move books and papers that she didn't want to touch with her hands. If she found something not to her liking, she'd shriek as if she'd seen a tarantula, make the student stand up, exhibit the forbidden object, and then throw the offending item into the rubbish.

This day she was triumphant—a lipstick was found hidden behind a math book. Biddy took the gold case, slowly, from the girl's hand, and unwound it sensuously until the long tapered end of Kisses of Rubaiyat appeared, crimson and dewy. Biddy put down her pointer and basket. She took the girl's white face in her hand, pinched her chin hard, and without a word, smeared the bright red paint over the girl's lips like a clown's; on her cheeks she drew two large circles, colored in to look like apples.

"So, you want to wear lipstick, do you, girlie?" Her smile was like a snake's. "You can wear it like that for the rest of the day."

Biddy came in my direction. I was on my way to becoming a laughingstock. How did everyone else keep their desks so neat? My hands were trembling as I held up the lid of my desk. I'll probably be expelled, I thought. Lunch money was strewn among gum wrappers. Spelling tests were crumpled under dirty gym socks. There were pencil shavings, a hairbrush full of hair, popsicle sticks, index cards, a bottle of Elmer's glue that had opened and leaked and stuck together three nickels, four rubber bands, a paper clip, a red rubber eraser and a half-sucked fireball. My books had tumbled into piles as though an earthquake had rocked a badly made building that could never be realigned. I could never find anything without a struggle. It had always been like this.

Biddy stood with her back toward me, smiling grimly over at my neighbor's neat desks, berating the rest of the class. Her hand held my desk lid like a lectern. I was next. I stared at her ugly hand, freckled with age spots. Her forearm was plump, with a little pillowing of flesh around the elbow. The skin under her short sleeve wiggled like jelly as she talked. I closed my eyes. I was as good as dead.

All at once, beyond the crook of her elbow, I saw a soft light coming through the window. The sky was just as blue as it had been all morning. How could I have forgotten that? Then I remembered Moses in Genesis calling on God. Moses said out loud, *Lord, Lord,* and the great God Jehovah responded out of

the vastness of Heaven, *Here I am*. Tears came to my eyes whenever I thought of God hearing Moses in the depths of his
despair, and saying kindly, gently, humanly, *Here I am*. It was
not like a man and his God at all, but two brothers who were
walking in the woods together, momentarily losing sight of
one another, and one calling out, a little afraid, *Where are you?*
to which the other replied, for comfort, *Here I am*.

Lord, Lord, I cried to myself, a tear falling from my lashes. I
was carrion, the devil's spawn. As Biddy's voice cackled and
stormed through her tirade, her cast-iron rump in my face, the
room was dissolving into a single spot of golden light, no bigger than a pinprick, and I was falling into it like a well-shaft,
down, down toward its flaming center, my hands clenched on
the desk lid, my lips moving, forming the words that might
save my life, *Lord, Lord.*

Suddenly Biddy left my desk and strode to the front of the
room. Her voice, laced with sarcasm, filled the air like some
kind of sticky poison that you put under the sink to kill mice.

"Well, well," she said, rubbing her hands together, grinning
like a witch in a fairy tale who had created something deli-
ciously ugly. "Some of you little monsters have actually been
listening to me! None of you has the brains God gave little
green worms, and yet, lo and behold—I can scarcely believe
it—the devil himself hasn't found much of a foothold among
you." Biddy glared at the lipsticked girl, who blushed, and then
went over to the window, letting in the cold air.

My mouth was open and so was my desk. I quickly closed
the lid. The kids in the class looked over at me. They knew
my desk was always a disaster and that Biddy hadn't seen it.
Would one of them tell her? I held my breath, not daring to
believe I'd been saved.

The bell rang and the kids trooped out for lunch and recess.
Biddy stalked off to the teacher's room. I put my head on my
arms and cried like a baby. Things were too confusing. I
couldn't hang on to myself. I felt like a goat in a roomful of

sheep, trying to scramble up a hard-scrabble hill, slipping and sliding unsteadily on stones that would not stay put under my hooves. Everything was such a mess—my desk, my home, my heart. I wiped my nose on my sleeve and got up to find the wastebasket.

I threw out spelling papers, the glue, and some pine cones, tossed out a fistful of broken crayons, three hair ribbons, wads of scrap paper, an old report card, a map of Finland. I wiped my nose and threw out lunch bags, a sardine can full of paper clips, an old snot rag. I worked through recess, organizing the desk until the spines of my workbooks were lined up perfectly, my books were stacked, and my pencils were nesting in the pencil tray. I didn't know how long it would stay this way, but I would try to keep it neat.

It was Friday afternoon. On my way home I sat sullenly on the bus, staring out the window. I sulked all through supper. On Friday evenings my father gave up his place in front of the old Zenith and we were allowed to watch TV for two hours, but I couldn't stand the silliness of the "Man from U.N.C.L.E." and "Star Trek," so I went to bed early, putting on my heavy wool socks, pulling up the army blankets over my head in what Granny liked to call my skunk's nest. I wanted to defy the day. My scorn knew no bounds.

Biddy was not the enemy, I decided. She was crazy as a loon. The real, more insidious enemy was boredom. Home and school were the same: I had to waste my time on repetitive, stupid, meaningless activities, performed with the same reluctant and furious obedience. I hated being such a good girl, but I didn't have the nerve to be rebellious. I was a mouse and I knew it, and I hated myself. I might look like a quiet child with perfect penmanship and nice manners, but under my jumper I was molten, a criminal with a wish to murder as big as a mountain, a secret pyromaniac who'd like to burn down the school and reduce the farm to a pile of ashes. And yet, twinned with all this fury was a bursting wish to sing, to praise, to leap like a young goat from crag to crag and see the world, to weep for joy, to seek out its unexpected beauty, rich and wildly perfect. But no one understood this, not even me. The hateful words that flew out of my mouth were not the words I'd meant to say. I curled up in a ball and cried. Life was so humiliating. If something didn't happen soon, I would kill myself.

I plowed through the weekend in a stupor, doing my chores like a sleepwalker, but no one noticed. Everything seemed to be normal. My grandparents made their weekly visit from Boston. My father flew into a rage the minute Granny spoke to him, and stormed out of the house with his first beer, slamming all the doors behind him. Flap stayed out back until lunchtime. Granny rearranged the china cupboard in the dining room— the farm had been her summer home and she moved through it as if it were still her house. My mother, furious and silent, looked on. I made two platters of baloney and cheese sandwiches, put the kettle on for tea, and set the table. My sister was nowhere to be seen. My father and grandfather stood around the open-hooded cars in the yard, discussing their mysterious and greasy work, my brother kneeling on the bumper against the shiny chrome grille with his tow head over the engine. I watched them changing the oil, rotating tires, replacing spark plugs, the same as last weekend and the weekends before. Nothing would ever change, I thought, things would simply be moved around, taken out, and put back, like everyday dishes. I filled the bird feeder, cursing under my breath. *Nothing would ever change. We would go on like this forever.*

And yet, as the day wore on, I felt something strange in the air, some perturbation, an odd humming. A storm? It was November, and we'd already had a few flurries, but the days were still fairly mild, though the temperature would drop considerably when the sun went down. Today the sky was clear and cloudless. Was I getting sick? I could always tell when I was coming down with a fever, because a medallion-shaped scar under my left breast would begin to ache. When I was

nine, I had fallen off Dorrie Moore's bike in her steep driveway
and landed hard on the handlebars, cracking one of my ribs. I
tested the scar with the palm of my hand, and for a minute I
imagined a twinge, the shadow of an ache, but it never really
started throbbing, so I shrugged it off and went about my
chores. However, in the turmoil of my body, I knew that something was about to happen.

I had nightmares all night, as usual. I yawned through ten
o'clock Mass the next morning. My mother and father sat at
the kitchen table in stony silence reading the *Boston Sunday
Herald-Traveller* while I knelt in the bathroom, scrubbing the
toilet and swearing under my breath. I was trying to finish
Wilkie Collins's *The Moonstone* so I could get started on *The
Woman in White*, but reading on weekends was especially forbidden because there were so many chores to be done, and I was
supposed to be "making myself useful." One day, I thought, my
father will say that to me once too often, and I'll beat him to
death with my broom.

Busy work, busy work, busy work. It was just like school. I
attacked the tub with the same white fury, only my fury was
whiter than the tub would ever be. I washed the curling linoleum with Spic and Span and a wire brush, knowing it would
never come clean. Busy, busy, busy. I swept the kitchen, the
pantry, the back hall, out into the breezeway, the mat, and the
outdoor bricks of the terrace. My parents continued reading
the paper. I swept the front hall stairs with the handbrush and
dustpan, banging the wooden-handled brush between the
stone-cold rungs of the radiator so they would hear that I was
busy working. I changed all the sheets, made up the beds fresh,
and carried the bundle of linen down to the cellar. I felt like a
slave, but I relished my martyrdom. It was an identity. Whenever my father noticed me pouting—which I did with great
drama, lots of sighing, and flouncing from room to room with
a bucket of water in my hand—he would mock me, calling me
poor little Cinderella. I'd turn on my heel in a rage and make a

tcchhing sound of pure hatred with my tongue on my teeth. I'm not your slave, I'd think to myself, sweeping furiously under the kitchen table. Someday I'm going to show all of you who I really am, and it isn't this! And anyway, Cinderella went to the ball and married the handsome prince and lived happily ever after, and so will I! And into that tcchhing sound went all the hatred and scalding epithets that I wanted to but didn't dare say. If something didn't happer. today, I was going to die.

A premonition came over me as I was peeling vegetables at the kitchen sink. Carrots, potatoes, cabbage, and turnips were to be boiled in a pot with some indescribable, fatty, and disgustingly tough cut of meat. The feeling was so strong that I stopped mid-stroke with the peeler. It was wonderful, whatever it was, a silence full of palpable longing, like the minute before a great symphony begins and you know in a heartbeat that you'll be hearing amazing music, almost as if the instruments themselves were anticipating the remembered notes in waves of sweetness. It was like waiting for the Decoration Day parade on Main Street, when the trees rustled slightly, and the full skirts of the women answered back. A baby stroller squeaked from being rocked up and down to keep the baby drowsing, and people talked, almost reverently, as they gazed down the street, and the wine-glass elms moved in time to the music that no one else could hear, like dancing in a silent movie. Soon there would be the faint percussion of drums. The horn would remove its mute and come up Main Street with its golden note, pure as ambrosia, followed by the snap of flags and the pounding of feet in unison. But it would still not be audible, though we could feel it like an ocean's undertow, pulling through the air like a current. Something was coming to me at the kitchen sink, some kind of music, some rapturous sound, and I couldn't move. I stood at the sink, listening, dumbstruck, a half-scraped potato in my hand.

Suddenly the room was suffocating. I threw on Flap's plaid work shirt, flung off my shoes, and jumped into my boots to

take the vegetable peelings to Rosita. I had to get out, my heart
was bursting. Something was passing through my body—
excitement or terror or bewilderment—coursing through my
flesh like white water rushing through a mountain gorge.
Everything had crystalized: colors, sounds, my body poised for
flight.

Rosita was standing under a pine tree in the muddy snow.
There'd been a thaw, and the sodden slush under the tree was
pockmarked with her peculiar hoofprints. Donkey's hooves are
not shod like horses'. They have to be trimmed every year, but
for as long as we'd owned her, the vet had never been called,
so her hooves had grown until they curved around and in upon
themselves. She was like an ancient holy man of the east who
sat under a sacred tree for years without moving, whose hands
rested on his knees in silence, in meditation, whose fingernails
grew and kept growing until they cut into and through the
palms of his hands. Rosita's hooves curved like rams' horns
until she had to hobble on her fetlocks. It was cruel, pitiless.
And the longer it went on, the more impossible it was for the
vet to ever be called. It was like the year I had poison ivy and
lay in my room for days without a doctor, or the five winters I
went to school every day with tonsils so infected that I could
hardly speak, and still no doctor was called. Rosy's feet made
me cry, but how could I call a vet without betraying my family?
My parents' motto held sway: *If you ignore something long enough,
it will go away.*

I gave Rosita the peelings and stroked her long, soft face. I
understood her gratitude for small acts of kindness. I felt
wretched for not being able to help her. A mild breeze came
up from the valley and moved over my cheeks and bare hands.
The pale sun was white and impassive, but I opened my jacket
and the air was like a caress. I felt warm and happy and out of
breath.

The family ate dinner in silence. When there wasn't hollering or plate smashing or tears, it was deadly quiet, but for the

hollow sound of forks on plates and chewing amid a heavy, ponderous vapor of unspoken feelings that could never surface through the dense air. I bolted my food. I had to get away from the weighty, dark, inarticulable storm that was brewing inside us but would not break that day. I put down my fork and waited for the others to finish so I could clear the table, hearing one tine touch the plate like the plucking of a harp. A single bright note and the tone died, though the aftertone lingered, clear as a bell, in my mind. Something was coming that I didn't know about, and I was waiting for it, clenching my hands in my lap.

My sister and I did the dishes in the same silence while my father closed himself off in the living room with his beer, and my mother sat at the table, ruffling pages, a cigarette burning down to its filter in the ashtray. My sister wiped the silverware, as sullen as I. My brother snapped a dish towel on my fanny but when the crack! on my dungarees resounded, sending them both into peals of laughter, I didn't react. It was as if what was happening all around me—my sister banging dried plates into the cupboard, my brother crashing pots and pans in the pantry, my own hands in the gray soapy water—was occurring some-where else, far away. Someone was washing the dishes, but I wasn't there, and the childish hoots filtered through a dream that was passing over my face like a fog, a vision, the shadow of a vision, yet more real than life itself. I drained the soapy water and scoured the sink. I wiped the grease off the top of the stove. I put away the food like a sleepwalker.

On Sundays my brother, sister, and I all had to take naps. It had been the custom since we were babies, but I thought it was ridiculous that I still had to take naps—I was eleven-and-a-half years old! The three of us would trudge up the narrow stairs to our rooms like prisoners returning to their cells. My mother would close her door and read historical fiction all afternoon. My father would snore in front of the television, and Flap would read murder mysteries from the library under his gooseneck lamp, moving the due-date card over the print, line by line, so he wouldn't lose his place. My brother would work on his model cars. My sister would plug fat white ear-phones into her tiny black transistor radio, lie on top of her blankets with her back toward me, and be instantly absorbed in rock 'n' roll. I'd throw myself face-down in my skunk's nest and pull a pillow over my head.

I envy my sister, I thought, burrowing deeper under the feathers. She will be one of them. She'll be popular with boys. She already knows how to surrender herself to the music every-body likes. I envied her the way I envied girls in my class who seemed to know so many things I didn't, about growing up, about boys, about belonging. My grandfather had given us all transistor radios for Christmas, and because it was the very latest thing, I was excited to think that I could discover what all the commotion was about and could be more like the girls in my class: Jody, Linda, Karen, Marie, girls who were pretty, who devoured *Seventeen* magazine, who raved about the Beatles, Donovan, the Dave Clark Five, the Supremes, and who knew the same anecdotes, howled at the same jokes, watched the same television programs, shopped with their mothers at Rog-er's and R. H. Stearns. I had listened to my little radio for almost a month, trying to understand what they liked and why they liked it. What was I missing? I felt as though I were drowning at the bottom of the sea, hearing strange incanta-tions through the waves from a lost civilization. I couldn't com-prehend them at all. I imagined one song—"Downtown," by Petula Clark—to be describing my life as a writer living in glamorous New York City when I grew up. But even that tune palled after a while, and when the batteries ran down in the radio, it never occurred to me to replace them.

Sunday naps were a kind of luxury, actually, though I resented the hell out of being sent to bed as if I were a two-year-old child. Sometimes I really did sleep, though I didn't know which was worse—my nightmares or my waking life.

Sometimes I read. Sometimes I looked out the window for
hours, thinking about everything and nothing at all. Today
I was restless, I couldn't get comfortable, I couldn't focus on
anything. There was still a vague thrumming in my ears.

I leaned over the edge of my mattress and a curtain of hair
fell over both sides of my face to the floor. Under my bed was
just like my desk at school. I was a slob. I saw dust kittens as
big as ocelots, three shoes, a pair of red tights, my gym bag,
paperback books with cracked spines left open where I'd
stopped reading them, a balled-up towel, a headband, a mocca-
sin, a couple of dead wasps. And, of course, my treasure chest
of paper: a cardboard carton full of spiral notebooks, two reams
of Boston Naval Shipyard bond, a box of onion skin, three
steno pads—all that beautiful pristine paper. I'd always been in
love with clean white paper, the way it smelled, its smoothness
in my hands. I lived in fear that we would have another
Depression and there wouldn't be enough paper. For years I'd
been cadging an extra notebook out of my mother at back-to-
school time, so I would always have paper to write my stories
on. It was a great thing to be a writer, I thought, because no
matter how poor you were, there would always be paper and a
stub of pencil somewhere. Thank God I wasn't a painter or a
sculptor who would need a studio, expensive paints, canvas,
tools, and stone. As a writer, I could be as destitute as a church
mouse and still be able to work. And if the house ever caught
fire, I could throw all my writing out the window into the snow
and it would be saved.

It was starting to sleet. I turned over on my side and watched
a knifeblade of ice scoring the glass. A shiver went through me
and I closed my eyes. The house was quiet except for the faint
scratching sound of my sister's radio and the sleet on the windowpanes. The anxious, exhilarating sense that something was
coming had gone, and in its place was a peace so sweet that I
wanted to cry. I sank into it, slowly, sleepily, the way one
would sink into an old-fashioned feather bed and drowse.

Suddenly I heard a voice, then another voice, two voices, a
conversation. What was it? It wasn't a dream. I was not asleep.
I could still hear the static from the radio and the sleet whispering on the window sill. I kept my eyes closed, listening. It was
the voice of a fifteen-year-old boy, Danny Hanks, talking to
his one-year-younger sister, Becky. It was the fall of 1837 in
Freedom, New Hampshire. My heart was in my throat. I heard
a cowbell's lazy clanging. The fields outside their farm were
bronze and green, and the yellow birch leaves were drifting
gently through the mild air like a light golden snowfall. I heard
the door to the summer kitchen open, squeak on rusty hinges,
and bang shut as they went into the house. Their grandfather
was sitting by the fireplace with a long white beard and suspenders, his arthritic hands clutching a wooden walking stick
with a carved English spaniel as its head, his bad leg resting on
a three-legged stool before him. He'd been wounded in the
Revolutionary War and had walked with a terrible limp ever
since. In the borning room beside the kitchen, a young woman,
his daughter Mae, the children's mother, lay on a pineapple
maple bed under a patchwork comforter, her fever not quite
broken. Her dark hair was spread out over the pillows. Her lips
moved quietly in prayer. She was dying. I could see her white
nightgown, soaked in sweat, and her long thin fingers picking
fretfully at the lace near her throat. There was a braided rug
on the floor and a blue-and-white covered chamber pot under
the bed. The end-of-summer light was coming in through the
muslin curtains. Becky and Danny stood silently at the foot of
her bed. Becky wiped her hands on her calico apron and placed
a bunch of black-eyed Susans in a vase on the night table by
the window.

Who were these people and how did I know so much about
them? My heart was pounding. A curtain in time had been torn
and I was witnessing a scene that had happened over a hundred
years ago. I could smell the old man's pipe smoke and the sour-
sweet odor of the sickroom. I could hear the creak of the

Windsor chair as the grandfather turned to throw a chunk of maple onto the fire. I saw sparks fly up and some tumble onto the hearthstone like a summer star shower.

All at once, I understood. It was this, this, that I had felt in the air, in my body, in the tiniest thoroughfares of my heart. It was this that I had been waiting for. It was not a dream. It was a book! These were people in a book that I was going to write! I lay very still, my eyes shut, afraid that if I moved a muscle, the idea would disappear like a mysterious and shape-shifting mirage. But after a minute, I knew it would never leave me, that these were characters in an imaginary family who would stay with me as long as I needed them, until I had written their story. I leaned over the bed, pulled a yellow spiral notebook out of my cardboard box, opened to the first page and put the date: November 17, 1965. Then I began to write.

School was never the same again. I'd been forbidden to read books during Biddy's classes, but no one had said a word about writing one. I opened my yellow notebook inside my reading workbook. Boys were making spitballs. Girls were braiding their gum-paper chains. Biddy was in the middle of a civics lesson. If I didn't stop myself, I would be grinning from ear to ear like a fool. Every day I had two whole hours to write and to figure out what being a writer meant. On Mondays I wrote in ballpoint; on Tuesdays in pencil; on Wednesdays in pen again. Each day's work was set off in a block headed by a date. That way, by the end of the week, I would have some way of gauging how many pages I'd written in a day. Sometimes the words flowed out in a fountain and I had a hard time writing fast enough to get them all down. Other times I just stared out the window, tapping the eraser end of my pencil on a blank sheet, wondering what in the world was coming next, and whatever possessed me to think I could write a book. Sometimes I didn't write at all, but simply watched my characters go about their lives. It seemed then that I was sitting in a plum-velvet orchestra seat in a cavernous old theater with gilded

chariots and cherubs and clouds flaking from the ceiling and
cobwebbed chandeliers twinkling in near-darkness. All of my
characters were actors on stage. I was there, not as author, but
as audience. It was their drama, not mine; they spoke lines of
dialogue that came naturally, words I had not put in their
mouths. In the darkened theater beyond the footlights, I copied down everything they said and did and thought. They were
creating themselves.

Part conduit, part carpenter, the torrent of ideas and descriptions poured through me in a glorious supernatural rush.
Where was it coming from? And why was it coming to me? I
had no answer but to keep taking everything down as though
I was divining it from God. And yet the words needed my help
and understanding. They were rough, unfinished, and bumped
awkwardly along my lined paper like one of the old logging
roads that ran from the top of Barker Hill to the abandoned
quarry. I had to smooth them out, plane their bumps and hum-
mocks into a clear, clean passage, which is how I learned the
value of details. An exact and careful detail pinned the sentence
to the paper the way an entomologist's pin made fast a butterfly. To write that the dying Mae Fowler was musical wasn't
interesting or descriptive. But to say that Mae Fowler played
the West Randolph, Vermont, Congregational church organ
when she was sixteen and met her ne'er-do-well husband-to-
be, Jedediah Wilton Hanks, at the Ladies' Day Picnic after
she'd finished a particularly melancholy version of "Abide with
Me"—now, that was interesting.

All that year I opened myself to the flood of inspiration and
tried to temper it always with real things. I learned how powerful simple words could be. I wrote "The woods were brown"
and knew that it was early November before the winter rains
came, that the trees were dark, the sky overcast, and the fallen
leaves were frost-sodden and no longer crackled underfoot. I
erased it and wrote, "The woods were gold" and saw a crisp
October day, a flawless azure sky, the silver birch and white

maple leaves fluttering still on their stems and spilling a faint
gold light over the stone walls and fields and farms. It was
thrilling beyond the saying of it. One word could change
everything.

I also discovered the pleasure of research. I had to find out
who was president in 1837 and learn a little about the people
of New Hampshire and what they thought of Andrew Jackson.
I found a book called *The History of American Costume*, and made
drawings of what they wore in the margins of my notebook.
Another book on nineteenth-century farm life led me to
recording the kind of buggies they drove and the sort of tools
that farmers had back then on 4 × 6 index cards. Stories came
to life in the details and I wanted to get them exactly right.

Aunt Amelia Fowler Duffy, the children's aunt, lived in West
Randolph, Vermont, with her two sons—Irwin, who wore
glasses and threw balls like a girl, and Bennet, who was a bully,
picked his nose, and liked to strangle frogs with his bare hands.
Aunt Duffy wore whalebone stays. She had a mole on her right
cheek with three white hairs growing out of it. Jedediah Wilton Hanks, Becky and Danny's father, sold snake-oil patent
medicine in his day and passed himself off as a surgeon and
dentist. He left Mae Fowler when the children were toddlers,
having married three women in succession without divorcing
any of them, and was reported to be a riverboat gambler like
Gaylord Ravenau in New Orleans. The grandfather was called
Colonel Fowler. He smoked Virginia tobacco, read Horace by
candlelight until the wee hours of the morning, and drank only
a cup of hot water for breakfast.

But the book was really about the children, Becky and
Danny. After a while they were as real to me as any playmates
I'd ever had. I became intimate with them in ways I could never
be with my own brother and sister. Becky and Danny loved
each other. Each one knew what the other was thinking without a word passing between them. They spent their days
together, the way country children do, because there were no

other children near. Becky was tiny and shy and afraid of
snakes. She had fallen out of a wild cherry tree on Baldwin's
farm when she was eleven and had a five-inch scar on her ankle
because old Doc Mulgrew had been hung over when he
stitched her up. She prayed every night for the soul of her
mother, and prayed, too, that her father would come back to
them someday. Danny was almost six feet tall with a shock of
chestnut hair. He trapped rabbits. He had perfect pitch,
though he rarely sang because singing reminded him of his
mother. He was good with a gun. He and his friend Beanie
Warren sometimes rode their horses out past the waterfall at
Jameson's Mill and shot pheasant and grouse.

Every morning when I opened my yellow spiral notebook
and read what I'd written the day before, I was faced with the
question, *And then what happened?* It wasn't enough to fall in love
with language, or write long descriptions of what things looked
like. I had to know what happened next, what people did and
why. I came to the part where the children's mother dies and I
had to imagine the whole scene as if it were happening to my
own mother. My stomach turned over at the thought. What
would it be like? Who would be in charge? What would we
say to one another? To her?

So I had Mr. Alfred Wingate, the postmaster, summon Aunt
Duffy and her boys by telegram to take over the sickroom and
death watch. When Aunt Duffy walked through the door, the
house was in a state of confusion. Colonel Fowler was pacing
in front of the fireplace, muttering about a battlefield under his
white walrus mustache, his spaniel-headed cane thumping on
the hearthstone as he passed. Aunt Duffy took off her hat,
plunged two ebony-ended hatpins into its crown, and brought
him a brandy, motioning for him to sit in his chair by the fire.

"Pa, it's Amelia. I'm here to take care of Mae." He blinked at
her like an owl and didn't seem to know her. She sent Danny
into town on Major, his gelding, to fish Dr. Mulgrew out of
his stupor and bring him to the house at once. Becky had been

trying to get her mother to sip chicken broth from a ladle, but she was so fretful that the soup kept spilling. Amelia stood at the foot of the bed, looked at her sister and knew it would not be long. Mae's face was gray and clammy, she was shivering with cold, her brown eyes glazed with pain. She kept calling for her own mother, long since gone. She died in Becky's arms without a word before Doc Mulgrew and Danny returned.

The next part was harder because I'd never seen a dead body. Aunt Duffy had Becky bring her a pan of warm rosewater while she undressed her sister modestly under the white sheet and washed her stiffening limbs. Becky rummaged through her mother's clothes cupboard and bird's-eye maple dresser looking for her prettiest chemise and drawers, the shift with the handmade lace, her best white stockings, and her sky-blue merino dress with the bisque collar and three-quarter sleeves. When the clothes were laid out on the bed, she began to cry.

"Child, your mother must wear Grandmother Eloise's cameo. Can you find it?" Aunt Duffy said, steering the child away from the deathbed to the dressing table. "And get her box of hairpins."

Becky sniffled and stopped to touch the silver-backed mirror, comb, and brush set and the squat glass-covered hair-receiver that her mother would never use again. She found Grandmother Eloise's pink-and-white cameo with the figure of Liberty carved on it, and in a cloisonné box she found the ivory hairpins. When she turned back to the bed, her dead mother was dressed. Aunt Duffy had parted her sister's long chestnut hair on either side of her limp shoulders.

"Now, child," she said matter-of-factly, but with kindness, "You must brush your mother's hair until it sparkles and then braid it. You can braid, can't you? Mae always had the most beautiful head of hair. When I was a girl, mine grew so long that I could sit on it, but dear little Mae—hers grew until it hung past her knees."

Aunt Duffy reminisced while both of them brushed and

braided until the room grew dark. She turned up the wick in the kerosene lamp on the night table, lifted the glass chimney to light it, and replaced the white globe with the blue irises on it that had been her sister's favorite.

"Give me the braid," Aunt Duffy said when Becky was finished, "and find her box of violet powder and the pearl earrings she wore when she got married." Becky found the powder box on the lace runner and the earrings wrapped in tissue paper carefully tied with pink ribbon in the smallest top drawer. She undid the knot and gingerly unwrapped the paper. The two pearls were breathtaking in their delicate filigree settings of gold.

"Mama hasn't worn these since her wedding day and now she is dead," Becky sobbed.

"Come, child," Aunt Duffy said, a bit sternly. "Give me one and you take the other."

Both figures bent over the dead woman, whose thick braids had been set with the ivory hairpins into a crown on her head, and gently clasped on the earrings. Aunt Duffy powdered her sister's already white face. With tears in her eyes, she opened her arms to her niece, and they both cried quietly for a long time until friends came to view the body, carrying food and wine and cakes.

The day of the funeral brought a black November rain, and mourners under umbrellas gathered around the grave at the top of Ford Hill. Colonel Fowler sat in a folding chair brought by the mortician Mr. Busbee, while Irwin and Bennet held Amelia's gloved hands. Becky and Danny stood side by side in their stiff funeral clothes and not a word passed between them. Neither shed a tear. Becky was gazing at the beautiful arrangement of flowers that covered her mother's coffin, tied with satin ribbon like a wedding bouquet. She thought of the small bunch of Queen Anne's lace that she had threaded through her mother's fingers before the coffin lid was nailed shut, and the soft kiss she'd put on her mother's brow, cold like marble. The minister finished his prayers and the gravediggers awkwardly lowered the coffin into the grave with ropes. The minister gave the shovel to Colonel Fowler to lift earth into his daughter's grave, but he could not. Danny took the shovel from the old man's trembling hands and shoveled twice, once for himself and once for his grandfather. He handed the shovel to his sister, and she shoveled twice, once for herself and once for the father who was lost to them. Colonel Fowler, Aunt Duffy, and her children rode back to the house in a carriage. Becky and Danny walked home through the woods, hand and hand, in silence.

When I finished this part of the story, I put my head down on my desk and cried. It was so sad. Poor beautiful Mae, with her long hair once past her knees, was under the ground forever. It was strange to walk out into the sunlight at lunchtime and discover that I was still a child. When some of the kids teased me about crying at recess, I lied and said I had a cold. I shuffled over to the swing set to get away from them, and pumped and pumped my legs until I was very high. As I swung back and forth, in an arc of fury, an arc of exhilaration, I thought about what I had just done. I was crying for the characters I had made up. They weren't really alive, so how could they die? And how could I mourn for them? At home when I sobbed at movies on television, my father would snort impatiently, "For Chrissake, it's only a movie!" And Granny always said, "That's just ketchup, you know. The director is telling her to fall down like that. It's not real!" I could never explain to them that I knew it was only a movie. What my family couldn't understand was that it was fiction, yes, but to me fiction was truer than life. Somewhere, sometime, something like that had actually happened. A soldier is shot looking into the eyes of his enemy, and it is himself he sees. A woman loses her baby and never gets over it. Two lovers are parted by fate and yet their lives cross again and again but they are destined never to meet. My story was more real than real, because children do lose their mothers; old men do live long after the battles are

over and it is still the greatest moment of their lives; fathers do
abandon their families; children do grow up alone on farms,
confused and frightened, with only themselves to depend on.

I didn't show my book to anyone, not at school nor at home.
I dragged the yellow spiral notebook everywhere, and it bol-
stered me. When I suffered a dressing down in class, my mind
was always miles away—at the fishing hole below Jameson's
Mill with Danny and Beanie Warren, catching trout. When my
father slammed and swore in the mornings, his hair standing
up in the air and a wild look in his eye, I stood serenely at the
stove stirring the glutinous mass of Maltex that we had for
breakfast, hearing Aunt Duffy's soft voice as she placed a monogrammed silver spoon in a cut-glass bowl of fresh strawberry
jam. I forgot to eat lunch. I picked at my supper. My desk at
school returned to chaos, but none of that seemed important.
I wasn't at home in my real life anymore. I was at home in my
novel.

The rest of the school year passed uneventfully. Biddy never
discovered me scribbling in my yellow spiral notebook during
class, I was never caught at desk inspection. By June I had
written 178 pages. The following term I would be attending a
junior high school run by nuns in the next city while the rest
of the class went to North Middlesex Regional High School in
town. It was a turning point, and I knew it, and for the first
time in a long while I didn't feel sad about everything. Writing
this book had made me braver. I sat in the stifling auditorium
on the last day of sixth grade, listening to speeches and jumping out of my seat to walk on stage and receive an award, but
my mind was elsewhere.

Becky and Danny and Beanie Warren and Aunt Duffy's two
boys were up at the water hole above Jameson's Mill. Becky
put down a wicker picnic hamper under the shade of the pine
trees and watched the boys stripping down to their underwear.
She took off her dress, stockings, and button shoes and laid
them neatly beside the basket. In her chemise and pantaloons

she waited behind the boys as each one grabbed the end of the old rope swing, made hooting noises like wild animals, and raced down the slope. The rope swing flew out over the falls in a great arc, and the boy at the end of it hollered with glee and let go, waving his arms and legs in pure joy and plunging into the frothing water below. The rope swing flew back and the next boy howled over the falls and dove gracefully into the water. Becky caught the knotted end of the rope and sped over the cliff's edge in her lace pantaloons; the swing spun and spun as she flew over the water and fell, swift as a white diving bird into the sea.

My heart was in my throat, but I was with them on that hot summer day at Jameson's Mill. I was afraid of speed, of heights, of water, but I took the end of that rope and ran down the slope to the cliff's edge, and when the swing flew out over the falls in a great arc, I was airborne, I was free.

PRISM

GRANY TOLD ME how her in-laws met, suffered a long court-ship and were married, based on facts recounted to her by other members of the family. But hearing only the dry bones of the story, I needed imaginatively to flesh out the details of what life might have been like for my great-grandparents, in order to make them more real to me and, especially, in order to understand what happened to the generations that followed.

> *I am a child of the sea, I sang,*
> *from soldiers and sailors I come;*
> *And for as long as I live, the sound of the sea,*
> *will measure my heart like a drum.*

I was singing to myself at Granny's dining-room table—stripped now of the Irish lace tablecloth she'd soaked in a tub of tea to age it and covered with pages from the *Boston Herald*—under the prisms and cream-colored satin shades of the brightly lit chandelier. On a long sheet of paper, I was drawing our family tree.

It was snowing, the day after Christmas. Except for the pine-cone wreath wired with walnuts, pecans, hazelnuts, and a red velveteen bow that Granny had made and hung on the front door, I wouldn't have known the time of year. Our teacher had given us a mimeographed sheet with blurry blue lines and

arrows entitled "My Family," and we were supposed to fill in
the names and dates of all our relatives. But the night before I
had torn up the useless sheet into tiny pieces. I wanted to make
a family tree that looked like a tree, so I had spent the entire
evening sitting on the pantry floor in front of the bottom
drawer of an old bureau where Granny kept all her art supplies,
choosing my weapons.

I pulled out a roll of paper and laid it on the oriental rug
under the dining-room window with frying pans, a sugar
cannister, a coffee can heavy with nuts and bolts, and a stack
of dinner plates to press out the curls by morning. Then I emptied the drawer, inspecting carefully the pastels, chalk, watercolors, oil crayons, oil paints, pencils, charcoal, inks, pens,
rulers, French curves, brushes, compasses, templates, fixatives,
calipers, modeling clay, and tracing paper marked with flowers,
cherubs, leaves, and fruit. It all smelled so good. To write in
the names and dates, I chose a 4H pencil, a gum eraser, two
colors of india ink, and a pen with a perfect point. I found the
watercolors and a watercolor brush. I picked out a brand-new
box of Grumbacher's pastels and a can of fixative for the
branches and leaves. I liked to draw standing up, with everything spread out where I could see it. This was going to be a
beautiful tree.

I made a lovely blue wash with the watercolors, light at the
top of the sky for wisps of clouds, a deeper, softer azure in the
middle of the page, and a rich cobalt line at the horizon. Then
I made a wash in green and gently brushed the grass, leaf
green, olive, and viridian. With Granny's help, I made a list of
relatives—who married whom, who died when, and as many
maiden names as she could remember. Finally, I began to draw
the tree over the watercolor wash. It would be a magical tree,
I thought, not like an oak or an elm or a maple, but resembling
something from a myth or fairy tale. I gave it hardy limbs at
the bole that rose into delicate branches, twisting and crossing
into twigs, with a feathery crown. All the leaves would be a

different pastel color, I decided as I drew, the deeper shades spiraling up from the first limbs, growing lighter and smaller as they reached the top. Then, using a ruler, I drew lines in pen and ink and wrote out the names of my ancestors in pencil.

I knew my mother's family as far back as Hannah Rockett— a French Huguenot who had escaped across the English chan- nel in the hammock of a brigantine. I knew Granny's family, on one side, back to Henry Hudson Kimball who drowned in Lake Champlain, and Thomas and Hannah Watkins, the par- ents of her grandmother, Anna, from Barford, England, on the other. But the Greens were far less clear to me. As I drew, Granny gave me her version of how the Greens came to America.

"The old man, Jeremiah Green, my father-in-law—your great-grandfather—came over from Ireland with his mother when he was ten years old, right in the middle of the Civil War," Granny said. "Damned shanty Irish they were, the whole lot of them. His father, John Green, was lost at sea, so he and his mother came alone. But the sea must have stayed in the blood—Jeremiah left his mother at fifteen to be a cabin boy."

Now that I had all the lines drawn and the names in place, I began sketching in the heart-shaped leaves, and tried to imag- ine my great-grandfather as a boy.

Jeremiah was only ten years old. His father's body was never recovered. His older sisters settled in Brooklyn, New York, for the rest of their lives. How different from Ireland, from Castletown Bere outside of Kinsdale Harbor, it must have been. Had they lived in a row of sooty brick tenements? Or was their house in the country made of turf, with a peat fire and black-and-white-faced sheep nuzzling a stone water trough? Could his wizened mother, having survived the fam- ine, imagine anything worse than leaving Ireland? Did she weep or stand stony-eyed as she pulled her son by the hand up the gangway of *The Girl Aurelia* on its final voyage, knowing

she would never come back? Or perhaps she wanted to flee all
the death and suffering and start a new life?

And the young boy, not sickened by the pitch and heave of
the North Sea, did he climb every inch of the ship from bow
to stern, fall in love with the wave-swells, the danger, the mysterious workings of shrouds and ratlines, even the bandy-
legged tattooed sailors who taught him knots and politics, his
face reddened by sun and wind and insults as he ran behind
them, a sea-spray of excitement salting the corner of his mouth
as he bawled his replies?

And coming into Boston, a good Catholic boy drenched in
the stories of the saints, would he have known his new many-
tongued city had been named for Saint Botolph, patron saint
of fishing? Could he see the harbor, the wharves, the fleets of
ships crossing under the clouds and slipping like otters onto
the docks from the Charlestown settlement where he and his
tottering mother huddled in a dressmaker's attic under draper-
ies, hastily basted selvadge, and a mountain of serge? Did he
hear the anchors winched on board and watch the glistening
spars rock gently as the billowing staysails trembled above the
brightwork like petticoats, until the ships seemed to be moving
out over the water as gracefully as Sirens?

And later, hardened by work on the piers and signs posted
in windows everywhere, *No Irish Need Apply,* his back bending
over barrels, crates, flagons, and whores, did he, one afternoon,
pull off his watch cap and oilskin in his mother's rooms to see
her fillet yet another small cod to split between them for their
supper, one poached egg swimming in its broth? Could he
have stood, dumbfounded, hating her ice-blue cataracts and
twisted knuckles and the damning poverty of that single egg?
How was this better than Castletown Bere? Did she look at
him distractedly as she clattered down their plates? Did a soft
wind from the North Sea and all the meadows of his childhood, a half-remembered lullaby, purl from between her gums,
deranging him? Was she frightened when he hurled the bub-

bling pan against the wall and held her to him roughly, apparently in tears? Was she puzzled as he gently untied her sugarsack apron, lifted her black shawl from the peg by the door, and took her by horsecar to dine in Scollay Square at the glassed-in Palm Garden at Higgens' Famous Oyster House? Did her heart crack when he told her he had to put to sea, and he wouldn't come back until he was rich and she'd be able to live like a queen?

Granny said, "He went halfway around the world and back—to Calcutta, San Francisco, and around the Horn, they say, but once, as they were coming into port, he fell out of the crow's nest and broke his leg, so he ended up where he started—in Boston."

I bit my lip, watching my heart-shaped leaves grow smaller and smaller at the top of the tree.

On a full dreen tide in the autumn of 1867, Jeremiah signed on as a cabin boy to the schooner *Maria Consuela* bound for Halifax and Spain and returned five years later, his femur bound in oakum—the tarred fibers of hemp and manila rope used for caulking seams in planking—and he would not say what happened. Did the raucous voices of Babel undo him as the crew of the *Maria Consuela* rounded the Horn, the black seas pitching like mountains, the way Castor and Pollux, in lightning and thunder, leaped from mast to mast in their crackling, unearthly game? Or was it the rum-soaked days and days becalmed that finally bewitched him—the inviolable quiet, the endless silence of God? Did he pace the decks alone on the dogwatch, night after night, peering through the chesstrees and mizzenmast for the hoary equatorial moon where he always saw his mother's face and heard her voice, rheumed with pain, in the Judas-flap of a loose rope-end, saying, *Son, come home?* Perhaps a light wind rose, and with it, the stargazer, the small sail carried above the moonsail, the skysail, the royal.

And he leaped like a madman up the ladder they called Jacob's, hand over hand on the wooden rungs, the rope sides twisting with exertion as he fought for the topmost section of the mast and his angel at Peniel, but the only wing-beats he heard were his own as he plummeted like Icarus through the dawn-reddened sky, trying to fly.

The leg healed; he hobbled to daily Mass with his mother, both of them listing like two old scows, one needing as much support as the other. Still, sitting in the incense and melancholy of the Mass, he knew he could never describe what he had seen: glittering cities on seas of tourmaline silk, cathedrals held up on pillars of light where blood-red rose windows spilled history incarnate on marble altars, ʰthe alleys of shanty towns he'd reeled through, drunk on the smell of spices, strange cooking, fly-blown excrement, ditch water, and the rotting fruit of slatterns leaning out of dark doorways, with their children, ugly and wild in animal skins, begging for scraps like young vultures.

Granny said, "He ended up in Scollay Square without a farthing and started washing glasses in a barroom. All he could think about was money."

Now the leaves were delicately sketched. I dipped the pen carefully into the india ink, tapping the point gently on the lip of the glass, and began to outline the limbs and branches of my marvelous tree.

All for his mother, then, the fury of his love. Jeremiah found two rooms in a basement tenement in the West End where he could stoke the furnace day and night in lieu of higher rent. In winter his mother lay on a pallet near the coalbin, warmer than she'd been in years, content with the transom window where she could watch the snow and the flurry of sparrows and starlings at the feeder. In summer, when he'd dug up the overgrown terrace, she puttered among her potatoes, scallions, and herbs, leaning on a stick, her face turned toward the sun like a lily.

All day he scalded great tubs of glasses out in the alley behind the Grotto, his pretty tenor rising over the rooftops of Scollay Square and the ruffling pigeons in the rafters, catafalqued like popes. In the dining room, he held up the starched, pristine linens over the tables like altar cloths and snapped them open like sails. He parted his hair in the middle and grew his first mustache. He banged on the piano when the orchestra was late, his flashing black-Irish smile disguising his contempt for the ladies in satin and jet who put pennies in his cigar box. In his mind's eye, he saw a gaily colored abacus where every cent he earned was recorded in columns: rent, food, books, and business. Business was his dream.

Education. That was the thing. If he learned enough, he could make a fortune. He interrogated sailors at the bar. He eavesdropped on bankers and philanthropists. At night, when he swept out the aisles of the Old Howard theater, he took home and pawned everything he found: purses, gloves, umbrellas, and once a gold wedding band. He spent the money on books. The theater was upstairs from the Otis S. Neal Brewery, and the smell of hops on hot summer nights was unbearable. There was money in liquor, in spite of the Temperance League. Perhaps his business was liquor.

From the booksellers crowding Corn Hill, he'd buy tracts on engineering, building, commerce, and because he passed by Papanti's Dance Academy where Charles Dickens had once recited, he also brought home novels and poetry. Eventually he got an apprenticeship to a boilermaker, and his business account began to grow.

The limbs and branches were outlined. Now I had to write in the names and dates of my long-gone relatives with ink in my very best penmanship.

Granny said, "In 1872 the city of Boston caught fire. Jeremiah must have been twenty. They say he was rushing around, trying to help put out the fire when he met Emma Beckett at one of the relief tables—hard to believe the old bitch was ever that young."

I tried to imagine the city of Boston on fire.

It was a windy November. The only stars were chips chiseled from some celestial glacier. The first sparks ignited in the cellar of a four-story dry-goods store and hoop-skirt factory on the corner of Summer and Kingston streets and soon roared through Bath Street, Bussey Place, Leather Square, Lindall Street, and Morton Place. Huge granite mercantile buildings, carved out of mountains, surely could not be falling—fire burning upward to the timber mansards like some demonic whirlwind, leaping from roof to roof—to St. Stephen's Church on Purchase Street, to the Boston, Hartford and Erie Railroad depot, across the corniced fretwork and gargoyles of six banks. Iron shutters warped and melted. Granite columns crumbled and fell. Whole city blocks collapsed as if the buildings were made of sand. The noise was apocalyptic. A small freighting schooner, *Louisa Frazer*, was seared at her wharf on Broad Street, and the crackling wind whipped from spar to spar through seven other wharves. The sky above the water took on an unearthly glow, silhouetting in the eerie sunset a flock of flying geese which people mistook for meteors, they were so black against the sky. Sparks, driven by the wind, flew through the streets with the thickness of a snow squall. Large flakes of burning timber were carried down into the bay. Firemen dynamited sixty buildings ahead of the inferno on both sides of Federal Street, hoping to control the blaze. After two days, 776 buildings were ash, sixty acres of goods were consumed, and not a wool house in the city was left standing.

Emma Beckett, her hair in a long plait the color of roasted chestnuts, shivered at the corner of Kilby Street with six other young women, shaking out their winter coats and muffs like ducks ruffling their feathers. They hovered by the tables, shredding and rolling up linen to bind burns, and filling pails of water from a pump on Matthew Place. Callouses pierced their hands even through gloves, and hot cobbles singed the leather soles of their buttoned Adelaide boots. With kerchiefs tied over their noses and rings of charcoal smoke underneath their tearing eyes, they looked like bandits come down from the hills to scavenge the remains.

Emma was worried about the horses. The fire department had ninety-three of them, but they were all dying like flies in the stables. She was almost sixteen and thought she loved horses more than people sometimes. Buildings were crashing, debris was falling from rooftops in a flaming bombardment, and all around her, men were screaming obscenities while the women bandaged their burns. It was too much. She wanted to go home. She wept openly, in the smoke and wind and sorrow.

Suddenly, out of the heart of the reddest part of hell, a burning angel leaped out of the fire, his hair a corona of flame and blazing wings of fury flying from his shoulder blades. She thought she was dreaming. But a black mouth opened in the glorious face and an ungodly howl roared out of it. It was a man, not an angel, a man on fire, lurching toward her, his blackened hands aloft like Job's, the furnace of his pain so fierce it seemed to hollow out her limbs and open a crater under her rib cage. Black bees buzzed angrily before her eyes, and she knew she was fainting, but she held onto his cry as though it were a golden rope let down from Paradise, and she brushed away the bees and ran—for a full pail, a blanket. She threw water over his coronet and wings, and flung herself, full weight, against his sparkling chest, beating the blanket with her fists as their bodies fell, pounding out the syllables of her single, unextinguishable thought in the tumult: *this man will not die, this man will not die, I will not let this man die.*

He was suddenly still.

She sat up, frightened. Oh, God, had she killed him? She

heard a muffled sound under the smoldering blanket, a coughing, a snorting, a wheezing, and when she flung the blanket from his face, she saw his eyebrows were crisp and his mustache gone, but he was laughing. A great, deep spasm was shaking him—he was not dead, he was laughing!

She stood up, blushing, beating out the end of her braid with her hands. She cleared her throat and wiped one cheek with her sleeve.

"I'm Jeremiah Green," he said. "'Tis my very great pleasure."

The names were perfect. I stood before the brand-new box of pastels, my heart in my mouth. Why did the sight of so many beautiful colors in their arrangement of shades make me feel like crying?

Granny said, "Oh, the Becketts put on airs, you know. Lace curtain Irish! They fancied themselves country squires from Belfast—as if anything good ever came out of Belfast—and thought that living in Harvard Square made them royalty."

Emma hardly remembered going home from the fire. She stood in front of the enormous yellow house with the silver silk river curving behind it, trying to make sense of the snow perched on the rooftree like wedding-cake frosting, the chocolate-brown shutters, the stained-glass Saint Paul on the Road to Damascus in the oak door. Did she really live there? It seemed so peaceful, so safe. She was very nearly too tired to climb the six steps to the porch. Her body seemed to be somewhere else. The door flew open and Roberts, the butler, and Mrs. Graham, the housekeeper, ushered her into the foyer, and when she collapsed at the foot of the stairs, they carried her up to her room.

Her mother, Anne, and her mother's maid, Helene, stripped off her bonnet, her coat, stockings, petticoat, bustle, basque, and stays. Mrs. Beckett rolled up the rug where they'd dropped her clothes and ordered everything burned. They soaped Emma in a hot frothy tub, rinsing and rinsing her hair in vine-

gar and lemon to get out the soot and the smell of smoke, her
sister Charlotte trying to pour some brandy into her, but her
teeth were chattering so violently that she bit down convulsively and a seashell of glass came away in her mouth. Emma
was bundled under the covers with hot bricks and slept fitfully
for three days, making frantic little cries, tossing back and forth
in her dreams as though she were at sea. The night the fever
broke, she sat bolt upright in bed, pointed at the marble mantelpiece, and said, *Look, Mother, it's him—my burning angel!*

She was fine. She hated their fussing and cosseting, their
little coos of anxiety—the drawn shades, the hourly tumblers
of cool water, the doctor's waxy hands touching her, her
father's furrowed brow as he tugged at his mustache. She
wanted them all to go away. It was the city of Boston that had
been destroyed, not her. It was Jeremiah Green, a tall young
man with ice-blue eyes and a golden laugh, who had been
burned, not Emma Beckett. She undid the throat button of her
nightgown. *Go away,* she croaked, her voice still hoarse from
the smoke, *go away, all of you, and leave me alone!* Her mother
sobbed into her lace handkerchief as she softly closed the
door.

Emma sat gingerly on the edge of the bed until the room
stopped spinning. She reached into her bedside table, found
the gold pencil in its place next to the inlaid mother-of-pearl
paper knife and her embossed stationery, and began to write
to Jeremiah Green in a shaky hand. A Catholic. Her mother
would die.

For the next six months, with a secrecy and deceit she didn't
know she possessed, she posted and received his letters at the
hands of the maid, Helene, who was from Paris and knew
about things of the heart. *My burns have healed quite well,* he
wrote, *and I'm back at work, though my eyebrows are still growing in.*
And she answered, *I'm sixteen now and can wear my hair up—my
sisters would be shocked if they thought I had a beau!* Sometimes she
wrote two and three times a day. She couldn't imagine her life

without him. Could she come and see him? Would he come to
Cambridge and see her?

It was mid-May and the glorious weather made her so restless that she could hardly keep still. She scowled doing needle-
work on At Home days with her mother, dutifully pouring
tea for women from church or the Cambridge Beautification
Committee or the Ladies' Auxiliary Guild for the Betterment
of the Deserving Poor, grinding her teeth so loudly that she
thought they would hear. She spent as much time in the stable
as she could, brushing her mare, Circe, and riding her hard
through the pastures and woods beside Fresh Pond—girl and
horse lightly clearing the stone walls and low gateways of the
farms. She kept the Charles River in sight as she meandered
through the sleepy towns on the outskirts of the city, and one
day she found herself trotting through Boston Common as
bold as brass, an unexpected butterfly beating its wings in place
of her voice. She turned Circe's head toward the West End
where Jeremiah and his mother lived.

She maneuvered carefully through the crowds of children,
the dogs, the traffic of horsecars, carriages, and market wagons,
piled high with hay or crates of chickens, trotted slowly by the
black-bordered bay windows of shopfronts, the velvet displays
in their casements heaped with ribbons, laces, parasols,
brooches, and clocks, past a glover, a milliner, a shoe shop, a
corset-maker, past a draper and a gentleman's clothier whose
signboards swayed gently in the bright air, adrift with magno-
lia petals, the gold dome of the State House hovering in the
distance like an icon.

She came onto his street through an alleyway heaped with
refuse, toothless old men in urine-soaked rags, and running,
consumptive children who jeered at her and whose language
was so coarse that she knew her cheeks were as furiously red
as theirs. Three rack-ribbed dogs snarled and tore at a dead
pigeon. An evil cascade from a slop pail tossed from an attic
dormer splashed up on her skirt and Circe's flank. She could

barely see where she was going, and she was crying. What an awful place. She might be killed. What if Jeremiah weren't home? How could she possibly have been so foolish to travel unchaperoned to see a man in such a horrid part of town?

She found the address, tied Circe to a lamppost outside the tenement, and sped up the stairs, recoiling from even putting her gloved hand on the blackened, broken rail. Somewhere a child squalled. The foyer was dark and reeked of excrement and mildew and cabbage. She was sickened, terrified, and heard herself calling his name again and again, as though he or she or both of them were at the end of the world, and suddenly he was there, his soft brogue saying, *What's this, then?* and she clung to him the way a drowning sailor clutches at driftwood—for life itself. As she let herself be led into a fusty parlor, his strong arm guiding her by the shoulders, she knew she would marry him.

Jeremiah's mother, a rail-thin woman with ice-blue eyes as big as demitasse saucers, offered her thick bread and black tea, but barely spoke to her. She would not stop staring. Emma sipped her tea and nibbled the crusty bread, dumb as a statue, trying to remember fragments of the patter that she and her girlfriends would exchange at parties or what the twittering ladies of the guild, the committee, the church, or the league would say, but her tongue felt like cotton in her mouth. Bright, meaningless chatter would fall like stones into this curtainless, airless room, she thought, before the unfathomable glitter of his mother's eyes. But what she ended up saying opened a rift in the room the size of a burning meteor.

You're the only Catholics I've met, except for our kitchen maid.

The silence was deafening. It lasted a lifetime.

The old woman, blazing with the kind of hatred Emma had seen on the faces of the children in the alley, stood up stiffly, the beak of her nose as regal as a bird of prey's. She put one arthritic claw on Emma's arm, leaned forward as though to devour her, and hissed into her face, *My son will marry a Protes-*

tant over my dead body! She hurled her teacup through the window over the slovenly daybed and was gone.

Jeremiah was laughing as they bent together to sweep up the broken glass, but Emma couldn't speak for the shame of it. When she put on her bonnet and stood in the doorway, he set down the dustpan and came across the room, tall and graceful as a dancer. He held the blue satin ribbons awkwardly in his rough hands and tied them into a ,houghtful bow under her chin, then teasingly flicked imaginary dust from the velvet and fluffed up the twin ostrich feathers on the bonnet's crown. And just as she was about to turn away, he kissed her.

That night, she couldn't sleep. The year she was born, Jeremiah Green was running barefoot through fetid potato fields, starving. When the shabby *Girl Aurelia* landed in Boston and Jeremiah and his mother staggered down the gangway to be taken to the Islands for quarantine, Emma and her sisters, in white crinolines and hoopskirts with pantalets were feeding the swans at the pond in Boston Garden. When she was being given riding lessons at the exclusive Belmont Academy, Jeremiah was working like a pack mule on the Charlestown docks. He shipped off as a cabin boy on the *Maria Consuela* the year she was reading *Hans Brinker* and *Alice in Wonderland*. He was in Spain with typhus the night that she and her family dined in a brass-and-mahogany room at Delmonico's in New York City after their carriage ride through the beautiful, nearly completed Central Park and an afternoon of shopping on Fifth Avenue. While she had frittered away her time at parties and cotillions, he had earned in a month what she spent at the milliner's in an afternoon.

She was ashamed. She was chastened. She loved him so much that it hurt. She would marry him, no matter what she lost, because in him there was a strange, other, desperate world that she wanted to know. Her money wouldn't save him. He was going to save himself. And perhaps he would save her as well.

I ran my finger over all the colors, arranged like piano keys in their box. The darker pastels would be beautiful at the bottom of the tree, and I would make the leaves grow lighter and more delicate as they rose into the mild paper sky. Pastels were so soft, so fragile. I had to work very slowly and quietly to get the colors right. My eyes were getting scratchy.

Granny said, "The Becketts lost all their money in the Great Panic of 1873—they got their comeuppance. They lost everything, even their house—can you imagine? And them, putting on such airs!"

Emma stood across the street from the yellow house with the chocolate shutters and the stained-glass Saint Paul on the Road to Damascus on the oak door. If she squinted her eyes, the world grew blurry, and she could see black ants marching in an orderly row up the right-hand side of the steps and into the house, and on the left-hand side, another orderly row of black ants coming down, awkwardly carrying crumbs four times their size on bent backs and setting them on the lawn where other ants, gesticulating wildly with their antennae, directed them. It was a picnic of sorts, wasn't it, after all. The ants were doing what ants do everywhere, foraging and carting away, boring into whatever food has been carelessly left behind, this time a handsome wedding cake that someone had placed on a green blanket under the apple trees. The Charles River behind it was the wedding knife's silver blade, set down within reach, while the bride and groom were elsewhere, dancing.

Emma stopped squinting. Thank God none of the family was here to see the portly sheriff ride up on his chestnut gelding, wipe his forehead and burnsides with a sweat-stained handkerchief, and bark at the black-suited men who ran around the yard in a flurry of confusion. Mother and Father were at Charlotte's, with her new husband and baby boy. Mother was heavily sedated. Father had been dead-drunk since the bank-

ruptcy had been declared, waking occasionally to pull down
Uncle William's rifle from the War Between the States above
the fireplace and threaten to blast his hot-blooded ignorant
soul to hell. Roberts, the butler, was kindly staying beside him,
out of loyalty and without pay, until Emma could find him
another position. Mrs. Graham, the housekeeper, had tearfully
gone to her niece's in Montpelier. The understaff were scattered to the four winds, taking the last of the Beckett's money
with them.

The Panic had hit in October, but things went on as usual
until one night in January 1874 when Richard Beckett had not
come home. He appeared two days later with half-moons of
exhaustion under his eyes, a sweaty pallor, and a fistful of
paperwork that explained everything. There were eleven pages
of creditors. He'd lost every cent that he'd kept in the bank.
Stocks he'd held in the municipal gasworks were worthless.
They would have two months to find an apartment and gather
a few of their belongings, because the house and most of the
furnishings would have to be sold at auction to pay off the
debt. Mother fainted dead away. Emma stood stock-still, while
the magenta fleur-de-lys wallpaper in the front parlor shimmered and the intricate pattern seemed to creep up toward the
carved ceiling and disappear.

There was no one to help. Charlotte was preoccupied with
the welfare of her own family as well as Mother and Father.
Their oldest sister, Anne Marie, was in Buffalo, carrying her
first child, and in bed most of the time. Emma was staying with
her best friend, Eliza Minton, whose family had not lost a cent
in the Panic, and realized that it was up to her to set about
resurrecting a life out of chaos.

She was surprised at her self-possession. No one would have
guessed she was only sixteen. She dealt with the sheriff, the
auctioneer, the creditors, landlords, carriage drivers, wagon-
eers. She hired boys off the street to load the trunks into which
she had packed some of their most precious heirlooms. If they

were going to be poor, she thought, they were not going to be
without beautiful things. She saved her mother's music box,
her jewel case, a Japanese fan of ivory and silk, a favorite
ormolu clock. She carefully wrapped the tea set her grandmother Emeline McKinley Beckett had brought with her from
Antrim in 1834. She stuffed the trunks with heavy winter
clothes, capes, shawls, blankets, and boots. She knew the poor
were often cold. In fact, she couldn't imagine ever feeling warm
again. She arranged for the ebony horsehair sofa, three beds
and mattresses, four mahogany dining-room chairs without
the table, a dresser for each of them, and the rosewood tea
table her mother loved, to be delivered to an apartment on
Garden Street. The rest had to be sold. She brought one of
her mother's finest diamond pendants to a jeweler on Brattle
Street, and was shocked when he would only give her half its
worth. With the money, she paid the landlord rent for two
years.

Emma stood across the street under the shade of a beech
tree, not wanting to be recognized. Gossip was such a filthy
thing. A crowd was beginning to gather. People loved misfor-
tune when it was not their own. The auctioneer rapped his
gavel on the lectern and began his high-pitched incomprehensible speech, and Emma watched as the buffet, the sideboard,
the dining-room table, the chandeliers, the highboys, lowboys,
hassocks, her own dressing table, daybed, and piano were sold.
The silver went quickly, as did the Lowescroft wedding service, the paintings, the gilt mirrors, and the Aubusson carpets.
When the auctioneer began pitching the parlor drapes, her
mother's satin ballgowns and moire afternoon dresses, even her
underthings, Emma turned away. A piece of paper, blown back
against the root of an old beech, caught under her boot heel.
She bent to pick it up, and the first tears she had shed since
this whole disaster had begun slid down her pale face. It was
half a week's dinner menu, written in Mrs. Graham's hand and
initialed by her mother:

MONDAY

Thin potato soup
Roast pheasant (nestled in brown crumbs and fine fat raisins)
Purée of chestnuts
White bread sauce, currant or grape jelly
Alligator pear and grapefruit salad with cheese biscuits
Pineapple sherbert with chocolate leaves

TUESDAY

Crabmeat with Russian dressing
Squab en casserole with mushrooms served on green noodles
Artichoke   Black cherry tarts (rum flavored)

WEDNESDAY

Chinese "egg drop" soup
Roast saddle of lamb
Mint sauce, green peas
pan roast potatoes
Mixed green salad, Camembert cheese
Strawberry flan

THURSDAY

Terrapin stew, Baltimore style
or a fish mousse
Roast boned leg of veal
Whipped sweet potatoes
String beans with dill-butter sauce
Hot sliced oranges with grated rind,
sprinkled with a little burning brandy
Vanilla wafers

Emma wiped her eyes and slipped the menu into her pocket.

I sighed. I hated to put the pastels back into their tray—azure, crimson, peach, lilac, magenta, and malachite—but all my leaves were done. There were deep shades on the lower branches, growing lighter as they rose to the top of the pale blue paper sky, and the tiniest leaves, barely brushed with color, had been blended with a tissue wrapped over my finger-tip. Time seemed to be passing so slowly as Granny talked. My tree was ready for the fixative.

Granny said, "Emma's mother's hair turned white overnight and she took to her bed for the rest of her life, out of shock. Her father couldn't work anymore, he'd lost his nerve. Varicose veins had kept him out of the Civil War, and after the Crash, he couldn't walk without a cane. Emma had to work as a dress-maker to support them!"

At first, though they tried to live frugally, there was an air of gaiety in her father's spending, as if he'd forgotten that they were nearly destitute, as if he thought, since the ship was foun-dering and there was no hope of rescue, they might as well go down in style. Emma took over the accounts. She haggled with the grocers at the farmer's market. She sent out the laundry. She learned how to starch, scald, bake, broil, braise, hem, sweep, polish, and disinfect. If Jeremiah could do anything to keep his family alive, so could she.

Most of their friends had deserted them, either suffering their own humiliation in private or refusing to acknowledge the Becketts' new condition, since it might have been theirs. Emma still went to church, but she no longer believed in God. She was chosen as the soloist for the dedication exercises at the new Christ Church in Harvard Square, and when she looked out over the feathered hats and derbies of her neigh-bors, she felt a thousand years older than any of them. She sang, *Swift to its close ebbs out life's little day; / Earth's joys grow dim, its glories pass away; / Change and decay in all around I see; / O thou who changest not, abide with me,* pouring all her sorrow, despair, and courage into each pure note, so that for as far as she could see, ladies were bending their heads over their handkerchiefs and the stalwart men who had been her father's friends were sniffing and blinking their eyes. She spoke to no one as she strode down the aisle with her shoulders held back. Then, in the spring sunshine, she saw Jeremiah standing on the church steps.

You're lovely, he said. *I want you to be my wife. When can we be married?* For the first time in ages, she gasped with hilarity and burst into a long, trilling laugh. *What, the blind leading the blind, or rather, the poor leading the poor?* she'd managed to say between hiccups. *How on earth would we live?*

I've saved enough money to buy a tavern on Stuart Street, he said, *and in a year, I'll be able to buy another.* He was beaming.

And shall I be a barmaid as well as your wife? she blazed.

But, Emma, this is only a start. Money makes money, don't you see? In a couple of years I'll be able to build us a house—in Cambridgeport near your parents. Or maybe I'll build a house big enough for all of us.

And what about your mother, she said, opening her parasol, turning sharply on her heel toward Garden Street. *She'll not welcome me with open arms. Over her dead body were her words, if I'm not mistaken.*

She marched off under the poplar trees, wishing she still had Circe on which to gallop away. Poor Circe. Was she happy in Lincoln with that family of nouveau riche? She blinked back tears. She would not look into Jeremiah's ice-blue eyes, she would not hear his golden words or his purer golden laugh. A tavern-keeper's wife! The very idea!

He followed her, turning her by the shoulders, so that she had to look at him. *Em,* he said softly, *I want us to be married. Here. See?* And from his waistcoat pocket, he pulled out a velvet box and opened it. Nestled in the plush maroon was a pear-shaped diamond and on either side, two delicate amethysts, her birthstone. She looked at him and thought him the most beautiful man she'd ever seen. Something caught in her throat and she couldn't speak. *Em, I want you for my wife. I don't care how long we have to wait. We may be old and gray before we're married, but I will love you until the day I die.*

Her face grew hot, then white. This was silly—her knees were so weak that she had to lean against him. His eyes were bright as tourmalines. *Look, Em,* he murmured, taking the gold ring from its box and slipping it onto her finger. *Now we're engaged.* And so, with a kiss, they were.

⚜

I took my family tree out the back door and laid it carefully on the grass. There was no wind, so the fixative would spray evenly. I'd put masking tape at the top of the page so that later I could write in "My Family Tree" and not have to worry about the fixative interfering. I straddled the paper, shook the can, and waved the gentle mist over the branches and leaves. I didn't let Granny see I was crying for Emma.

Granny said, "Can you imagine that girl—who had French lessons, riding lessons, went to the opera, to Europe, and never lifted a finger in her life—had to become a dressmaker so they wouldn't starve! Serves the old bitch right."

⚜

Inside Madame Odessa's shop, Jane and Irina were lighting the lamps. They lifted a large globe in the drawing room, the trimmed wick caught under the glass chimney, and the room filled with the royal blue and citron of the Japanese irises etched there, brightening two satin gowns on mannequins, the silver tea service on the rosewood table, the velvet benches and ladies' chairs where Madame's customers sat. The opaque lamp by the fireplace brightened with fiery peonies, and its reflection shone back into the room from the gilt mirror above the marble mantelpiece. The girls moved into the hall, and the squat abalone-colored sconces bathed the flocked wallpaper and stairway with a wash of peach light.

In the left-hand parlor, the tallest girls, Flossie and Nan, on two open ladders that made a wooden M before the shelves, were storing bolts of paisley challis, Henrietta cloth, and mousseline de laine. The younger children were putting the racks of Chantilly, Mechlin, English, Maltese, and mermaid's lace in order, red-headed Bridget was sweeping up scraps of chambray and zephyr cloth, while little Lucy was straightening veils and

ribbons on the bonnets at one of the six clawfoot tables. Dear
Lucy always looked carefully over her shoulder to make sure
that no one was watching, and then, tenderly, concentrating
with her tongue inside her cheek, she would lean forward over
the magenta-velvet Rembrandt hat and stroke the tiny wing-
tips of the stuffed gray wren, forever making its nest in silk and
satin.

Emma turned to look at seven-year-old Abigail McGuffy,
the youngest Thread Girl, cranking up the pink-and-white-
striped awnings for the night. The dusk-rose sunset blushed
on the mid-winter snow, softening the ballgowns, bonnets,
gloves, shoes, lace, and linens displayed in the bow windows
on either side of the front door. Emma's fingers made two fists
inside her muff. For six years this was how her evenings had
ended. She wouldn't see it again, now that she was leaving for
good.

Tears sprang to her eyes. She had been with Madame
Odessa when she'd chosen Lucy at the almshouse five years
ago. The child had been a starveling then, a pitiful urchin in a
scorched pinafore whose lank hair fell defiantly over one eye.
She had put up her chin stubbornly when the matron had
called her out of the flock of rustling, chattering girls and Lucy
had walked across the foyer of the workhouse with the dignity
of a duchess. She was four years old. Madame fell in love with
her and took her to her house on Brattle Street. All the Thread
Girls had come from the almshouse, but Lucy was the one
Emma favored. She was careless, slovenly, chattered like a
magpie all day long, but she was full of life. That's how
Madame chose her children. They must be full of life. Emma
would miss the child as if she were her own.

The front door flew open and a fractured square of yellow
light spilled onto the shoveled path. It was Madame herself,
standing in the doorway in her black bombazine and jet-strewn
bosom, looking like a figurehead at the prow of a ship.

Miss Beckett, she rasped, her hoarse voice billowing out in a feathery cloud in the cold. *Go home, get married, be happy.* She waved the lavender-scented square of lace that she kept tucked inside her cuff, gave an odd salute with it, and gently shut the door.

Emma had thought to laugh, but a sob caught in her throat instead. Could she really be leaving the shop and her rich life there? How could so much time have passed so quickly, like a comet through the night sky of her youth? A street lamp sputtered over her shoulder, and she turned to look up at it, wondering whether it was she or the flame that was winking unevenly. She shook herself, as though a goose had walked over her grave, unlatched and stepped through the wrought-iron knee-high gate to the street.

Through the oval glass in the oak door, she saw the Thread Girls trailing up to bed, the edges of their petticoats drifting out like the tide. When she had first come here to work, it had been spring. She was eighteen and secretly engaged. She had paused then, too, at the wrought-iron knee-high gate, watching the ubiquitous Mr. Dooley sweep dogwood petals from the bricks, nodding to him as he lifted his cap, never guessing that the stooped, gray-haired Irish ex-soldier with the walrus mustache was married to Madame Odessa, a French-Russian Jewess. Emma had teetered down the walk then, thinking how odd it was that she and her mother and sisters had been patronizing Madame Odessa's for years, had been fitted for dozens of gowns and coats, and that the even-younger Emma—carefree, spoiled, not thinking of anything but a new bonnet—had no way of imagining what was coming, in fact could never have conceived of a world in which the eighteen-year-old Emeline Louise Beckett would be approaching Madame Odessa to ask for employment.

Frances, one of the cutters, had opened the door and curtsied in confusion to see a much-valued customer who had not been scheduled in the appointment book.

Oh, Miss Beckett, Frances wailed, her mouth opening and clos-

ing like a trout's. I don't have you written down for this morning—I
must have forgotten to—oh, dear, oh, dear—please, do come in—I'll get
Madame.

Frances left a mist of anxiety behind her, so potent a dampness that Emma felt obliged to take out her handkerchief and
wipe the girl's distress from her own person—her chin, her
forehead, under the looped braids of her chignon. She sat in
the parlor and heard sounds that she had never noticed as a
patron: the clattering feet of a child racing toward the attic on
carpetless stairs, the slamming of a door, a hissed quarrel from
the fitting room, the clanging of shears, the squeak of a man-
gle, and over her head, the sharp heels of the head seamstress,
Mademoiselle Ferré—whose pinched white face and wild matted bangs gave her an air of a woodland creature that always
made Emma want to add a T to her surname. Mademoiselle
dropped something hard on the floor, and from the sewing
room Emma heard a shrill *Mon Dieu*, followed by a furious *merde*.

It was the strangest thing. She felt as if she were waiting in
the wings of a tiny, intimate theater, hearing all the props
being moved, the lines practiced, the jarring mishaps of a
rehearsal that would somehow right itself on the night of the
performance, actresses scurrying around in their petticoats
tearing costumes from the rack, ransacking trunks for feathers,
hats, scarves, boas, and lorgnettes to complete their disguises.
She half-expected Madame Odessa to come flying out in her
corset, her flaming red hair done up in rags, with cold cream
on her face, clutching the gap in her sheer nainsook dressing
gown while she scrambled to find the ends of the sash, wondering what on God's green earth could warrant her being called
on stage before the curtain went up. Emma only knew the shop
from the dresses she ordered that were always ready on time.
How could she not have understood the bustle, the energy,
the work of so many hands that went into the making of just
one of her gowns?

Madame Odessa finally entered the parlor, not as an actress

caught out of costume, but bearing herself like a marchioness. She betrayed no sign of annoyance or surprise at Emma's unexpected appearance, but smoothly carried in the japanned tea tray laden with a silver chocolate pot, a basket of croissants and jam, and set it on the gate-legged table beside Emma's chair with a smile.

Bon jour, bon jour, ma petite, she expostulated in French, bussing Emma extravagantly on both cheeks, and then, holding her at arms' length, in her graver, more awkward Russian-English, *It givez me zuch zadness to know zat your mothair iz being so eel. And your papa? Ah, I can zee it een your faze. Zit, darling, eat. We vill talk.*

Emma allowed the chocolate to be poured, the croissants to be broken and buttered for her. She held the plate on her lap like a child, and for a minute, tears stung her eyes—she did not know how much she missed being mothered. Madame looked at her steadily, with kindness, without pity, knowing Emma's shame, and seeming to say without uttering a word, *My zweet, I know what haz happened. I too have been poor. I too have been ashamed to azk. But you may azk anything of me.*

Emma burned her lip on the chocolate. She returned the cup shakily to its saucer and placed it to the tray. The mantel clock rang the half-hour. Emma covered her face with her hands and filled her palms with tears.

And so she was hired and sewed for Madame Odessa for six years, moving through the ranks like any other apprentice. She was too old to be a Thread Girl, but in the large butler's pantry in the back of the house, Emma began her education. The children were up at dawn, clattering down from the attic dormitory for tea and porridge, and before Emma arrived sleepily from the apartment on Garden Street, the orientals had been beaten, the hardwood floors swept, the brass polished, fresh flowers put in all the vases in summer, and in winter, silk ones shaken daily and replaced once a week. The Thread Girls ran errands, modeled children's clothing, made tea, covered buttons, replenished supplies in every alcove, brought kindling in neatly tied bundles into the drawing room, parlor, fitting room, and sewing room. During the day, Emma sat with them as gentle, soft-spoken Miss Phinney taught them basic stitches, how to embroider their own handkerchiefs, to keep fringes, tassels, and ribbons in order on their racks, and to know the names of everything. She taught them rudimentary French and basic mathematics while they sewed. The littlest ones napped over their samplers and were not scolded. Emma marveled at the complexity of it all, amazed that such small, rambunctious children could be taught to be careful and precise. There was a place for everything at Madame Odessa's, and the children took great delight in shyly leading Emma by the hand through their orderly kingdom.

Thimbles were kept in tiny oak apothecary drawers, marked gold, silver, brass, celluloid, bone, ebony, and ivory. There were drawers for bone, jet, leather, ivory, and mother-of-pearl buttons. Spools of thread in every conceivable color were kept on racks of dowels against the back wall, stacked almost like books in gaily colored bindings. Emma was most bewildered by so many different kinds of needles, but the children explained them simply by showing her six psalm-book sized pillows. On the rose pillow were darners and straws, used for bonnets. On the cornflower pillow were the long-eyed sharps, used for embroidery. On the yellow pillow were the ground-downs, shorter than sharps. On the lilac pillow were the betweens, shorter even than the ground-downs. On the ivory pillow, shorter still than the betweens, were the blunts, used for making stays, and on the dove-gray pillow, used only for embroidery in silk and wool, were the Whitechapel and Chenille. Emma wondered how she would ever keep them straight, but she did, magically, thanks to the children's elfin whispers guiding her along.

Emma became a cutter after Josephine Driscoll left the shop to get married and marveled at the astonishing fabrics that were brought to her table in the upstairs front parlor to be spoiled by her shears: duchess satin, albatross cloth, cotton with a Bengal stripe, ice wool for shawls, and once, for a winter dolman cape, yards and yards of velvety penguin skin. Emma learned to chalk, pin, cut, and baste a garment together for the fitters across the hall, arranging the complex pattern pieces so carefully that nothing was wasted. She stoked the stove to keep the irons hot, pressing seams, ribbons, and finished garments— there was always something to be pressed—and when there was not, she steamed, through a wet chamois cloth, the delicate yards of lace hanging on the racks downstairs. Her fringe of bangs was a froth of curls when she went home at night.

Two years later, Marianne Walters, the first fitter, died of consumption at age twenty-six, hurried along by a deliberate ingestion of too much laudanum. Madame Odessa, regardless of her own beliefs, paid for a lovely Episcopalian funeral, and Emma was given Marianne's position. She learned to make respectful allowances for their patrons' busts, bustles, trains, and crinolines, recording their measurements in a kidskin ledger along with the kind of gown each woman favored, and the colors that suited her skin tone, hair color, and age. Customers left Emma's fitting room feeling pampered and understood, and just a bit proud of their figures, imagining themselves resplendent in verdigris, royal blue, purple, and garnet, the most daring colors from the Continent.

Night after night Emma stood before the dressmaker's forms, whom she addressed as Mistress Anne Boleyn, Katherine Howard, and Mary, Queen of Scots, straining her eyes by a kerosene lamp to match the checks and stripes, ribbons, braids, tassels, black lace, and knotted fringes of a hundred gowns, secretly wishing that she could behead Mrs. Eugenia Gibson, the Misses Isolde and Rowena Charlton-Huff, the scrawny crow of a woman who drank absinthe, smoked clove cigarettes, and called herself Comtesse di Rimini, and at least seventeen other odious women in Madame's clientele.

Some nights she was so tired that she could barely hobble

home. Her mother had been diagnosed with Bright's disease shortly after the auction and she never left her sickbed. Emma had become an expert on patent medicines and herbal curatives, her wages siphoned off to stock the shelves with Baker's Stomach Bitters, Lydia Pinkham's Vegetable Compound, Ayer's Sarsaparella, paregoric, Dover's Powder, and Jayne's Carminative. Often when she entered her mother's room to wish her good evening, she heard a drugged, off-key warbling, and the odor of alcohol and tincture of opium nearly gagged her as she stood in the doorway. Emma's face burned, and she imagined herself becoming an Amazon, a breast-plated Valkyrie, who had the strength to fling open the windows in a fury and hurl the tray of bottles, spoons, and tumblers out into the alley, the shattered glass splintering the sanctity of the sickroom and the stuporous self-involvement of the patient. She heard herself shrieking obscenities that she knew would come to her in such a moment of passion, and saw herself shaking the dazed old woman who had once been so full of life, and shouting, *Help me, Mother, I can't do this by myself.*

But she never broke. She fluffed the pillows, cleaned the bedpan, tenderly washed the sagging flesh she could no longer love, spooned Arrowroot blanc mange, Iceland moss jelly, and baked milk into the helpless mouth. She settled into the straight-backed chair beside the bed and opened the latest romance by Mrs. E. D. E. N. Southworth and read aloud until her mother fell asleep. Then she tended to her father, whose varicose veins needed a nightly massage with liniment before his withered legs could be covered by white elastic stockings. Emma gave her father his supper, never knowing if he recognized her or not.

Emma began to wear a pince-nez on a velvet ribbon. She stood quietly before the customers at Madame Odessa's side as her first assistant, showing them rich curtains of cashmere, satin, taffeta, moire, and velvet faille for winter; surah, mohair, and foulard for summer; and for evening, lace, beaded jet tulle, ribbons, silk flowers, white ostrich tips, and aigretts for their hair. *Yes, ma'am, one Scotch caitlin silk full dress, Stewart, trimmed with black velvet. Lovely on you. Yes, ma'am, one vraie couleur de rose gros-de-Naples, with richly brocaded flounces. Perfect for a woman of your figure. Two silk grenadine dresses, trimmed with Valenciennes lace and velvet, two bodices to match, blue and green. Yes, ma'am, ideal for your daughters. One ponceau silk dress, violet, trimmed with llama fringe and gold balls. Certainly, Miss, in time for your birthday celebration.* And the sumptuous fabrics slipped through Emma's hands like the glorious colored rivers of Paradise, the sparkling clear waters of Lethe, the freshets and rills of her own youth, flooding swiftly away.

She had worn Jeremiah's engagement ring on a gold chain around her neck, so that it hung between her breasts like a bright gold flame, still burning after six years. He had bought a second tavern in South Boston and was speculating on a real-estate development on Linnaean Street in North Cambridge. One day he came to Madame Odessa's with a gift for her, a fabulously expensive, buttery kidskin purse, his ice-blue eyes soft with affection and mischief as he pulled her under the Japanese beech in front of the shop.

Please accept this, Miss Beckett, he said in his pompous banker's voice that he sometimes used to tease her. *I hope it meets with your approval.* He bent in an exaggerated, courtly bow.

Inside the purse, wrapped in gold paper, was enough money for her to buy a secondhand sewing machine and start her own dressmaking business out of the apartment on Garden Street, and to be available to her parents, since no nurse could manage to stay longer than a week.

Emma sighed distractedly, taking his hand. It was true. She was needed there. Madame Odessa had taught her everything she knew. It was time to go home. She looked into his eyes with worry, then fear. Would there ever be enough money for them to marry? Would there ever be enough time?

And so, on a winter's night in 1881, Emma watched the

lights wink off one by one in the shop with the pink-and-white-striped awnings, heard the brass key turn in the lock for the night, and saw the lamp-enveloped shadow of her beloved friend and teacher float up the curving stairs to the landing, turn, and disappear into the darkness.

Granny said, "Jeremiah's mother was a mean old thing. She hated Emma and wouldn't let her come as far as the front door. They had to meet in secret or on Sunday afternoons—they were engaged for twelve years before the old devil finally died."

I shook the paper to make sure the fixative was dry. The page was neat and clean, without smudges. I took my family tree back into the house and laid it on the dining-room table where I thought about how to write the title.

In the breathless moments before the first birds stirred and tentatively sang the world awake, it seemed infinitely quiet, as if some eternal clock had slowed and stopped, the great cogs and wheels of the universe that ground so purposefully, inexorably onward, now paused, and Emma thought that she could see the restless stars turning in their sleep. The morning sky was an unfurled bolt of cobalt silk, and the virginal palm of the moon was cupping the wedding sapphire, Venus, the Pleiades above it soft as a veil of mist. Emma lay on her stomach, her fists under her chin on the pillows, and stared without blinking at the impossibly beautiful sky.

Suddenly, she understood how people could take their own lives.

Quilting. Hemming. Tacking. Gauging. Felling. Binding. Braiding. Shirring. Ruching. Pleating. Thousands of miles of thread, enough to weave a path to Venus, and she was alone in her bed on a summer night, lace wavering shyly at the window, her body with its monthly aches. What would she give for a pair of strong hands to rub her back at the end of the day? Everything.

That's what the struggle was for, wasn't it—love? Elusive as smoke and solid as the chimney hearth from which it burned. It had been promised to her, and yet it did not come. Something dark moved through the tops of the trees—the wind, a bird, the breath of God. It had been years long, her waiting.

She was going through her life asleep.

Monday: soak sheets, towels, handkerchiefs, undershorts, shirts, and nightgowns in hot water, using the plunger and washboard; wrestle the copper washtub to the old Sterling range, fill it with laundry, add soap and stove-hot water, boil the clothes for thirty minutes. Drain, rinse with bluing and clear water, wring, hang. Make three meals. Bathe Mother morning and night. Change sheets. Massage Pa's legs. Sew after supper by the kerosene lamp until her eyes burned.

Tuesday: Send out the ironing. Put clean clothes away. Bake bread, muffins, tarts, johnnycake, try to sieve the bugs out of the cornmeal. Sit by the kitchen stove, make over old dresses for herself, knit socks and scarves for her parents. Dust, clean, trim, and fill lamps. Sweep parlor, hall, and stairway. Make three meals. Change sheets. Bathe Mother morning and night. Massage Pa's legs. Sew after supper by the kerosene lamp until her eyes burned.

Wednesday: Go to market. Pick through shriveled potatoes, winy apples, cabbages with worms deep in the whorls. A carp, or cod, or haddock. A piece of salt pork. White beans. Molasses. Suet. Rice. Tea. One-half pound of sugar. Make three meals. Bathe Mother. Change sheets. Wrestle Pa into the tub for his weekly soak. Massage his legs. Sew until blind.

Thursday: Pay laundress seventy-five cents for ironing. Pay three dollars to druggist for bill past due. Wash windows. Clean pantry. Make three meals. Bathe Mother. Change sheets. Pa's legs. Sew until blind.

Friday: Baking again. Suet pudding. Mending. Shake rugs. Shovel ashes from the fireplace and stove. Make three meals. Bathe Mother. Change sheets. Pa's legs. Sew until blind.

Saturday: Charlotte sits with Mother all day. Customers come to the parlor from nine to one. Offer tea and scones. Fit, measure, baste up, tack. Show the latest Godey's fashion. Take new orders. Do accounts. Set aside money for food, medicine, rent, doctor, and laundress. Put savings in a strongbox. Lay out patterns, cut, and baste. Bathe herself and wash her own hair. Sew until blind.

Sunday: Sleep until eight. Make up three trays for father to take to mother. Bathe Mother. Change sheets. Dress for church. Meet Jeremiah after the service—wild, uproarious roller-skating arm in arm in a bright maple-floored arena for twenty-five cents and hot chocolate afterward, a long walk beside the Charles no matter the weather, a picnic in Mount Auburn Cemetery, a ferry ride to lawn tennis at the summer resort town of Winthrop—risking her reputation by participating in the scandalous new sport, bicycling—wearing her shocking new "Londonderry" made of gray-green hopsack, a coat with long full sides, worn over knickerbockers, cloth vest, leggings, hat, doeskin gloves, and low cycling shoes. Sometimes they took a ride in his carriage out to Lexington, Concord, Lincoln. Checked on Circe. Sat by Walden Pond. Drove by the Cambridge house Jeremiah built for his mother and, by extension, for her, his bride-to-be, the old woman watching them from behind parted curtains. Supper at Jake Worth's. Too much sherry. Kissing under the linden tree on Cambridge Common. Tears. Recriminations. Quarreling, returning his ring. Letters in the mail. Apologies. Jeremiah asking for patience, he simply cannot put his mother in an asylum. More letters. Kisses under the linden tree. The ring back on its velvet ribbon between her breasts. The same quarrel over and over. The engagement broken. The giving in. Did she even love him anymore?

There was a sewing furrow between Emma's brow and silver filaments in her hair. Once she'd heard a trap spring shut in the cupboard and a gray field mouse, back broken and bloody, was frantically trying to swim from the pain with its tiny front legs, but the creature could not get away, no more than she.

Emma lay on her stomach, her fists under her chin on the pillows, and stared without blinking at the impossibly beautiful sky. Venus and the moon were drifting apart. Clouds like yards of crepe were draping the conch-shell pink of the horizon. Why get up at all today? When the tears came, she turned over on her back. Her life was going on without her, somewhere else, and she was growing older without ever having been young. Her body had changed. Her breasts were heavy, hips wide, stomach no longer flat. She had sciatica and rheumatism in her knees. Love had not changed her body. She had not borne children. Years of work had done it. In the afternoons when Mother napped, Emma knitted bed-size wedding blankets made with the complicated stitches of an Aran sweater and long lovely fringes. Knit five. Purl six. Cross over. Drop stitch. Knit one. Purl seven. Rows and rows of attentive stitches. Hour after hour. Day after day. Week after week. A beautiful honeymoon blanket for Jenny, for Margaret, for Edith, for Mildred, for Gladys, for Sue. Each one took months to make, and as she was steaming the heavy patterned wool before boxing and wrapping the gift, she invariably discovered that she'd knitted strands of her own hair into the cables and braids. And then came the soft, pearly pastel infant blankets— how many? ten? eleven?—lamb's wool against the tender skin of other women's babies. She would never be married at all.

Emma lay on her back and let the tears come. Charlotte had tried to tell her about her wedding night with Frank, but she had blushed and stammered so much that Emma wasn't sure she'd heard her sister properly. Nothing with Jeremiah could ever be so ugly, so primitive, like animals rutting in a field. Loving a man could not be so base a thing. There was too much she didn't know. Her own body might as well have belonged to a stranger. But when Jeremiah kissed her, a fierce current ran from her lips to her bosom, her flesh shivered hot

and cold, and—she could not even say the words—a slow dark
fire swept over her and the hunger she felt was like nothing
she had ever known.

She was shocked at her passion. She did not understand it.
Even more shocking was the wish she had sometimes to touch
her own body, the worst kind of evil. They said people could
always tell when you "did it"—the clues were as clear as day:
indolence, pale cheeks, tenderness of the spine, backaches,
nervousness, peevishness, irritability, moroseness, disobedi-
ence, and unnatural appetites for mustard, pepper, cloves, clay,
and salt. The temptation was almost overwhelming sometimes,
and yet she could not bear exposure, so she did not give in.

She never laughed. She was angry all the time and carried
in her waistband a jet hatpin that she would push into her arm
when Mother was querulous and Pa critical and argumentative.
She could never do enough, it was never done right, there was
always something she'd forgotten to do. How could one person be expected to take care of everything? And Jeremiah
would not send his mother away. The old witch was going to
live forever. At night, when she begged God to let that terrible,
self-centered, son-crushing woman die, Emma tasted metal in
her mouth, a poisonous alloy of hatred and bitterness so deep
that it made her retch. She thought she might go mad with
fury. She was twenty-nine years old and still a child, but older
than she thought she'd ever be.

One Sunday morning as Emma stood in the kitchen prepar-
ing the breakfast tray to bring to her mother, there was a knock
at the back porch door. She tightened her robe around her,
took the shrieking kettle off the stove and poured it over the
tea leaves in the pot, then padded to the door in her socks. It
was Jeremiah, his eyes so red and cheeks so white that she
nearly laughed, he looked so much like a rabbit. He crashed
into the kitchen, crushing her in his arms.

Jeremiah, what is it? she cried because he was trembling.

His mustache, wet with tears, tickled the nape of her neck
as he whispered, *Mother's dead.*

Her knees gave way and she nearly fell. Was it shock? Relief? Guilt? The burden of his grief made her light-headed. He sat her in the chair by the stove, poured a cup of tea and crouched beside her on the footstool, holding the cup carefully in his hands until she could take it from him. It was too hot to drink. She stared at him through the steam, his face so full of suffering that she thought her heart would crack in two.

Jeremiah. Oh, my darling, I'm so sorry, she said in a gasp, and to her surprise, she was sorry. She set the cup on the table and held him to her breast like a child.

Shh, shh, she hummed while she rocked him, snippets of a lullaby she sang to Charlotte's boys slipping from her tongue. *It will be all right, my love. You'll see. It will be all right.*

And now she knew it would be. She moistened her dry lips thoughtfully. She would make his mourning coat. She would move Pa and Mother to the house that Jeremiah had built for her, his bride-to-be. They would be married within a year.

I found an old book that had what I took to be a title page in Old English script. I copied it in pencil the best I could, with extra flourishes and serifs on the M, the F, and the T. Then I drew over them with very black ink until it said 𝕸𝖞 𝕱𝖆𝖒𝖎𝖑𝖞 𝕿𝖗𝖊𝖊. I put my initials on the bottom right-hand corner of the page.

Granny said, "Well, they finally got married after all those years and moved into the house in Cambridgeport that he'd built for his mother. Jeremiah was making money hand over fist, and—you know how the Catholics are—they started breeding like goddamned rabbits! Imagine—Emma had ten children in twelve years, all of them after she was thirty years old."

Emma stood before the pier glass, trying to get ready for the service. Her bones seemed weighted with lead, and her hands trembled as she picked up the silver-backed brush. How white her hair had grown. Where had the radiance gone? She twisted the long skeins into a chignon and pinned it with the jet hair-pins of interlocking hearts that Jeremiah had given her. She felt as if she were arranging garments on one of her dressmaker's forms. Her fingers were clumsy. She could not do up the onyx buttons on the front of her paramatta gown. She'd sent Charlotte out of the room in a wordless fury—if she didn't do this herself, she would never get through the day.

She gazed into the pier glass and pulled the veil carefully over her face. Through the crosshatching, the world looked stranger than ever, tilted, awry. She patted the glass-topped bureau with her gloved hands until she found her ivory and jet fan, her crocheted reticule where she put her handkerchief, her smelling salts, and her tiniest pair of gold sewing shears. She glanced out the window. It was hot for late summer. Anvil-colored clouds boiled over the rooftops and chimneys of Cambridge. She could hear the low rumble of trolley wheels in the distance.

Emma closed her bedroom door, then stopped on the landing, surprised that everything could look the same: the aubergine oriental under the leaded windows, the Boston fern in the jade and plum-blossom jardiniere. One of her tasks as a child of three or four had been to comb out the long creamy fringes of the Aubusson carpets in her parent's parlor and dining room. She remembered kneeling there, humming contentedly, with hoops and petticoats around her like satin wrapping the bottom of a Christmas tree. Could she have ever been so young? Someone had combed these fringes today. She wondered why they had bothered with such a little thing.

She heard the buzz of guests in the parlor and saw at the foot of the stairs the mahogany and marble hall tree hung with umbrellas, parasols, derbies, and walking sticks. Reflected in the beveled mirror was a tall vase of fragrant roses—white, of course. The silver card-receiver was overflowing. She would have to go down now.

She took two steps, careful of her unaccustomed train, and peered through the balusters like a child up past her bedtime, spying on a grown-ups' party. The front drawing-room mantel was banked with daisies and ferns. Two knee-high vases on either side of the fireplace were filled with pink and white hydrangea, and a basket of tiger lilies tied with white ribbon sat on the hearth. In the sitting room under a wide mirror the mahogany table was draped in lace under Mother's cut-glass punch bowl and cups. On either side of it stood a high bouquet of lavender and bisque-colored roses whose soft, faint pink petals like smooth porcelain of cream seemed to exude light as they opened. Candles were burning on the sideboard behind platters of food, beside vases of pink clover blossoms. It was like a dream—the linen napkins precisely laid, the too-bright silver. Emma blanched when she heard the organ music summoning her to the drawing room, and held on to the balustrade until she reached the foyer.

She could not go in, just yet, though they were waiting. Charlotte and Anne Marie were hovering again, alarmed by her inability to speak. She couldn't explain how the words seemed to feather apart like split milkweed pods, or puffs blown from dandelion stems at the end of summer. She could see their mouths moving, puckering with concern, but it was as if she had grown suddenly deaf as well as old, and heard nothing but the sound of hundreds of bumblebees buzzing in honeysuckle. Which struck her as enormously funny, and when she began to laugh, she could not stop. Anne Marie appeared with a tumbler of sherry and had to hold the glass while she drank.

From the corner of her eye, Emma saw Jeremiah standing in front of the malachite fireplace in his black tie and tails looking grim, and people, white faces an ocean of moons, parting like the Red Sea to make it possible for her to walk through them. She heard the sound of someone strangling a kitten, and knew it had come from her throat, heard the splintering of a fallen sherry glass, and sailed through the front door like a ship leaving port.

It was starting to rain. She held up her face to the cool,

forgiving drops that fell from the orange bells of the trumpet vine along the eaves of the porch. She wanted her fan, but couldn't think how to retrieve it from her reticule. Heat lightning flickered over the Charles. When Jeremiah touched her elbow, she did not turn, but suddenly found that she could speak.

Did you know that whenever rainwater falls on crape, it leaves a mark—white, you know, like a scar. Look, she said, showing her sleeve, *here, all the black has been bleached out. But I know how to fix it. You hold a piece of old black silk under the stain and with a camel's hair brush dipped in ordinary ink, you go over the stain and wipe off the excess with a little bit of soft silk. It will dry right away and the scar will be gone. And of course, you know, in this hot weather, crape leaves black stains on a lady's arms and neck that can't be washed off with soap and water, no matter how hard you scrub. But I know the remedy for that too. I have a box full of cream of tartar and oxalic acid that takes it right away. And you know,* she said, looking at him for the first time, *it's poison. If I swallowed it, I would die.*

Em, he said softly, *oh, Em,* and he cradled her like a child. Tears ran quietly down her cheeks behind her veil. She could not return his embrace.

Emma, Jeremiah said with a catch in his voice, *it's time. We have to go in now.* And she let him lead her into the parlor until they stood before the malachite fireplace and the draped mahogany table with the griffin-claw feet. Two silver candelabra stood on either end, eight curved branches wound with silver ivy, blooming into white wax and a flickering petal of yellow flame. A garland of pink roses hung to the floor on either side of the tiny coffins, set side by side like some terrible centerpiece. The organist was playing "Lead, Kindly Light, Amid the Encircling Gloom," and Emma, surprised at the firmness in her voice, said, *Please stop that damnable music.* The room became deadly quiet, except for her own rustling crinoline as she stepped up to the table's edge.

She put her fingertips on each of her baby's coffins, rosewood and white with brass fittings, and soft pink satin pillows with edging as fine as Queen Anne's lace. Yes, these were her children, her twins, Madeline and Emeline. Five months old. How small they were, like porcelain dolls with rosebud lips and eyelashes that left shadows faint as spider webs on their waxen cheeks. Madeline and Emeline. Had she ever carried them in her body, alike as two rose petals curled into one another, or held them tenderly at her milk-heavy breasts? She couldn't remember, it seemed so long ago. How strange to see them both so still. They had never slept so peacefully in their cribs. Now they lay in their christening gowns, further away and purer than angels, tiny sprays of violets and a rosary of seed pearls—so pale as to be nearly translucent—interlaced between their ivory fingers.

Madeline, her first born. Emma smoothed the scalloped collar and straightened a pleat. A happy child with a sweet disposition and bright ice-blue eyes like Jeremiah's. She touched a vein that ran like pale violet ink through her temple. How had all the light gone out of her child's face? And Emeline, the frailer, second born. Solemn. Cautious. Calmer when she could touch her sister. Emma's forefinger rested in the dimpled cleft of the baby's chin, and a note so faint that it was almost inaudible passed through her—the sound of the last white key on the piano.

They'd gotten so sick, so suddenly. Emma and Jeremiah were up all night, each cradling a feverish child, pacing, frantic. The children could not even keep down chips of ice. Vomiting. Distended, sensitive stomachs. Convulsions. Madeline died at eleven o'clock on the second night of it, and Emeline, as if sensing that her twin sister was gone, stopped struggling two hours later. Summer sickness. *Cholera infantum*, Dr. Morrow had written on the death certificates. Germs in milk could cause it, he said, but no one really knew.

The priest coughed discreetly. The service was about to begin. Emma looked at him, feeling nothing. How like her wedding this was. Candlelight, white lace, organ music, the overpowering smell of roses, sandwiches, and dainties laid out on platters, loved ones in their finery come to take part in the ceremony. She'd been so happy that day and more in love with Jeremiah than she thought possible. He stood next to her now in his black suit, his hair parted in the middle, nervously stroking his mustache, and he could have been a porter at a railroad station for all he meant to her. She would take a trip by herself when this was over, sit in a deck chair wrapped in a tartan and let the sea breeze lift her sorrow out over the waves. She might never come back.

The organ started once more, the dirge-like notes like a fog-horn in the harbor. She fumbled with her crocheted purse but the strings didn't want to come undone. Grudgingly, she let Jeremiah hold the bag while she opened it. It didn't matter. It would never matter. She unfolded the lace handkerchief and laid it on the table. She took her tiniest pair of gold sewing scissors and clipped a white lock of hair from Madeline's crown and placed it on the lace. Emma kissed her stone-cold forehead. She bent over her namesake, her Emeline, and snipped a curl from behind her ear, kissing the dead cheek, wiping away one of her own tears that had fallen there. The curl was laid on the handkerchief alongside the other, and she carefully tied the ends of the hankie together, placed it and the tiny gold scissors in her purse, and pulled tight on the strings, like her heart.

Granny said, "Winthrop was a very popular seaside resort in those days. At one time there were sixty hotels. After the babies died, Jeremiah brought Emma to a cottage down at Point Shirley so she could rest, and Emma liked Winthrop so much they decided they'd build a year-round house. Look, there it is, right across the street. It took them almost three years to build it and move out of Cambridge. By then the Greens had three children—your great-uncle Tom, your great-aunts Lillian and Anna. You can see how much money they had. Your grandfather was the first baby born in that house, in 1894."

It was a beautiful white house with a turret I wanted to write in, not as grand as Nanaquaket, not a mansion like those big houses on Washington Avenue that looked out across the water, but a pretty house all the same. It made me sad to see it falling apart with just my great-aunt Emeline living there with her mangy Airedales and Yorkshire terriers. I'd see her hanging laundry on the back porch in a ratty nightgown with a man's flannel shirt thrown over her bony shoulders for a bathrobe, her hair standing up in the air. She was stone deaf, like all the Greens, with a beak for a nose, and when she hollered for the dogs across the yard she sounded like sandpaper scratching through a bullhorn.

I wanted her to come over and be part of our family, but there was a feud going on that had to do with money and property. None of my grandfather's brothers and sisters spoke to one another. Emeline, the youngest girl, had stayed home to take care of her father and mother and sister Annie. After Jeremiah and Emma died, all the money and property was left to Emeline. The rest of the Greens felt cheated.

I was nearly finished with my family tree. Gingerly, I picked through fifty grease-and-dust-blackened picture frames standing beside the oil tank in the cellar until I found one that would fit it. It was old-fashioned, with a little bit of gold leaf, but not too gaudy. I took it up to the kitchen to wash off the years of filth.

❧

It was a perfect Indian summer day. The sea was a blue cloak sewn with stars. Instead of dew, the morning had scattered gold dust over the fields, the soft feathery fragmites nodding like helmet plumes along the curved stretch of beach from Grover's Cliff to Great Head, the water glittering like a shield. The air was so clear that Emma could distinguish each gilded

maple leaf apart from another, like single, newly written pages
from a medieval psalter hung to dry, the gold leaf burnished
by a dog's tooth in an old monk's hand. It was Anna's first
birthday, and they were going to take a picnic down to the
cliff.

The children were finishing breakfast, all three in high-
chairs—Tom chiding Jingo very seriously in a boy-whinny, as
though the pony were in the seat beside him; Lily, plucking
petals from a black-eyed Susan and arranging them thoughtfully around the crusts on her toast plate; and Anna, cheerfully
banging out a primitive song with her silver spoon and porrin-
ger. Emma stood in the pantry surveying her fruit jars, tallying
the count of jams, jellies, and marmalades on the papered shelf
with the notebook she'd been keeping since berrying began: *5
quarts strawberry jam, 20 quarts black raspberry jam, 4 jars currant jelly,
8 ½ quarts red raspberries and currants, 10 quarts raspberries, 12 jars
peaches, 14 jars beach plum jelly, 2 quarts currant juice, 5 jars quince
marmalade, and 2 jars cherries.* It had taken all summer and halfway
into the fall, but she'd worked at it every afternoon when the
children were napping. She thought she'd never be finished
straining berries through the cheesecloth, measuring sugar and
simmering it down, filling the endless rows of scalded jars.
She'd burned herself quite badly when she'd tipped the granite-
ware kettle and spilled boiling water on her instep. Once,
when she was cutting sheet tin into circles to fit over the white
paper dipped in brandy for the tops of the jelly jars, Anna had
stumbled into the kitchen, rubbing sleep from her eyes, and
said, *Look, Mama, blood,* pointing to Emma's berry-stained hands.
Emma wiped them on a dishrag and knelt to explain to Anna
about the berries, but when she put our her palms to mollify
the child, she saw a ruby jet of blood pumping out of her
thumb. She hadn't felt a thing. Dr. Morrow had come to the
house to suture it which Anna had insisted upon watching.
Hurt, Mama, hurt? she'd asked, her face furrowed in consterna-
tion. Emma thought she was the brightest child she'd ever
known, walking at nine months, curious but not frightened,

but then, mothers were supposed to think that their children were extraordinary.

It was a perfect day for picnicking. The children were dressed and washed without fussing. Emma found their sun hats, their shovels and pails, hooked the wicker basket over her arm, and they straggled out across the lawn to the stable. She hitched up Jingo to the pony cart, rubbing his velvet muzzle and reached into the pocket of her long smock to find him a crabapple. She lifted the children into the cart one by one, settling them between the basket, the blanket, and umbrella. The little Shetland took the bridle easily, tossing his rum-colored mane with joy, and Emma walked him out of the stable into the sunlight.

She led him by a rope past cottages where morning glories studded a tacked-up fishnet like garnets and a screen door gently wheezed shut, past the Cliff House, a stately private home behind a stone wall owned by Mr. H. H. Hutchings—the mullioned windows in its tower so stained with light that it looked like an abbey, though Emma had never seen one—past a wooden fence that ran along the cliff's edge, wreathed with the last of the *rosa rugosa*, the fragrant pink beach roses, blooming through mid-October this year. The pony knew the way to the sweetest grass, and Emma dropped the lead, letting him wander toward the top of the hill. With the soft clop-clop of the pony's stride like a kind of percussion, Emma heard the leaves overhead shuffling like sheet music, readying for the rhythm of the sea. A Great Black-backed gull flew high above the pony cart, the guttural shriek of the scavenger startling the children, followed by the sweet kip-kip-kip-killick of a least tern somewhere on the sand below, together sounding like an orchestra tuning up before a symphony. She spread out the tartan, opened the umbrella, and watched her children scramble off through the knee-high grasses, searching for treasure. Later, after lunch and a nap, they would go down to the sea, now at low tide where the air was pungent with salt.

Emma sighed contentedly, settling herself on the blanket,

lifting her face for a moment to the sun. Butterflies swept over the cliff in a spiral, a waltz in the wind, and three-year-old Tom, with his platinum shoulder-length curls, was standing like a soldier holding up a stick, patiently waiting for a monarch to perch on it. Anna, her eyes closed in rapture, was spinning in circles, her arms outstretched to the cloudless azure sky, her white dress ballooning out as if she believed she could fly. Dark-haired, dark-eyed Lily was stepping delicately through the brambles, pulling up her pinafore to keep it from being torn. She bent over to pick up a flower, and the breeze blew back the ribbons of her smock, the edges of her petticoat ruffling like surf. Emma unbuttoned the top of her blouse and remembered when she and Anne Marie and Charlotte had gathered armloads of shore mallow, Little Bird Orchids, sea lavender, and Grass of Parnassus to bring to their mother on a day such as this. She rested her hand lightly on her belly, thinking of the new child she was carrying there. It felt so good to be out of mourning. The muslin underdress was cool, the smock soft and unconstricting.

For a year after the twins died, Emma was numb and lay in bed, silent and useless. She was ashamed now to think of how much trouble she'd been, with Pa hobbling around on his cane, Mother so frail, and Jeremiah out erecting blocks of apartments and buying shops, office buildings, and empty lots. Her sister Charlotte had been a godsend. The next year Tom was born and Lily nine months later, and for one winter they were a family again. Pa got up from supper one night in March, half-turned back to the table as if to say something, and fell down dead without a sound. They had all been thinking that Mother would go first; she'd been sick for so long, the flesh slowly disappearing from her body until her skin barely seemed to cover her bones. She died later the same year, right before Thanksgiving. When Emma's third child came the following October, she named her Anna Katherine, after her mother, and she told Jeremiah that the next boy would be called Richard after her father. The house in Winthrop was finished. They could finally leave the heartache of Cambridge. The sea air would be good for all of them.

The children returned to the tartan, hot and cranky. Emma fed them, sang them silly songs, made them laugh, and they curled up like little commas to sleep, the sea breeze gently lifting their curls from their damp faces. She lay down beside them, listening to their sweet breathing, heard Jingo tearing the grass nearby with his strong yellow teeth, and the slow, soft slide of the tide going out.

She was thirty-six years old—not so ancient, really, though her hair had turned white after she'd lost the twins. Jeremiah continued to hold her tenderly at night, and when he winked at her from across the dining-room table sometimes, her silly, middle-aged heart still did a girlish two-step. Her figure came back easily after each child, and now that she was not sewing or managing the sickroom every day, her headaches had disappeared. Winthrop was quiet, clean, and healthy. She spent a lot of time in the garden, with the children on the beach, and on the wide porch that ran around the house where she could see the ocean in all seasons. Winthrop. Yellow leaves were falling past her gaze, gold leaf tumbling over the grass. She put her hand on her belly. Richard Winthrop Green would be the name of this child. A strong name for a strong boy.

The train whistle woke her sometime later. She sat up, blinking, momentarily lost, and looked down to see three Narrow Gauge cars and the engine purling smoke as it rounded the curve of the undercliff and puffed its way up the incline toward the Crest Hotel. The children woke up as the whistle shrieked again, and pointed excitedly as it headed for Locust Street and Rocky Beach, vanishing through a tunnel of trees, leaving only a plume of smoke. Emma stared at it, and for no reason that she could fathom, she found herself trembling. *What in the world was the matter with her?* She shook herself impatiently. The little train traveled the length of the beach, past St. Leonard's Hotel to Point Shirley and the ferry, then back around through town to Cherry Street and the Highlands as it did every day, on schedule. Why did she feel like a cloud was passing over the sun?

She stood up suddenly, tipping over the picnic basket and stepping on Anna's fingers by mistake. She picked up the squalling child and held her tightly in her arms, feeling a chill. Something of her life was being taken away on that train, leaving her behind, and it would never come again.

The children sat without complaint in the pony cart, Jingo happily heading homeward, Emma wiping her eyes furiously with a handkerchief. *What in the world was wrong with her?* This was Anna's birthday. It had been a perfect day. She was overwrought. She was with child. She was losing her mind. It must be the changing season. She hated to watch the leaves come down. She turned to look back at the children. Tom was saluting, a soldier with a willow stick over one shoulder like a rifle. Lily smiled, holding out her armload of asters and tiny tickseed sunflowers. Yellow leaves were falling softly behind the wagon as it traveled home, a gentle golden snowfall under the colonnade of trees. The sea and the horizon faded to a mural in the distance. Anna reached for her mother's hand, and Emma, walking beside the cart, leaned down and kissed the child's fingers with a buzzing sound that made both of them laugh, her sadness and panic forgotten.

When Jeremiah came home for supper that night, stashing his hat and gold-tipped walking stick in the hall tree, the children, who had been playing quietly in the front parlor, tumbled like puppies over the rug to be the first to greet him. *Papa, Papa,* they cried, as though he had been away for years at sea. He tickled them fiercely with his walrus mustache, growling their favorite bear sounds into each of their collars, picking up Anna under the arms of her pinafore and heaving her toward the ceiling so that she could touch the angels painted there. They were cherubs, really, in an azure heaven with suns and moons and garlands. Emma had copied the design from a book. She'd had a difficult time making the wings, once telling Jeremiah she thought their fat little bodies looked like toadstools with faces, but Anna saw only the angels, and wanted to fly with them every night.

The dining room was bright with candles and flowers. Gaslight in the ivied sconces made everything glow, and Emma came to meet Jeremiah in her plum-colored watered silk dress. She blushed like a bride when he kissed her cheek, and she impulsively took him by the arm, wanting to tell him so many things—*that they'd had a wonderful picnic, that the cake was done to a turn, dinner was nearly ready, and that she'd been frightened at the cliff today but didn't know why.* But Tom and Lily were quarreling tearfully over a toy, and Anna was fussing to see her cake, so they were called away from the moment, and Emma didn't have the chance to say any of the things she'd intended.

Dinner was over in a trice. The cake was brought out of the pantry and the children oohed with excitement. They sang Happy Birthday to You, and Anna, knowing what was expected of her, puffed out her cheeks and gave a tremendous blow, clapping her hands gleefully when the flame went out, for having done it so well. Jeremiah went to the back hall to fetch her present while Emma sliced the cake—the silver lifter with lilies-of-the-valley etched in the handle that cut the angel food like butter—and soon returned to the parlor with an enormous package wrapped in brown paper and set it down in front of the fireplace with a great smile, calling gently, *Anna, come here, then, this is yours.* Anna toddled over timidly, because the package was twice her size, and awkwardly began to unwrap it.

Emma watched from the dining room, her arms across her chest, the silver cake lifter still in her hands. She was trying not to smile. It had been Jeremiah's idea. Evelyn Etheridge's father down the Point was an expert woodcarver. He'd made some of the most beautiful merry-go-round horses at Revere

Beach, with flaring nostrils, fire in their glass eyes and luxuriant flying manes, powerful as lions in mid-roar, muscles rippling as they galloped and shied, their hooves seeming to throw off sparks as they raced around the track of the calliope. Jeremiah had paid him handsomely to make Anna's present.

The paper came away in her hands, and her pink mouth made an O of astonished delight. It was a rocking horse made of wood, but so alive that it seemed to be already in motion, the fluted nostrils breathing heavily, the chest rising and falling, a gold bit between his teeth and gold-braid bridle looped over his wind-blown mane, with a red-and-turquoise saddle and real stirrups. Jeremiah touched the rocker with the toe of his boot, and the horse seemed to spring in the air, his gleaming hooves leaping for a fence, a stone wall, a gateway, and the children squealed with joy. He set Anna gently on the saddle; she put her arms around the horse's neck and kissed him under his blown-back ear.

Circe, the child murmured gratefully, *my Circe.*

Emma was dumbfounded. She'd been telling the children stories before bed ever since they were born—because she'd read somewhere that the sound of the mother's voice before sleep contributed to the child's mental health and security and was better medicine than anything devised by science. So every night she recalled her favorite fairy tales and spun adventures from her imagination on the spot, which she couldn't have repeated if her life depended on it, told them stories of her ancestors arriving from Belfast, stories about her own childhood, of being courted by Jeremiah. But never in her wildest dreams did she imagine that the children might remember them. She thought they would remember the safety of being snuggled in bed with her, the soft candlelight, or the lavender scent of the sheets, but Circe! Anna was so little. How in the world did she latch onto the name of the beloved horse from Emma's childhood?

Emma bent over the cake again, tears on her lashes. It

seemed to be her birthday all of a sudden, and she had just been given a marvelous gift. The tea tray would be ready as soon as the kettle whistled, and she went into the kitchen to fetch it. She could hear the children laughing as she made the tea and brought it to the table. Jeremiah was at the piano, playing "Camptown Races," and Tom was riding Circe the way he would one day ride Jingo, hell-bent-for-leather. She spooned sugar into the cups, smiling again, poured in milk, and waited a minute for the tea to finish steeping. When she looked up once more, prompted by the sound of Jeremiah's sweet tenor voice singing *doo-dah, doo-dah,* Tom was standing on the saddle, gripping the bridle like a bareback rider in the circus, the horse at full gallop.

Emma screamed and dropped a saucer. Jeremiah bolted from the piano and grabbed his son in a fury, shaking him until the boy cried out in terror.

Don't ever, ever stand on that saddle again, his father bellowed, taking Tom over his knee and walloping his behind. *Do you understand me, you little bastard? I'll take the goddamn thing and hurl it over the cliff and you after it, do you hear me?*

Jeremiah, Emma pleaded, but he did not hear her over the wails of his three children, and continued pounding the boy. Emma's heart burst—he'd been drinking again—oh, God, the babies were so frightened!

Jeremiah! She screamed. *Stop it, stop it!*

And her husband looked up, so like a stranger, as if he didn't know where he was. In a daze he set down his son, blinking, and ran a hand through his hair. Tom raced howling for his mother's skirts.

It's all right, lamb, it's over now. You must do as Papa says and not ride the horse that way. You have to promise to sit properly in the saddle, hmm? It's all right, now. It's all right. Come, children, come and have your cake.

They were subdued as they climbed into their chairs. Tears glistened on their cheeks. Tom wiped his nose on his sleeve and Emma didn't have the heart to correct him. She passed around the cake, gave Jeremiah his tea, and sat in silence while they ate. She'd ignored it so often. *Just a dram o' whiskey wi' the boys, Mother,* he'd say, in his merriest brogue. *Stopped off t' see the fellahs on A Street and met up with me old chum, John Barleycorn.* His temper came and went like lightning or a flash flood, but she'd never connected it to his *bit o' porter* or *his wee drap of ale.* All at once, she covered her face with he. hands. *Oh, God, how could this have happened?*

Like an automaton, she picked up the silver cake lifter with the lilies-of-the-valley etched in the handle and cut her husband another slice that he'd asked for meekly, by way of apology, but she could not look at him. From a long distance she heard Lily say, *Look, Mama, look at Anna,* and as she slowly turned toward the sound of Lily's voice, she saw Anna in the parlor in front of the fireplace, standing on Circe's saddle, gripping the golden bridle like a bareback rider, the horse in a frenzy of rocking. Emma was up, the cake lifter flying from her hands as she ran for the child, but everything seemed to be moving as if she were underwater—she was wading through a deep sea in her heavy skirts, Anna was laughing like a beautiful tropical fish, bubbles of delight floating out of her mouth, the bridle slipping slowly from her hands, and for a moment the child was airborne like one of her angels, and she was falling forward over the carved mane of the fabulous horse, her petticoats like the surf crashing over a rock before it disappeared forever into the sea. Emma heard a horrendous, ungodly sound, and knew it was Anna's skull on the fireplace fender. Suddenly she could move, and she was cradling her daughter, screaming for Jeremiah to call Dr. Morrow, the child white and limp in her arms, blood pouring into the lap of Emma's plum-colored dress, blood all over Anna's starched pinafore, and the older children screaming.

Jeremiah ran for a towel and ice, packing it under the little girl's head, rang through to Dr. Morrow—*an emergency,* he

shouted—then wrenched Anna out of Emma's arms and carried
her upstairs, the sobs of a mortally wounded animal racking his
chest. Emma stood up in the front parlor, feeling faint, tore off
her soaking dress and dropped it over the hearth to hide the
running blood, knowing the children had already seen it. She
shivered convulsively in her chemise and shift, lifted Tom and
Lily to her breast, then raced them upstairs. She washed their
terrified faces, talked to them soothingly as she got them into
their nighties and tucked them in. She sang the same lullaby
she always sang, waiting for the doctor's bell, crooning them
in her arms until their crying slowed, frantically listening for
the carriage outside, softly, softly, mewing nonsense rhymes to
calm them to sleep, trying to quiet the thrashing of her own
heart. Hours seemed to pass. She sang quietly until her throat
was raw and the children were like stones in her arms, her mind
fierce and electric, willing the doctor to come. When the bell
finally rang, she slipped the children under the covers, ran for
her robe, and flew down the stairs to fling open the door.

They sat up with Anna all night. Dr. Morrow wanted to take
her to Metcalf Hospital immediately, but Jeremiah wouldn't
hear of it. Emma clutched the child's dead-cold hand and
prayed to God to let her live, burying her face in the bloody
sheets as the doctor shone light in Anna's turned-back pupils.
She could not watch as he cut away the baby-fine hair and put
fourteen stitches into the top of her head, the child never rising
into consciousness as the needle pierced her scalp again and
again. Jeremiah had to leave the room. Emma heard him retching in the bath. He came back, white-faced, with a tray of
sherry and three glasses. He held one glass to his wife's icy lips
and made her drink. It burned going down, but her mind
seemed to reattach itself to her heart. She did not take her eyes
off her daughter again.

Anna came to three hours later, not recognizing anyone, not
knowing where she was. She was too weak to cry. The doctor
had hemmed and hawed over his little black bag, wanting to

give her something for the pain, but also wanting to keep her awake so he could monitor her condition.

For Christ Almighty sake's, man, give her something for the pain, Jeremiah bellowed. Anna looked in her father's direction, but didn't respond to him, only to the sudden, loud noise.

The doctor left at dawn, writing out detailed instructions about the dangers of concussion and what to watch for. He wanted to be called immediately i. the child vomited or fell into such a deep sleep that she could not be roused. He left laudanum on the night table and gave a bottle to Emma, insisting that she go to bed. After some argument, Emma took a dose of the medicine, but pulled an armchair next to Anna's crib and refused to move from it. After a while, exhaustion overcame her, and she fell into a dreamless sleep.

Early the next morning Jeremiah called a neighbor, Gladys Peacock, to have her come care for the children. He'd never been so frightened in his life.

Anna seemed more alert after she slept. She cried a little, rocking and holding her head. Emma kept ice on her skull until she thought that she'd never have feelings in her fingers again. Then, in the late afternoon, Anna became restless and feverish, crying piteously, fearfully about *a horse, a horse that was coming to get her.* She went on for hours. Jeremiah stormed out to the stable with the beautifully carved Circe in his arms. Emma watched from the window, weeping, as he struck it over and over with an ax, attacking it as though it were a living thing, cracking its noble head into pieces, smashing its graceful legs, the red-and-turquoise saddle, the muscled flanks, until it had been broken into kindling and his fury was spent. He stood, swaying, and finally dropped the ax, sat down heavily in the stable yard and wept, his arms over the brutalized carcass of the wooden rocking horse.

The next six months were the worst of Emma's life. Anna began to have seizures, her eyes rolled back in her head, her legs banging the sides of the crib, saliva running from her lips.

Emma stuffed gauze into her mouth so she wouldn't swallow her tongue and held her hand until the tremors were over. When Anna came out of it, she didn't recognize anyone and slept deeply for several hours. Then she'd wake up and know people once again. She'd even sit up in bed and play quietly with the other children. Days would go by with no sign of illness. She was quieter and rarely spoke, but after a time she began to smile and started eating and acting like a normal child again. But there were odd things. She'd be in the middle of something—playing or singing—and suddenly she would stop and seem to fall into a trance. Nothing could bring her out of it—not a voice or smelling salts or a slap on the cheek. A few minutes later her eyes would refocus, and she'd be back in the world, confused. Once, on a sunny afternoon, she was sitting on the window seat in the parlor, happily telling a story to her favorite doll, when a look of terror came over her face so profound that it frightened Emma to death. *What was Anna seeing?* The child began to scream in a frenzy of fear, screaming and screaming, her eyes wide and glazed with some horror that she couldn't articulate, a dreadful thing beyond words.

Dr. Morrow returned for several visits, and each time he'd tell them about epilepsy. Jeremiah would leave the room because he couldn't bear to hear it. *Anna may grow out of her seizures,* the doctor said, *but we won't know for a while. If she doesn't grow out of them, the best thing would be to put her in a place where she can be looked after properly. Invariably,* he said, *epilepsy leads to insanity, and she could give herself a permanent injury during one of her seizures.* Emma stood up in a fury, handed the doctor his black bag and hat, and told him that no child of hers would ever be put away. They would care for her at home.

And so began a hellish set of rituals, all designed to protect Anna from herself. She was never left alone during the day. The children were instructed to call Emma at once if their sister began to act oddly, and when a day passed with no outbursts, no rages, no seizures, the family breathed a collective sigh of

relief. Meanwhile, Emma had all but lost her sense of who Tom
and Lily were. They were her other children, but she didn't
seem to see them very clearly any more. Mrs. Peacock stayed
on, Jeremiah went back to work, and Emma never took her
eyes off Anna.

Nights were the worst. Dr. Morrow insisted that there was
no cure for epilepsy, even if the seizures disappeared after a
time. There were only doses of bromides, which did very little
to stay the course of the disease. So at night, for Anna's own
protection, he showed Emma how to tie her in bed. He opened
the child's mouth and placed a wad of gauze on her tongue as
big as his finger. He closed her jaw by wrapping a long strip
of cotton several times around her chin to the top of her head
and back, tying it in a knot, until the poor child looked like a
woodcut from an old medical textbook of a Man With a
Toothache. Then he tied her wrists and ankles to the bars of
the crib. Now, he said, if she did seize in the night, she
wouldn't hurt herself or swallow her tongue. Emma was in such
a state of agony and grief that every night she tied Anna
mechanically, as if her heart had been placed in a cone of
ether. Her distraction was so complete that she'd nearly forgotten she was carrying yet another child.

In April, Anna seemed a little more like herself. She picked
daffodils and brought a scraggly bunch to her mother. She
stopped pulling Lily's hair. She let Tom take her down to the
beach and back in the red wagon. Emma could hardly move,
the child inside her had grown so big. The baby had dropped
down, so she was due any time. The house seemed so peaceful
with Mrs. Peacock around that Emma sat rocking on the porch
in the mild weather, wrapped in a tartan and looking out at the
sea, hypnotized by its consistency, its dependable comings and
goings. She did not think of anything, only how serene it was,
at last. Maybe the nightmare was over and Anna was well.
Maybe they could be a family again. Maybe she could sleep
for a thousand years.

Then a tremendous crash woke her, and a shower of glass
from the curved front window broke over her shoulders and
hair, and Anna's terrible screaming began—a keening, an inhuman shrieking that went on and on and wouldn't stop. Emma
sat stunned, covered with shards of glass from the window and
the vase of flowers that Anna had thrown through it. She tried
to rise from her rocker when a pain so fierce that it took her
breath away sliced through her body. She tried a second time
to heave her heavy body out of the chair, but the pain came
again, stronger. Her water broke. *Oh, God, she was in labor.* The
screaming went on and on, and she couldn't bear the noise of
her sick child and the labor pains, it was too much. She staggered to the front door, clutching her belly, and leaned on the
doorbell until Mrs. Peacock came. She was half-carried
upstairs, put to bed, and suddenly the doctor was there with
Jeremiah, and the screaming went on and on. She pulled on
the sheets that were tied to the bedposts and tried to push, but
her screams were coming from somewhere else. She was pushing away the terrible thing that was hurting her, and she was
screaming, and in her heart she heard Anna screaming too, and
after a while she couldn't tell which inhuman sound was hers
and which was her child's.

The baby, when it came, was a strong and healthy boy.
Emma, beyond caring about anything, lifted the weights of her
eyelids with one last thought. *His name,* she gasped to Jeremiah,
his name is Richard, after my father—Richard Winthrop Green. Then
she fell down the long tunnel to sleep in the echo of Anna's
screams, which seemed to Emma like someone begging to die.

Carefully, I dried the frame and glass with a dish towel. I laid
the family tree upside down against the glass, trimming the
page's edges so that it would fit. I cut a piece of cardboard to
size and put that over it. With a little hammer, I gently
pounded tiny nails around the border of the frame so that the
picture was held in place. I glued a piece of brown paper bag

to the edge of the frame. Then Granny helped me twist in the eye-screws and cut the wire for me, which I threaded through the screws so that it could be hung above the fireplace. I had finished my Family Tree.

Granny said, "And so, that's the story of how the Greens came to Winthrop." She got up to wash her hands and make us some tea.

I was sitting on the porch after supper, waiting for Boppa to come out so that we could have tea together until it grew dark. It was a mild summer evening in Winthrop, and after-supper tea on the porch was our custom.

His sister, my Great-Aunt Emeline, was standing under the apple tree in the yard of the big white house across the street, her hair wild, her enormous beak in the air, wearing a man's ragged plaid bathrobe over her torn nightgown, calling for her flea-infested Yorkshire terrier, Jolly. There was a graveyard out back for her other, long-dead Yorkies, all of whom had been named Jolly. My aunt was a terrifying woman. All the kids in the neighborhood were afraid of her, but still brave enough to be mean. They'd run up the high stone steps and ring the door-bell, then scatter hilariously down a side street before she could come to the door. Emeline was stone deaf—she couldn't hear the doorbell. Only the dog would go into a frenzy. So the kids broke the windows on her sunporch with stones. At night they soaped the beautiful rounded glass entranceway. They cut her clothesline into pieces and tossed the ragged ropes high into the branches of the apple tree.

"Jolly! Jol-l-l-ly!" Emeline called in a voice raucous and rough as a crow's.

I could hear the creature routing around in the hydrangea bush, and dashed over to get the dog before he ran into the street. Jolly was no bigger than a rat whose coat stood up in points, and he smelled. Silently, I handed the wiggling rat to my aunt. Emeline had bright, fierce eyes, a massive head with thin hair pinned up hastily with tortoiseshell combs. Her teeth were as huge and yellow as the horses that she doted on all of her life. She talked, loudly and gruffly, out of loneliness, to whomever happened to stumble into her yard—the mailman, the cabbie who delivered her groceries, the paper boy, little girls selling cookies. She talked at them, as if holding them in place with her hoarse voice would keep them from disappearing before she'd finished telling her story. It was impossible to get away from her, the neighbors said. No one wanted to get nabbed by Aunt Emeline. Patient, disconcerted tradesmen were treated to rambling, disconnected stories—of people long since gone, trips she'd taken, horse shows she'd attended, riding trophies she'd won, tenants she'd tangled with in court. Sometimes Emeline would call Granny on the telephone and launch into a long, uninterruptable monologue, to which Granny would respond, "Uh-huh, uh-huh" and "Yes, I know" for several minutes, then put down the receiver on the kitchen table and go into the pantry to make lunch. Every so often she'd pick up the phone and bellow, "You've already told me that!" and go back to slathering mayonnaise on the sandwiches. I thought it was awful.

Emeline, cuddling the rescued Yorkie, started to tell me a story I'd heard before—about one of her cruises to Europe between the wars when she was the only white woman on board who wasn't seasick during the crossing. I hated to leave her, alone and bedraggled in her yard, so old and hungry for company, but I had to go have tea with Boppa. Impulsively, I kissed her leathery cheek, patted the ratty dog, and ran back across the street to our porch.

I remember being inside the big white house only once when Emeline had invited me over "for luncheon." Granny, who hated her sister-in-law ferociously, insisted that I go. She was convinced that if I were nice to Emeline, the old bitch would leave me something in her will. I felt like a hostage, a fraud, a cheat as I climbed my aunt's steep stone steps. I wanted to like my aunt, to know her, to listen to her stories, to ask her questions about the family, but all I was supposed to do was smile and cozy up to her so she'd leave me some money when she died. I hated Granny sometimes so much I couldn't see.

The house was full of beautiful woodwork, a high domed ceiling with a hand-painted sky-blue mural of cherubs and angels and flowering vines. Curled petals of paint were scattered on the foyer floor. The chandeliers were ornate and spun with spider webs that Pip might have seen at Miss Havisham's. Oriental rugs stretched from one parlor to the other, but the elaborate and faded designs were marred by dried urine stains and piles of dog turds so ancient and dry that they were white. The dining room was stunning—the table a mahogany lake where scalloped plates floated like water lilies anchored by bright monogrammed silver, starched linen napkins with lace trim, exquisite porcelain cups and saucers. I was afraid to sit down.

I never had a meal like the one I had at Emeline's. She was a splendid cook and a gracious hostess, asking me about myself as she ladled lobster bisque out of a large tureen patterned with irises, served dandelion green and endive salad on scrolled clear plates, and offered me oil and vinegar in cut-glass cruets. She had prepared cold sliced Cornish hen with a sweet pink sauce, Duchesse potatoes, green beans with sliced almonds, and crème caramel for dessert. The teapot had a cosy of an English countryside with riders running to hounds.

She was kind and sane, and did not frighten me. She seemed to remember the gentility of another era, as if, only when surrounded by fine china and lace and generous helpings of elegant food was she able to find her bearings. She sat taller in her chair, and the years of loneliness seemed to slip from her shoulders like a shawl, her eyes sparkled, and she became a warm and enchanting storyteller. I was utterly charmed, though I had to shout to make her hear me.

Sometime during the meal, I had discovered that her birthday was the following week, so when the day arrived, I gave her a rose-colored African violet in a brightly painted ceramic pot with a thank-you note attached. I did not know that she would keep the plant for years, thrilled and touched because it had been so long since anyone had remembered her birthday. Still, I was not invited to luncheon again, and Granny never forgave me for not ingratiating myself into Emeline's lonely existence so that eventually I'd inherit everything.

In Winthrop on summer evenings after an early supper, Boppa and I would sit out on the piazza. At the farm we called it the porch, but Boppa called it the piazza. It sounded so grand. Long tubes of matchstick blinds, hanging from hooks over the enormous shingled archways, could be rolled down when the afternoon sun beamed directly on the wicker furniture and the paper-thin gray-and-rose rug. Red geraniums spilled over clay pots and saucers on each tier of the porch stairs, as well as from two gaily painted terra-cotta Mexican urns on either side of the doorway. Winthrop didn't have a black-fly season and there weren't many mosquitoes because of the salt air, so we could sit comfortably outside until dark. Granny would bring out a tray with tea and cookies and leave us alone while she did the dishes.

A neighborhood was a wonderful thing—so unlike the isolation of the farm—where people who had known each other since they were children would run over to borrow clothespins or dress patterns. Housewives would stand on the corner in their aprons gossiping, and bring over pies and casseroles when someone was sick or died. Kids went clamming together at low tide. The same things happened, day in and day out. Boppa and I would watch people come home from work, keys jingling in their hands, their gaits buoyed by cooking smells. We'd hear the clatter of pots and pans and screen doors slam as they went in to eat their suppers. Mr. Doig walked his dog by our house at a quarter past five every night, and Boppa would holler at him *to make his damned dog crap in his own yard, for Chrissake*, and

Mr. Doig would mildly take his dog away. Some people came up onto our porch to say hello and see how we were. They noticed that I was growing up and would ask me about school and what I wanted to do later in life. I was a person to them, related to someone whom they liked and seemed to respect— my grandfather.

Of course, I wasn't allowed off the porch. But just knowing such a camaraderie existed made me happy. I felt I belonged, at least a little bit. And so we'd sit on the porch on midsummer evenings, my grandfather smoking his pipe while I absent- mindedly picked at the scabs on my knees, drinking tea. Who was this tall, silent pillar of a man, wearing ragged clothes and wire-rimmed glasses, looking for all the world like an intellec- tual scarecrow? Boppa reminded me of a marble bust of some forgotten emperor with his large white head, his Roman nose, his strong jaw. Even his pale blue eyes were beginning to bleach out from old age, and I imagined one day that I would look at him to find the irises had disappeared altogether. His skin was whiter than any I'd ever seen. It wasn't the pallor of illness or a life spent indoors; his skin was naturally white, smooth and free of wrinkles as a baby's. Sometimes I'd put a towel around his shoulders, tuck it into the frayed collar of his old plaid Pendleton shirt, and trim his hair. His hair was also very white, not the buttery-colored hair that some old men have, but pure and soft as swan's down. I'd trim the bristles in his ears and clip the hairs in his enormous nostrils, while he'd sit perfectly still, knowing I wouldn't nip him with the scissor's sharp point. Over and over I'd run the comb through his hair and cut carefully along its teeth, trying to make the time go by slowly, because this was one way that I could love him and be with him.

He was so old. He never complained of pain. He was still over six feet tall and strong as an ox, but he was a very ancient man. I was sitting beside him in a brown wicker chair with faded flowered cushions, watching his huge white hands gently cup the bowl of his pipe, lighting match after match, champing on the pipe stem to get it lit, tossing the dead match into the arbor vitae. We'd look across the street at the big white house where he was born—the rounded glass foyer, the turret and wide piazza above the stone foundation, a froth of syringa at one corner and, like a large heavy drapery, a swag of hyacinth-blue wisteria at the other. I could smell it from the porch, the scent of dusk, the soft, faint, gray-purple light sifting down from heaven, and I thought of him growing up there so long ago.

That boy, whoever he was, had become a husband, a father, and finally my grandfather. That man, whoever he was, had worked, fought, loved, laughed, and grown old, but the boy was still inside him somewhere. I thought of the way Granny folded egg whites into the yolks with a spatula when she made her famous sponge cakes, how the egg whites would change into something completely different. I thought of the way my favorite little forgotten mammal, the eohippus, still existed inside the thoroughbreds that won steeplechases, danced in parade rings, and raced for the roses of the Kentucky Derby. I would never see an eohippus in my life, but I thought that if I looked closely enough, I could imagine one in the muscled flanks and fetlocks of Roger St. Cyr's palomino, Sugar.

I thought of all the truths in the world, ones that fought and contradicted each other, but still stood up on their own. The eohippus was dead; but the eohippus was still alive in the American quarter horse. The egg whites were folded into batter and disappeared; but the batter could not become a cake without them. Boppa was an old man, but the boy he once was would have his own shape inside him for as long as he lived. It made my head hurt to think about it.

How could one person ever really know another? And what was history anyway but one version of a truth so large and complicated that no one could ever understand it? Whenever I thought about Heaven, I hoped it would be—not a place, but a way of knowing. I did not want white wings—I wanted to be able to fly back to any century of my choosing since the beginning of time. And it wouldn't be like watching a movie of Joan of Arc, or the pioneers sailing across America in their prairie schooners, or Balboa discovering the Pacific. Heaven would not keep me outside history, it would let me inside, because I believed that in Heaven, history was not in the past but always in the process of happening.

This was my favorite dream, the one that rocked me to sleep most nights. My mother's vivid stories, all my secret reading, every painting I'd ever seen, all made me believe that someday I'd be able to know what it was like to be a peasant during Charlemagne's reign, to be a slave working on the pyramids, to be Nefertiti; Cleopatra; Mary, Queen of Scots; Artemisia Gentileschi; Florence Nightingale; Margaret Bourke White. In Heaven, I would spend all eternity being other people— famous, infamous, sad, sick, powerful, hungry, victorious, beautiful, deformed—and live their lives down to the last detail—the rope-soled sandals, flies, plague, rich brocades, and ambrosia in silver goblets encrusted with rubies. I would squat in the gutter to shit, eat a cat if I was starving, be a mapmaker's apprentice, pose for Leonardo da Vinci, be Leonardo da Vinci, be a fifteenth-century herbalist burned as a witch, feel the fire and smell of my own flesh roasting. I would mix my own colors, sit under the groaning board in some medieval keep, and snatch the greasy bones from the mouths of dogs in the rushes. I would be a moth flying into a candle flame, a black child dying a fierce death in the hold of a slave ship; I'd be a solitary, gigantic polar bear lumbering across the frozen tundra, sailing through the Arctic on a blue ice floe. I did not believe in Hell—I had already felt that endless burning—but I did believe in a glorious Heaven. After a while I would understand why Eve had taken the apple and I would know as much as God.

Now, with a strange, urgent desperation, I wanted to know about my grandfather's family and what had happened to make all those beautiful young people hate each other in their old age. So after supper one night, I stood in Boppa's room with the brown plaid wallpaper and stared at the two photographs on his dresser—one of his mother and father, Emma and Jeremiah, together in an ornate silver frame, the other of his entire family taken when the boys were still in uniform from World War I. I had heard all kinds of stories, mostly from Granny, about the character and exploits of the Greens, but she was so angry at them all that I knew I wasn't getting the whole truth. It was like pulling teeth to get Boppa to tell me anything, but it was always worth another try.

"Boppa," I said, settling into the wicker chair, cradling the picture in my arms like a baby. "Tell me who these people are again."

He tamped Prince Albert into the bowl of his pipe and struck a match before he spoke, puffing and puffing to keep the tobacco lit. I put the tea tray on the rug at my feet, stood up the photograph on the wicker table between us, and pulled my chair closer to his. I loved this more than anything.

He tapped the hot pipe stem in the left-hand corner of the frame. "That's me, after I got back from Pensacola. I fixed airplane engines during the war, you know. I think this picture was taken about the time I married your grandmother."

"Why isn't she there with you?"

He paused. *Ma had opened the door of the glassed-in foyer and looked down at us, her eyes blazing at poor Ellen who clung to my arm, trying to smile. We'd been married by a justice of the peace in Townsend that afternoon. Ma stared at Ellen's royal blue suit, the little hat and veil with a scowl. She'd gotten so deaf the last couple of years, I had started to shout, Ma, this is— And she hollered loudly enough for the whole neighborhood to hear, So this is what you left me for!*

"Well," Boppa said after a while. "My father wanted it to be just the family." He cleared a frog in his throat and pointed the pipe stem at the man beside him. "This is my oldest brother, Tom. He rode along the Mexican border under General Per-

shing when they were chasing Pancho Villa. He was Judge
Advocate General at Pearl Harbor during the Second World
War."

I liked Tom's crooked smile and the way his ears stuck out
like Clark Gable's.

*Tom, you skinny s.o.b. Who knew you'd be the one to get away, to
make use of your life, and leave all the rest of us in the dust? Well, I guess
I must've known it—I tagged after you so much growing up, you called
me Shadow. Mike and Ike, we called ourselves. Seems like we were always
together in those days. The girls stayed in, and Ollie was sniveling—we
ditched him whenever we could. Ma always wanted us out of the house—
Christ, we spent half our lives at the beach, in the woods, skating, fishing,
sledding down Temple Avenue to the boat landing, sneaking onto the train
without paying, jumping off at Shirley Street to buy day-old bagels and
sweets from the Jewish shops. Strange how Ma and Pa saw fit to raise
us—they gave us the best clothes, piano lessons, dancing lessons, plenty of
spending money, and then let us run wild through town. We did whatever
we felt like doing, and when we were caught—remember the time we painted
all the back windows of J. J. Dromgoole's market at Magee's corner—Pa
rumbled down in his open Marmon and gave him the old Irish blarney and
paid Dromgoole twice what he was owed "fer his tribble." He expected us
to be in dutch and was proud of us when we were, the old fool.*

*You had more patience with the rest of the little kids than I did. God,
when I think of the years we took Jingo to school, you leading the parade
like John Philip Sousa, trotting along the beach and up the hill to Almont
Street. Your rule was whoever rode in the morning had to walk home in the
afternoon. You'd put me and Lily on Jingo's back, and you and Ollie
would walk beside us. At the schoolhouse door, you'd say, Home, Jingo,
and he'd turn around and trot back to the stable. At three o'clock he'd be
waiting for us just like a bird dog, and you and Ollie would ride back,
while Lily and I would walk.*

*I saw you get mad only once, when Walter tried to get Jingo to buck
and rear like a bronco. He pulled on the bit till Jingo's mouth was bleeding,
and you tore him off the blanket like he was a tumor and whaled hell out
of the little bastard for mistreating a beautiful animal. You never raised
your voice—it scared the shit out of us to see you act like Pa.*

And even though Annie never got over being afraid of horses, she'd let you put her in the pony cart and take her all over town—I can see her now, in summer under one of Ma's old parasols, riding around as proudly as any grande dame on Beacon Hill with a sunshade. When it got cold, you'd bundle her up in blankets and ride up and down the boulevard, with the sea on one side and all the big white hotels on the other, because it was one of the few things in the world that made Annie laugh. Honest to Christ, when she'd have one of her spells and go out of her mind, biting, kicking, struggling in your arms, we'd have to practically break her wrists to get them into the restraints. She'd look at you, terror-stricken, with those wide, guileless eyes—it killed you to have to do it, didn't it, Mike? Practically a grown man and you'd lock yourself in the bathroom when it was over and cry like a baby.

Emeline was your favorite, though, probably because she could ride practically before she could walk. Remember the day—Emeline must have been about two years old—you put her up on Jingo, she hung on to his mane, laughing, and we took her all the way to school? When you said, Home, Jingo, off he went with this tiny child on his back, and brought her back to the yard. Ma nearly thrashed the skin off your hide with the rug-beater when we got home, but it was worth it. She said she looked out the kitchen window and saw Jingo grazing, with this little bundle on its back, and the bundle was wailing like the dead were after it. It took her a minute to realize it was Emeline, and she was crying because she didn't know how to get down!

Jesus, I learned everything from you—golf, tennis, basketball, squash, swimming, cards. Funny, the only thing I could ever beat you at was poker—you were an honest man, Mike. You were better at everything than I was and I had a terrible temper. I'd miss a stroke and wrap a nine-iron around a tree, and you'd laugh which only made me madder. Pa thought Ollie could do no wrong, you were Ma's favorite, and Lily always protected Walter—I always felt like I was fighting for something, attention, praise—whatever. But I knew you loved me. When I was fourteen and started hanging around the yacht club, drinking with my pals out behind the back door where they put the rubbish—you were nineteen, in the army, I couldn't run after you any more—I came home, reeling drunk, in the middle of the afternoon, and you steered me upstairs and held my head over *the commode while I puked up my guts. You tried to talk to me about drinking, but I was so broken up about you leaving home, I lay on my bed and wouldn't answer. I'm sorry now that I didn't listen to you. You were my best friend, Mike. My best friend.*

Boppa was very far away, his face furrowed as he stared at his oldest brother's face. I knew I could never understand what they'd been like together, growing up, or what Tom meant to him. I poured him some tea and pointed to the tiny young woman standing next to Tom.

"Who's that, Boppa?" I asked softly. He waited a minute before he spoke.

"That's Lillian, my oldest sister. She gave piano lessons. She was pretty but very, very shy. She stayed home with Ma and Annie until she finally married a dentist. Funny, we always called her Mrs. Tobin after that. She lives down at 52 Highland in the white house with all the black shutters."

I knew the house, but I'd never been there. I'd never even seen my great-aunt. Lillian seemed as fragile as a bird—so tiny between her brothers, all of whom were over six feet tall.

Lily. God, I almost forgot we ever called her that. She was never a rough-and-tumble kid, though she played with us sometimes when she was small. But after Pa and Ma took her to New York to see Paderewski when she was eight years old, she thought of nothing but music. She talked to me about it once, years later. "Dickie," she said, "I never dreamed anything could be so—so—transporting. His white hands flew over the keys like doves. He was beautiful—like an archangel—his golden hair to his shoulders—and every note struck my heart like some kind of heavenly chord until I was weeping. Nothing was the same for me after that." Ma got her a piano teacher, a rotund, oily little Italian named Maestro Pompeo, but I think Lily learned as much as she could from him in three years. She wanted to be a concert pianist, but Pa wouldn't hear of it. She had to stay home and take care of Annie. That's what girl-children were for.

Lily. Poor Lily. You were so good at standing up for the rest of us, but you couldn't stand up for yourself and tell Pa to go to hell. Walter always ran and hid behind your skirts when Pa was after him, and you came

between them like some cool white goddess—Athena, was it?—protecting a
loved mortal from the wrath of Zeus. And the way you went from one bed
to another when we all came down with influenza in the big epidemic right
after the war—people all over town were dropping like flies, and we almost
lost Ollie—you didn't sleep for a couple of weeks, feeding us broth, coming
in with cold compresses and clean sheets, and rubbing us down with alcohol
to bring down the fever. I never felt such kinder hands.

And Christ, how would we have lived in that house if you hadn't been
so good with Annie? That awful day when she looked in the mirror and
screamed that she saw a demon with flaming hair, and ran from room to
room breaking all the mirrors in the house except for the one over Ma's
dressing table—it took Tom, Walter, Ollie, and me to carry her into her
room, Annie screaming like a banshee that her eyes were hot coals, that we
would be burned to cinders if we tried to tie her down to the bed. And after
we did tie her down—Walter getting a bloody nose and me getting my
glasses broken in the bargain—she was still screaming that she saw us
through a red mist and that we were burning up and going to die. You
came in and held her while Dr. Morrow gave her a shot and stitched up
her hands and wrists. She turned to you with crazed eyes and cried heartbrokenly, as if only you could understand, "Lily, our four handsome brothers are pillars of fire, and flesh will keep falling off their bones until their
bones are black—it's my fault, and I can't do anything to save them."

She could explain her madness a little, when she had come out of it, but
mostly she spoke to you. "Lily," she'd say in her calm, little-girl voice, "I'm
not afraid when you're here. You sing such pretty songs. I can hear you
quite clearly, except when I slip under the water. Your voice goes away,
and I feel the soft ssh-sshing of the tide, it rocks me gently, gently, until
I'm weightless as seaweed, and I'm drowning in peace. Anna, my real self,
is calling me down to the bottom of the sea. She is so far away and so
beautiful. I don't remember how we were torn apart—do you?—but I know
I must be with her. She says I have to find all the medicine in the house
and take it, so I can sleep with her forever in the bright blue sea." And you
would tuck her in and rock her to sleep and quietly search the house with
a candle until you'd found every bottle and pill and locked it away. You
wore the key around your neck for years.

*And later, when she was grown—it happened so many times it was
almost funny—Annie would sneak out her window, tiptoe across the porch
roof, and climb down the trellis in my old raccoon coat, and walk bold as
brass to the Highlands Station to take the ferry over to Rowe's Wharf.
She'd go through Jordan Marsh and Filene's and Gilchrist's and put things
in her pockets—necklaces, little clocks, pairs of gloves, silk scarves, earrings, and walk right out of the store because she thought she was invisible.
When she came through the front door in that enormous coat, you'd gently
take her upstairs to look at all the pretty things she'd "found." You'd help
her drape scarves over the lamp shades and hang necklaces in garlands over
the fireplace and arrange the earrings across the mantelpiece between the
shells she'd collected to make them sparkle. She explained to you why she
needed three clocks on her bedside table. One was to tell the house's time,
the second to tell the dream time with Anna, and the third was the timepiece
of the black gods who made her have fits to punish her. And when the
shopkeepers discreetly called the house "concerning Miss Anne's purchases,"
you always made sure Pa sent a check over right away by messenger. You
didn't have the heart to tell her the pretty things ought to go back.*

*Ah, Lily. I never had time for you. I was too busy fighting or brooding
or worrying about Annie. It was me she asked for in the mornings. She'd
wake up and find herself tied down and want me to come in and hold her
so she wouldn't fly away. Annie was our child, Lily. We stood on either
side of her, holding her together, and never saw each other. We hovered
around her, still children ourselves, like moths around a porch light—and
everything else between us was dark.*

"Boppa?" I asked. Maybe this was too hard for him. I should
have left the picture where it was. But I wanted to know. I had
to know. I held my breath as he straightened up in his chair
and lit his pipe which had gone out again. He coughed for a
bit and pointed at the photograph with his pipe stem.

"That's Walter, the baby, next to Lillian. My father was
always bailing him out of scrapes. When Pa bought the Highland Garage and set up the two of us to run it, Walter wouldn't
get out of bed until noon. He was a lazy son-of-a-bitch. Never
did a day's work in his life. He was too goddamned spoiled."

I looked at Boppa in surprise. Not because he swore—he was always swearing—but because he so clearly hated his brother Walter. Walter looked sweet to me—young, and very handsome.

Walter, you little shithead. You'd have been a lot better off if you'd kept your mouth shut and your fly buttoned. Always had to be wild, didn't you, Sam? Sam Houston, they called you, the way you rode Napoleon up and down the cliff's side, whooping along the boulevard like a goddamned cowboy. Maybe you would have been better off out west, like we talked about. I guess you figured that if Pa wouldn't give you a handshake, a hiding was the next best thing. You never took responsibility for anything in your life—it was always someone else's fault. You little conniver, you knew Lily would take your side, no matter what. You only came to me when Tom was away, and you didn't want Lily to know about the trouble you were in.

You came crashing into the barracks at the top of the house where all of us boys slept and paced back and forth, smoking and swearing—mad at the whole Christly world. You were raving about how abused you were, that Annie was a devil and you hated the crazy bitch. I let you rant and rave so you wouldn't haul off and hit somebody.

"Ma and Lily are the only ones who give a rat's ass about me, and you know it, Dickie, and even then it's only when they can spare time away from 'Eleanora Duse.'. Christ, the stuff Annie gets away with—'Ma, I'm going to kill myself if you come any closer—Ma there are snakes crawling in my hair—Ma, I don't need to eat, the gods are giving me ambrosia.' Jesus God, what a scam! The whole effing family is supposed to jump when she threatens to sneeze. And Pa thinks I'm the one that disgraced the family! Right. Like they don't hustle Annie upstairs when company comes so she won't make a scene.

"Dickie, I'm telling you, Mary Alice Frobisher was asking for it—she's had a crush on me since we were in fourth grade. Everybody knows the Frobisher girls are tramps—all six of 'em. Mary Alice was so hot for me, it was embarrassing. One night I got so sick of being pestered by her, I went down to the little shack on the beach where she lived, asked for her politely at the door like it was Buckingham Palace, and took the little slut

down to the dunes. Did she say, 'Walter, stop!' when I opened her blouse?
Did she say, 'Oh, Walter, we mustn't' when I took off her skirt? Did she
scream and faint when I took myself out of my pants? She opened her
dainty little drawers and sighed, 'Oh Walter, let's make a baby!' How did
I know she'd never been with a boy before?"

The child was sixteen, you little shit. You knew better, Walter, but you
always took what you wanted, didn't you? The whole world owed you a
living and anything else you fancied. A few months later, when old man
Frobisher came to the door, hollering that Pa had raised an animal, that
his daughter was ruined, Pa took him out back for some whiskey to calm
him down—I looked at you across the dining-room table and you were
laughing! The girl was sent to upstate New York to have the baby, and
you never turned a hair. Pa came into the parlor, his face like a beet, and
snarled, "Come out here, you fucking little bastard," and you went after
him, your fists in the air, ready to kill him. He beat you with his belt until
he could hardly stand up himself, and when we got to the stable, Lily and
Ma banging at the door, crying, pleading, you were passed out cold on
the floor. I thought your back was broken. I smashed in the window and
crawled in to get you, but I could see then that you were lost and would
never forgive any of us.

The only other time you ever came to me was when Ditch Metcalf went
off to France. Ditch fought with Pershing in Mexico, chasing Pancho
Villa just like Tom. You hated him for that. No, you didn't hate him—
you were jealous that you couldn't have been there beside him. He was—a
corporal, I think—in the Winthrop Machine Gun Company until they
joined the 101st Infantry, 26th Division under General Edwards during
the war. Ditch came home on leave for a week—one week—before he was
shipped off to France, and Pa wouldn't let you see him. Poor kid—Ditch
was your best friend, and you'd have been in the trenches with him in a
minute, only Ma and Lily convinced Pa that you were too young to sign
up. It was just after the Frobisher business and Pa was punishing you—
he locked you in the barracks and wouldn't let you out. I came upstairs
one night and you were bawling on your bed, pounding the headboard
with both fists. "A couple of lousy postcards from Paris, Dickie, a couple
of raunchy postcards on his way to Chateau-Thierry. That's all I have of
him. They still haven't been able to bring his body back." And you fell

into my arms like a little boy, sobbing, "Ditch, Ditch, I'm sorry. I should have been with you. I wouldn't have let them kill you. Aw, Ditch. Ditch. I never got to say goodbye."

I'd forgotten. Lily is holding your hand in this picture, holding it like she wanted to take all your pain away. Something I could never do. Sorry, little brother. I couldn't talk any sense into you. You were as hardheaded as Pa.

Boppa scratched the stubble on his chin and said, "On the end there, in the white jacket, is Ollie, who was born after me. Pa sent him to Yale Law School, though I could never understand how he got through it. He was smart enough, but he was a dreamer. He wrote poetry. And he was always cooking up schemes to make money. He lives on the corner with your Aunt Cleora."

Another alarm went off. Boppa didn't like Ollie, either. How strange, I thought, that the beautiful officer in the white coat could love poetry at the same time as he loved money. The two things seemed at odds.

We hated each other from the start. Maybe it was the chaos in the house, Annie getting so much of Ma's attention, and you being the new baby. You were Pa's favorite from the beginning, I don't know why. Maybe he saw something of himself in you. As soon as Tom joined the army, even though I was next in line to learn the business, Pa took you under his wing and set me up to run the Highland Garage. I was a grease monkey and you were going to be a prosperous businessman. Funny how we always did what Pa told us. So that's how it was for years, me taking orders from Ma, and you riding around with the old man, counting the money, buying property, evicting widows and orphans. You had the stomach for it—maybe I didn't. So it was Dickie, come help John White fix the roof. Dickie, Pat needs you out in the stable. Dickie, go up to 93 Cliff and fix the furnace. Dickie, they need a load of coal over at the Henderson's. Dickie, hurry home and tie down your crazy sister. I was the gopher, the dog's body, almost like hired help. And Ollie, you were a prince among men. Smart, I'll give you that. But cold. A slab of granite for a heart. You would have sold Pa down the river and Pa would have happily taken the oar from your hand.

"Emeline is sitting next to my father," Boppa said abruptly. "She went to college and taught phys ed. But all she ever had on her mind was horses, horses—she won a lot of trophies, so I guess she was pretty good. You've seen her over there in the yard with her dogs."

She must have looked like a queen in her riding habit, I thought. She was so beautiful in this picture. I couldn't imagine how that breathtaking girl had turned into the old woman across the street who looked so horrible. It was too sad to think about. Boppa hated her, too. But why? They were neighbors and yet they hadn't said a word to each other in years.

Pa could never get enough of you, could he, his "darlin' girl." When Lil and Ma and I were trying to keep Annie from flying all to pieces, you were sent to Europe, given your own little car, the latest clothes from Paris, and all the while Annie was dressed like an orphan and Lily looked like some-one's dowdy old-maid aunt. He rented a stable in Swampscott and bought you horses, dogs, the best equipment. He pumped you so full of yourself that your feet barely touched the ground. He bought you like a slave, but you didn't see it for a long time. When Lily got married, he moved you right into her place—taking care of the house and Ma and Annie. Must've been a shock to come down off one of your highsteppers into the crazy house. Still, I have to hand it to you—you took care of Pa as well as any trained nurse, and then Ma after he died. Ma left you everything— everything—so that you and Annie would be taken care of for the rest of your lives. So there you sit, you old crone, pouring over your accounts, richer than Croesus. And you wonder why none of us will speak to you? Pa cheated us, Ma cheated us. Was it worth it, "darlin' girl"? There isn't a soul who cares about you. And it's nobody's fault but your own.

"My father and mother are sitting in the middle, and Annie's on the far right," Boppa said, as if he were in a hurry to get this over. It was growing dark. He puffed on his pipe. I could almost hear him thinking, sorting out his words carefully.

"My father came from Ireland, you know. He owned a lot of property in Cambridge and Winthrop. He was the president of three banks. Pa was very athletic, but you'd never know it from this picture. He played handball, squash, tennis, cricket,

baseball, and he was a great rider. Ma had her hands full, rais-
ing all of us. It made her, well, it made her hard. She was good
to us, but let's just say, she had her favorites."

I guessed that Boppa wasn't one of them. Still, she didn't
look mean. Emma looked strong and regal in her black jet dress
and pearls. Jeremiah seemed old or worried. Boppa was staring
off at the white house again. I couldn't guess what he was
thinking.

Ma and Pa both died of heart problems, about ten years apart.

*Pa took a long time to die. It was hard on him, being so sick, after
running his little corner of the world like a king for so long. I don't think
he and I ever had a conversation in our lives. He gave orders and I took
them. I could have been anyone to him, not one of his sons—just a big,
strapping hired hand. He had a general, all-purpose speech that he used on
all of us.*

*"Money," he would say, "is what I worked so bloody hard for all these
years. Didn't want any of you sleepin' above a whore's flat in Charlestown
like I did. Made a shitload of money and lost it all in the same day, but I
never gave up. Listen, boyo, never let yourself be bullied or swindled or
sweet-talked into a deal. I admit I pulled a few fast ones over the years, but
that's business. You have to watch your back, or someone'll stab you. You
have to lay on the malarky, the dear old Irish brogue—so that while you're
shaking a man's hand, you can pick his pocket with the other. They hate
the Irish here, but I've learned that there's not much use in being honest or
fair—the Yanks and the guineas and the hebes won't be. So, be tough and
cagey, and never let them know what you're thinkin'. And remember, boyo,
you can only spend your money once." We thought money was his god,
but when he died, he was crying like a baby for Emma. Pa ran my life for
so many years, I hardly noticed when he was gone. I just went through
the paces like a dumb animal, a plow horse who knows the routine and
does it by rote.*

*When Ma was dying, she called me to her bedside. "Don't cry, Dickie,"
she said, holding my hand, and I felt five years old again. "I'm old and
tired. You'll get along without me just fine." And then she started to ramble,
bringing up things from long ago that I'd forgotten.*

"Howard," she murmured. "My last baby. I was forty-three when he

was born, did you know that? Sometimes I think I didn't want another child. He was always sickly. It was hot that day, too, just like the day the twins died. Nanny was in the kitchen making my tea. I was cross and fretful. You came in and stood beside me, do you remember, Dickie? 'Mother,' you said, very earnestly, 'you must sit down.' Six and a half years old and already so serious! I sat in the window seat, hoping there might be an east wind, and smiled down at you, thinking how sweet you looked in your first Prince Albert suit with the celluloid collar and cuffs.

" 'I thought you and the other children were outside playing hoops,' I said, fingering your long white curls. 'Were you and Ollie fighting again?' We never could keep the two of you apart. You took my hand and squeezed it very hard. 'No, Mother,' you said, your bottom lip quivering. 'Our little Howard is dead.' Do you remember finding his body, Dickie? It must have been a terrible shock. I suppose I didn't have time to think about how it might have hurt you—there was always a crisis, one right after another—cholera, whooping cough, croup, scarlet fever, measles, mumps, diphtheria, broken arms, broken ankles. And Annie, always Annie. How did I ever live through it?"

I held her old white hand and let the tears run down my face. And then, Ma seemed to be talking to someone else sitting across the room.

"Dickie was probably my most sensitive child—he would wake up at night when he heard Annie crying and come downstairs to get into the crib with her—he was just a little boy then.

" 'But, Mother, I had to,' " he would say the next morning, " 'She was having one of her nighthorses.' He would untie her hands and feet and take the gauze from around her head, and I would find them with their arms around each other, sleeping like two little angels. It was terribly sweet. Even then, he couldn't stand to think of her suffering or being alone."

Then Ma seemed to know where she was again, and looked at me with such sorrow that I could hardly stand it. I wanted to put my fist through the window. She cried, "Dickie, Dickie, were you so much in Tom's shadow that I didn't see you? So quiet that Walter's antics took our attention away? Annie was my life, she needed so much care—you of all people knew how much. You just seemed to go your own way alone. I'm sorry. My handsome son. I didn't love you enough. I haven't been your mother."

She turned her head away in silence and I sat there, stunned, tears running down my face, holding her white hand.

Boppa sat still for a long time. His pipe had gone out again, but he didn't seem to notice. A breeze had come up off the water, and I could smell the salt and seaweed of low tide.

"What about Annie?" I said. "You forgot to tell me about Annie."

"No," he said after a minute. "I didn't forget Annie." *Annie. Oh, my Annie.*

"What was she like, Boppa?" I prompted.

My grandfather put down his pipe in the ashtray and stretched his long legs until I heard his bones creak. He rubbed his shoulder for a while, then he blew his nose into a madras handkerchief, honking loudly, a sound like the haunting cry of the geese that flew south for the winter, sadly, sadly, calling goodbye. His hands hung down between his knees, sharp elbows poking through the torn sleeves of his shirt. I could see the white stubble on his cheeks and chin.

"Annie was—well, she wasn't right in the head."

I didn't know what to say. "She looks okay in the picture, except for her funny haircut."

"She had good days and bad days."

"What was wrong with her?"

"A lot of things, I guess. They didn't know much about medicine in those days, you know. Maybe if she'd been born today, she would have been cured."

She was such a gentle thing when she wasn't frightened or sick. She had such a sweet disposition sometimes, it's hard to believe she once punched me in the nose, broke my glasses, and gave me two black eyes. She got quite a bit better after she started taking the phenobarbital. Christ, it was grisly before that. It gave me the damn heebie-jeebies to see that wild look come into her eye and know that we were going to lose her again.

Ma wouldn't let them take her away, even when things got very bad. We have to keep her at home, she kept saying, even though it costs us all dearly. For a long while Annie was depressed and locked herself in her room. She was probably thirty then, but she looked like a girl of twelve. She'd come to the door to take her medicine or a supper tray, and go right back to bed. Then it got so she wouldn't get up at all—she just got sicker and sicker until finally Tom, Walter, and I had to break down the door. She started screaming bloody murder and ran to throw herself out the window—we had to grab her and tie her, kicking and screaming, into the armchair while we hoed out the room. You never saw such a Christly mess in your life—food smeared on the walls, clothes everywhere, little piles of turds all over the rug, and swarms of horseflies, and the mattress so pee-soaked, we had to roll it out onto the porch roof, dump it into the yard, and burn it. We had to throw out most of her clothes, all of her bedding, and the rug. She sat there, tied like a lunatic, and laughed and laughed as we scrubbed down the walls and windows and floor with ammonia and disinfectant. Ma, Lil, and Ollie brought in a spare mattress and pillows and made up the bed as the room aired out, while Tom, Walter, and I wrestled her into the bathroom. Lil filled the tub and knelt on the mat, and we hoisted her screaming into the water. Tom sang to her and poured water from a pitcher over and over her hands, which seemed to calm her a little. Pa took the lock out of her door and put on a bolt which could only be locked from the outside, and put nails in the windows so they could only be opened a few inches. Tom sang, Lilly soaped her, and when she would sit still for it, I cut all the mats out of her hair. Ollie stood in the doorway, gawking at her breasts bobbing in the water. He turned so white that I thought he was going to faint and I grabbed for him, but he was gone— puking in the wastebasket in his room. He had his first three-day migraine that afternoon.

Annie, Annie. I used to sneak down from the barracks when I heard you crying at night, kneel on your bed at the curve of your underarm and unwrap the gauze from your head, untie your hands and feet, and snuggle up to you to keep you from crying. We'd cuddle in the blankets, our faces pressed tight together, and your little-girl breath on my cheek smelled like pears. I told you stories until you fell asleep.

Do you remember the one you especially liked, about our island? I'd say, "Once upon a time there was an island" and you'd say, "An Ireland?" and I'd say, "No, an island like Winthrop, only prettier." I don't remember the rest of it—something about soft grass and beautiful birds that sang all day and all night and bright flowers that grew as big as dinner plates because it was warm all year, and you and I slept out under the stars, and you never had to be tied down because you weren't sick any more, there would never be anything to frighten you, and we could eat apples and berries off the trees and bushes. I wonder sometimes if you ever knew how much I loved you.

"What was wrong with Annie, Boppa?" I persisted.

"She was sick—in her mind. She saw things. She heard things. She had fits." He stood up like a marionette, as if all the long bones in his tall body were attached by strings. He wobbled toward the door to get a bicarbonate of soda.

"Was she crazy?" I asked in a whisper, watching him go.

"She was sick—in her mind." The screen door slammed behind him.

I sat back in my chair with a thump. Well, I hadn't learned much that I didn't know before, but at least I'd heard it from him. *Crazy Annie,* they had always said to me—Granny, Daddy, and Flap. *You're going to be just like your great-aunt Annie,* my father would say with such a knowing look that I'd get goose bumps. I didn't think that I was the lost princess from Atlantis or hear sea gulls speaking to me, and I didn't have fits, but somewhere down deep I thought he might be right. I'd been told that I was brilliant, stupid, beautiful, ugly, talented, useless, hard-working, lazy, perfect, and the most self-centered brat ever born. I was confused and scared and hated myself enough to want to die. I guess that makes a person crazy.

I heard Granny and Boppa hollering at each other in the kitchen, followed by the crash of a cup or saucer breaking. They were at it again. In the old days, they used to fight all the time when Boppa was drinking. Once, when I was five or six, huddled behind the door in the little room, I heard them calling each other terrible names. I was afraid to come out, but it went on and on until I couldn't stand it any longer, and I flew into the kitchen in my nightie. My grandparents stood a foot apart, wild-eyed and breathing hard. It was like rushing between two lions roaring on the Serengeti—I was sure I would be killed—but I ran between them and cried at the top of my lungs, "Stop it, stop it, you two, you know you love each other!"

I stood under them in the long silence that followed, and it seemed so funny that I almost laughed. They looked stuffed— like the animals displayed in the Museum of Natural History— frozen, mid-roar, fangs bared, Granny's claws unsheathed and Boppa's big white paw ready to swipe at her. But their eyes, which had been red coals in the wild, cooled down in captivity to dull, lifeless glass.

"You know you love each other," I repeated bravely, and walked back to my bed.

I looked down at the old photograph and into the proud, angry, hurt, scheming, unforgiving, tender faces of the Greens. Their family was just like ours. Then I thought: it is ours. How did love get so mixed up with hatred? How did kindness turn to bitterness? Why was envy, resentment, fury, unhappiness, blame, and the deeply felt belief that life had cheated them, that they deserved better, at the heart of everything they said? Their blood was in mine. Their sadness and defeat and de-fiance ran through my veins until they joined like rivers at my heart.

I looked over once more at the glassed-in foyer, the turret and piazza where wisteria-colored shadows were gathering. Pigeons nested companionably on the copper ridgepole. The Highlands were quiet, and lights were coming on in the houses. I stared at my grandfather's face in the photograph, at his brothers and sisters. I thought about Emma and Jeremiah, wondering how everything had gone so awry—and especially, I thought about Annie.

Granny came to the screen door and said it was time to come inside. I hated to go in for the night, but it was too dark to

look at the photograph. I put it on the tea tray and took it into
the house.

I wasn't sleeping in Granny's room on the cot anymore.
Since I'd gotten older, I slept on the couch in the front room
in the winter and the sunroom in the summer. I kept my books
and papers on the coffee table and read by the standing lamp,
all night if I felt like it, and nobody minded. They even let me
sleep late in the morning. Granny would close the swinging
door between the dining room and the pantry so the noise of
their breakfast wouldn't disturb me. When she knew I was
awake, she would bring me breakfast in bed. Sometimes I
wanted to stay at their house forever.

That night when I'd settled under the covers, wondering if I
could be bothered with yet another boring Erle Stanley Gardner mystery, Granny came in with my nightly cup of tea. She
sat in the black-and-gold-striped wing chair and put her feet
up on the hassock.

"Your grandfather's stomach is kicking up again—those goddamned Chesterfields will be the death of him."

But it wasn't cigarettes, I'd heard Mama say, his stomach was
suffering from years of hard drinking. He had a bicarbonate of
soda every night. The doctor had told him he had to stop
drinking or he would die.

I put the book down on the coffee table, turned on my
elbow, and rested my head on my hand. One question from
me, and Granny would be off and running.

"Granny, how did you and Boppa meet?"

Her face, in shadow, lit up like a half-moon. "Well," she said,
and I could almost see her gathering up the scattered details
like windfalls in a basket. "In those days, you see, my grandmother was running a boarding house—a big old yellow house
with a wraparound porch—at 988 Massachusetts Avenue in
Cambridge. Probably gone now. Burned down, maybe, I don't
know. Most of her boarders were students from Harvard and
Tufts. I was taking a typing course at Burdett's Business Col-

lege—before that, you know I was a Flora Dora girl, like bur-
lesque, and a whole gang of us had gone touring through the
White Mountains—Flo, Maxine, Shirley, and I—you've seen
that picture—all of us decked out in sequins and boas and
fishnet stockings. We sang and danced and showed our garters
and had an awful lot of fun.

"One night, I was standing backstage at this dingy little dive
in Jaffrey, New Hampshire, waiting ior my turn to go on—the
men were all made up in black face, doing a minstrel show—
you know, Jiggs and Mr. Bones playing a banjo and playing
dumb. Well, I looked across to the other wing to see if Maxine
was ready for our number, and there was Gram, crooking her
finger at me. I ran around behind the set and Gram took me
by the collar and tore the feathers off my costume right then
and there. 'Time to come home, Ellen,' she said, and dragged
me out the backstage exit all the way to the train. I didn't even
get to say goodbye to Maxine or collect my wages. Gram
didn't speak to me for nearly a week.

"Well, anyway, as I said, I was studying at Burdett Business
College and came home on the tram one day, and there, at the
table, was the usual bunch of boys, smoking and laughing. Out
of the corner of my eye, I saw a tall nice-looking fellow with a
Chesterfield hanging out of his mouth. He stood up to leave,
grabbed his book bag, and said that he had to be going, he
was late for class. I hadn't even noticed him, really. But about
a week later I was in the kitchen, scrubbing the stove in a
grubby hopsack dress and an apron, my hair yanked up on my
head in a top knot, when the bell rang. It was that boy, the
one with the Chesterfield—and there was I, looking for all the
world like Mrs. Mag Snatch. Somehow, I remembered his
name was Dickie, so I said hello, wishing he would hurry up
and go away. Instead, he came in and sat down in the parlor
as if he owned the place. I asked him if he wanted a cup of tea,
and he said, 'No, thank you, Miss Kimball, but would you
marry me?' It was the funniest thing I ever heard. He wasn't

smiling, though—can you believe it? He actually wanted to marry me! I told him he was out of his mind, to go away and leave me alone. He put on his cap and walked out the door. The next week he came back and asked me again. Then he kept coming, once a week, for ages, until I finally agreed to go out with him."

"What made you finally decide to marry him?" I asked, trying to picture the whole thing.

"Well, you know I was never in love with him. I was in love with Winslow, the son of Governor Gates from Vermont. The summer I was sixteen, we were on Lake Champlain on Pa's houseboat, and I met Winslow at Fort Ticonderoga. We spent the whole beautiful summer together. Sometimes he'd walk three miles over the fields in the moonlight and he'd whistle up to me, wanting to see me just one more time before he went to sleep. Then he came to ask Pa for my hand. He'd even brought me a box of chocolates—I still have the cover of the chocolate box, it's in my sewing basket, you know that etching of ladies in old-fashioned evening clothes sitting around a spinet? Anyway, Pa raised a big stink, cursing and hollering like a crazy man, finally chasing Winslow out of the yard with a rifle. I was so mad that I didn't speak to the old son-of-a-bitch for two weeks—I just bided my time, packed my bag, then slipped out the window over the shed and ran to meet Winslow. I hated to leave Madeline alone with Pa, but I had to be with Winslow. It took the old bastard three days to find us. When he did, he dragged me into the house and beat me black and blue with a broom handle—it's a wonder he didn't break my back. I swore that day, when I turned eighteen, I'd shoot him dead with his own rifle."

Granny had told me the story a hundred times and I always sighed at this part—the handsome young boy walking over the fields in the moonlight to meet the love of his life, in a world so wicked that they had to run away to be together. Granny still kept Winslow's picture in a gold-leaf frame on her dresser.

She didn't have a picture of my grandfather there, and they'd been married almost fifty years.

"Anyway," she said, "I never got over Winslow. I never saw him again."

"Do you know what happened to him?" I asked, attracted and repelled by such a terrible wound.

"He died a few years ago. Dick took me up to see his grave. They say he drank himself to death."

"Because he couldn't marry you?"

"I don't know, really. I met his wife and son. She knew all about me, she said. Winslow had always talked about me."

I was getting a stomach ache.

"Why did you marry Boppa, then, if you didn't love him?"

"I wasn't in love with him, but I guessed I loved him. He was strong and kind. He liked my big bosoms. Didn't he hate skinny women! He liked me because I had solid flesh on my bones. I knew he'd take good care of me. It was Prohibition then, but all the people we went with were drunk all the time or having wild parties at Ko and Doug's or Ralph Halford's or Anna Tabor's, racing their Model T's up and down the beach like damned fools. There was always plenty of whiskey to go around. Somebody always knew somebody who knew somebody. Then one night in a hurricane blizzard, a rumrunner went down in the storm. The next day, when the tide was still high, cases and cases of whiskey washed up on Back Beach. Men in waders, standing up to their waists in freezing cold water, tried to keep the bottles from breaking open on the rocks, handing the crates to each other like a bucket brigade— to men on the shore, on the seawall, on the street, and into the trunks of their cars.

"I never drank—I just didn't like the taste of it—but the rest of them were always soused. And drunk as he got, Dick never hit me, but he hit Richie once when he was about four years old. He had come home drunk, and Richie was beating time on a chair leg in the kitchen. Dick hauled off and belted that child across the room, then stood there in shock—and without a word, Dick went down to the cellar, put his wrist in the vice, and pounded the hell out of his hand with a hammer until he'd broken four of his fingers. He never touched that child again.

"I was so mad that I put Richie and Gram in the car and drove all the way to California. In those days, there weren't many paved roads, mind you. We were in the middle of Nebraska, and Gram was still asking me if we were near Schenectady yet. Godfrey mighty! I drove clear to the edge of the Grand Canyon, and Gram wouldn't even get out to look because she was in her bedroom slippers and didn't feel like putting on her shoes. We ended up staying in Long Beach for two years."

"Did you want a divorce?" I asked her, gulping my stone-cold tea.

"Divorce? No. I just wanted to see California. I always had itchy feet. I used to leave Richie with old Mrs. Green all the time and just take off."

So my father had also been left on the doorstep like old luggage and picked up when she felt like coming back. *Out gadding*, Granny called her urge to travel. She was always going on a trip by herself or with her friend Mildred, for days or weeks at a time—to Montreal, New York Georgia, even Tampa in the days when it was practically a swamp. She pinched her household pennies, bought herself a monkey-fur coat, and took off for Europe in 1938, and never noticed a thing about the coming war.

"Your grandfather was damned frugal with money. During the Depression, when he was still working at the garage, he'd have butcher's string in his shoes because he was too tight to buy shoelaces, and yet he'd carry five thousand dollars in cash in his dungarees because he didn't trust banks. He used to play poker at the yacht club and come home, drunk but happy, and dump all the money on the kitchen table—piles of ten- and twenty-dollar bills, heaps of fifty-cent pieces, quarters, and silver dollars. He'd put the change back in his pocket and give me all the paper money. I don't think he ever lost a hand at cards. He was so damned clever at cheating that he was never caught.

"About this time, there was a gang of rough young kids who would hang around the garage, and one in particular took his fancy—a scrawny, black-haired, black-eyed boy who lived up on Summit Avenue with his grandmother and mother, both alcoholics. The kid was pitiful, and grateful for the least little kindness. Dick would bring him home for lunch, because the poor thing looked half-starved, and I never did like to see anybody go hungry. I was hungry enough growing up myself—I couldn't stand the thought of him not eating. Pretty soon, this boy was coming for supper too, then a bath and a change of clothes. After a while he came to live with us. So that's how Flap got to be part of the family."

Phillip Lincoln Flynn—such a noble name to me, and yet the Greens had shortened it, diminished him somehow, by calling him Flap. He stayed with them until he joined the navy, became a sailor drinking from port to port during the Second World War, and when it was over, my grandfather sent him to the farm as a hired hand to help start my father's egg business—also my grandfather's idea. My father always did what he was told. My grandparents had saved Flap from a sordid life by an act of kindness, and then, over the years, for reasons I could not understand, they came to treat him like an indentured slave.

Granny yawned loudly, stood up, and stretched. I realized the room had grown colder, and I snuggled deeper under my blankets. She came over to kiss me goodnight but stopped short when she saw the photograph of the Greens, upright on my Erle Stanley Gardner.

"What are you doing with that old picture?" she snapped. "The goddamned Greens had more money than anybody in this town and they didn't give a rat's ass for anyone but them-

selves. Your grandfather was the only decent one in the bunch.
The old man had a good word for me now and again, but the
rest of them wouldn't have wasted their spit on me if I were on
fire. Thank God old Mr. Green died before the Crash and
didn't see how his children fought over the property and what
was left of the money.

"Emma, the old bitch, went to law school during the Depression—got a law degree when she was seventy years old, can
you imagine?"

I'd seen a picture of Emma Green in a cap and gown, proud,
smiling, her face wrinkled as an old piece of satin. She didn't
look like a bitch to me. I wished Granny would stop calling
her that.

"Do you know why she went to law school? So she could
sue people! She was always taking somebody to court. The old
man had given houses to all of his married children, signed
over the deeds and everything, so this house had belonged to
us for years by the time she got sick. When the old bitch died,
we found out that she'd left every single house to someone else
in the family. We all had to go to court to get back our own
houses!

"And Lillian! She had the nerve to snub me in my own neighborhood. I haven't spoken to her in fifty years. Tom was the
only one with any gumption. He was Judge Advocate General
at Pearl Harbor during the war. And yet he won't set foot in
any of his brother's houses. Even now, he and Dick or Ollie
will chew the fat on a street corner for hours, but he won't
come into my house or your Aunt Cleora's. He spends his vacations across the street at your Aunt Emeline's. They always go
riding together. And don't get me started on her, that old horse
face."

Granny paused to catch her breath. I kept looking at the
picture, at those beautiful young people, trying to find the fis-
sures, the tears, the cracks that had broken the family apart.
The young Emeline was soft and pretty, and I didn't want to

know about her life beyond that moment, but I had no choice.

"Emeline stayed at home and nursed her father until he died, then took care of her mother until she died—and inherited everything, supposedly because she'd been such a loving daughter and would be caring for Annie the rest of her life. So the old bitch left her everything—blocks and blocks of apartment buildings in Cambridge, the South End, and South Boston. Everybody was furious. She put on such airs, always talking about her trips to Europe and throwing elegant parties—to which we were never invited, not in all those years— for people who arrived in limousines and Rolls Royces. She gave me a royal pain in the ass—the hunt clubs, the horse shows, the dog shows, those damned Airedales and Yorkies yapping all night long in the stable that she'd converted into a kennel. She wouldn't give me the time of day. Now all the houses are falling down, she's too damn old and stubborn to take care of things, and she won't sell a single piece of property. She'd rather let it all go to ruin than allow anyone else to have it. Dog-eat-dog—that's how it's always been with the Greens."

It was true about the houses falling down. They all had broken windows, sagging front steps, roofs with shingles blowing off, pigeons nesting under the rafters—house after house, including the one Jeremiah and Emma had built so long ago where the family was raised. Emeline's life distressed me—it was so full, yet so lonesome.

I knew Granny hated them all, but I couldn't see why. I had seen Tom the General in the street talking to Ollie, I had seen him on the corner under the big maple tree talking to Boppa. I'd seen him sitting on the porch after supper with his sister Emeline. Boppa wouldn't speak to Emeline or Ollie or Lillian or Walter. Emeline only spoke to Ollie and the General. Walter wouldn't speak to anyone. And nobody spoke to Lillian except Tom.

Granny was still wound up about the subject. She said, "And

Ollie, that old bastard. I could put a stake through his heart
for all the grief he caused poor Cleora, but I wouldn't want to
stand close enough to him to do it. He had six children by that
delicate little girl, the hulking brute. I don't know this for a
fact, but I heard that he used to spend all of his time down at
the yacht club drinking, then come home and pound the hell
out of her, poor little thing. Funny, none of the rest of them
had any children."

"What happened to Walter?" I asked timidly.

"He lives on Grover's Avenue. His wife Dot and I are very
good friends, but whenever I go over to visit her, the old bum
grunts at me and leaves the room. He never did a day's work
in his life."

"And Annie? What happened to Annie?"

"She's been dead four or five years. She wouldn't go to the
dentist, so all of her teeth were rotted in her head. When anyone talked to her in the street, she'd cover her mouth with her
hand and turn her face away."

I wanted to cry. I hadn't known she was dead. I'd imagined
her hiding up in her room in Aunt Emeline's like I did at home,
afraid to come down to see strangers. The last time I had seen
her, I was very small and she was hanging laundry with Emeline, but I could never tell the two of them apart. They both
looked like men.

"She got cancer of the throat and wouldn't let a doctor come
near her," Granny said. "The tumor kept growing and growing,
until she finally couldn't even swallow. All that money, and no
one tried to save her—she finally died of malnutrition."

I squeezed back tears, put my head on the pillow, and pretended that I was too sleepy to hear any more. Granny kissed
me goodnight and took the picture into my grandfather's
room.

The room was so quiet in the dark. Headlights shone
through the venetian blinds and swept over the ceiling like
searchlights. I felt so awful. I thought of how sad my grandfa-

ther must feel for all the waste in his life, and suddenly wanted to hug him goodnight one more time, to comfort myself or him or both of us.

He was sitting at the kitchen table playing solitaire with the greasy black Bicycle cards that he refused to give up. A bottle of liquor and a glass stood before him. I threw my arms around him and started crying.

"Boppa, please don't drink. It's bad for you. You'll get sick if you drink."

He held me for a minute and quietly told me to go to bed.

I fell into a rocky, restless sleep.

I woke up later, and every light in the house was on. There were men at the door, firemen and police, and they were taking my grandfather out of the house in a wheeled bed. There was a mask on his face, and Granny was in her bathrobe, holding his hand very tightly, saying his name over and over. They went out onto the front porch and left the door wide open. I could see the flashing red light of the ambulance and blue police lights sweeping eerily over the faces of the men, my grandmother, and my grandfather.

I ran into his bedroom—to get his slippers or his bathrobe or something—and I stopped short in horror. There was dark blood, so dark that it was almost black, on the pillows, the thrown-back sheets, dark blood pooled in the middle of his bed, bright red blood on the white George Washington spread, sprayed on the pale brown plaid wallpaper by the door frame. My knees began to shake, and I trembled all over. The photograph was on the dresser where it belonged. I looked down because my feet were cold, and I was standing in it, my white toes dipped in the terrible blood, soaking the hem of my nightgown. I screamed and screamed. I had done it. I'd upset him by making him talk about his family, and he drank because he was in pain, and now he was going to die. It was my fault, my fault, my fault.

Boppa did not die that night, but half his stomach was

removed. He ate nothing except Cream of Wheat and weak tea for the next six months. His pale blue eyes bleached out a little more each day, and I imagined that soon I would look at him to find the irises had disappeared altogether.

On the last day of sixth grade, I stood on the playground, sobbing hysterically, refusing to get in the car with Mama, my arms full of sweaters, notebooks, a book bag, report cards, drawings, one rubber boot, a mangled solar system made of hangers and painted Styrofoam balls, and all the other debris of my life at Spaulding Memorial School.

"Don't you understand, Mama?" I wept in despair. "This is my last day here, ever! Don't you understand? I will never be back here again!"

My mother clucked her tongue in dismay, as though she were wondering once more how on earth she had borne this alien child, hissing that I was making a huge fuss over nothing, and hustling me into the Chevy before I could embarrass her any further. I curled up in the front seat and cried into the locker-smell of my old blue book bag, resting my head between my turquoise Venus and my blood-red Mars. She didn't know what I meant. I would never be a student there again. The word never was terrifying. I wept inconsolably, watching the school with the bat on the weather vane disappear out the back window as we drove up Dudley Road. I had taken it for granted and now it was gone—the strange bat on the weather vane. The Spaulding brothers had given Townsend a free school, but the tight-fisted town fathers had crabbed so incessantly about how much it would cost to maintain that the Spaulding brothers, in a fit of pique at the last minute, substituted a bat—the symbol for Night, whose attributes were sleep and death—for the owl—symbol of Athena, goddess of wisdom, whose attributes were books and light. Even under the guidance of a bat, I had learned. I couldn't stand for my time at Spaulding School to be over.

I'd been hysterical on my tenth birthday, in just the same way. It had suddenly dawned on me, the morning I turned ten, that for as long as I lived I would always have two digits in my age—I would never live to be 100, and I would never be 9 again. Never, never, never. I wanted time to stop altogether, or to at least slow down, but that wasn't going to happen. How could there be such a monstrous thing in life as "never"? How did people get through an ordinary day with "never" hanging over their heads like the Sword of Damocles?

I was impossible at home after school was let out. For days I stormed and wept and threw temper tantrums over trivial things, picked fights with my brother and sister, talked back dangerously at the dinner table, knowing even as I made my snotty remarks that the rotten words boiling out of my mouth were not what I'd intended to say at all.

I didn't want my life to change. I wanted everything to be the same forever. In the fall I would be going to a new school in another town—a nun's school—and I'd have to wear a uniform and be a different person, almost grown up, a seventh grader. I hated meeting people. I hated new places. I was scared to death. I couldn't run away from home because there was nowhere to go except Granny's. In despair I packed my suitcase. Granny had argued and wheedled and wrung her hands until my parents agreed that I could spend the entire summer in Winthrop. I don't think that it took much convincing—I was in such a nasty mood that I wanted to be away from them as much as they must have wanted me gone. Between the shorts, sandals, and clean underwear, there were volumes of Dickens, Jane Austen, and Flaubert; the old Royal typewriter just fit behind the Buick's wheel well. I planned to finish my novel about Becky and Danny Hanks and life in Freedom, New Hampshire, in 1837. In Winthrop I could pretend that the future would never have to happen.

I lay on my cot in the sunroom and read, napped, and listened to the radio. I didn't go out, not even down to the beach

which had always been my greatest pleasure—I couldn't bear
to be seen in a bathing suit. But I was happy in the sunroom.
It was quiet and breezy, and I could daydream without too
many interruptions. I felt safe. I even half-convinced myself
that time wasn't passing at all. Still, the air tingled with something strange that summer. It was a little eerie. I watched from
the window—teenagers, a little older than me, were brightly
clothed in crazy psychedelic colors and tent dresses with daisies painted on their faces. Boys were letting their hair grow
past their shoulders, their dungarees were ragged and patched,
their music loud and angry. My friend Joycie Nolan had heard
about pills that could make you think you'd turned into a butterfly or a tulip, and another drug that made you believe you
could fly. I thought it was a crock, but it scared me to think
that it might be true. The old men on television seemed tired.
LBJ was beginning to look like a whipped old hound dog.
There were protests in Washington against the war, and every
night Walter Cronkite intoned the numbers of the dead soldiers like the Pope declaiming an encyclical of saints. I would
put my head down on the wooden arm of the chair in the little
room and weep because the world was too frightening a place.

I cried that summer over everything—the terrifying, explo-
sive combat footage, body bags being lifted into the wombs of
air force jets, civil rights marchers streaming toward the Capi-
tol by the thousands in the heat, their joyful faces running with
sweat as they sang "We Shall Overcome." I cried to see my
grandfather spooning Maypo into his sunken mouth, his teeth
floating in a glass like a specimen in a sixth-grade chemistry
lab. I cried over a neglected boxer named Ingie from next door
that lumbered up the back stairs out of pure love when Granny
tapped on the kitchen window with a spoon, even though the
dog's hips were so knotted with arthritis that she could barely
climb the steps. I cried when hair grew under my arms, and
when the late afternoon sunlight on the window sill caught the
iced tea in my glass and made it shine like gold—because I

knew that I would never be this young again, that whatever followed would be awful and dangerous and out of my hands. I had insisted on cutting my hair like Twiggy and Mia Farrow, but it was a gruesome mistake—without the vinyl go-go-boots, the mod Carnaby Street clothes, white lipstick, and false eyelashes, I looked like a stocky, short-legged paper boy with bad skin. I was mortified. Soon I was wearing long-sleeved shirts all the time, so no one could see where I'd been cutting my arms.

I'd been cutting myself for a long time. I don't remember how it began or how old I was when I began doing it in earnest. But when things were wild at the farm, or wild in me, I would slip into the bathroom (the only room in the house with a lock on the door), reach into the medicine chest behind Flap's cracked shaving mug and fossilized shaving brush for his razor, unscrew the handle, and take out a rusty blade. I couldn't help myself. I had to do it. The silvery blade shook in my hand as I slashed a bloody line across my inside forearm, but I didn't feel a thing. There was only a white seam filled with scarlet thread, and an enormous sense of relief.

When volleys of curses and fury flew around my head at the supper table—my father in an ecstasy of rage at some minuscule infraction—and I could sit still for it no longer, without a word I would take my plate to the sink and lock myself in the bathroom. The hollering bombarded the door like cannon fire, ricocheting there by accident. I was not the target—there was no target—but I was wounded just the same: they didn't understand me, they didn't love me, they didn't see me, and I was disappearing into thin air. The razor made a clean red line. *I bleed, therefore I am.*

When my sister and I fought, and words weren't hateful enough for the terrible hurt, and there was only an inarticulate hurricane blowing inside me, the razor spoke eloquently: *Here and here and here, look, the poison is out, you're free, it's over.* Sitting on the edge of the tub with battle lines drawn on my arms, I could put my head down and breathe again.

When I thought of the boys dying overseas, of my friend Carol Morrison whose leg was amputated from leukemia when she was eleven years old, of a man we knew from Maple Street who had shot himself in his garage, of a woman who came to Mass every Sunday in her Easter coat and flowered hat with a tiny veil and a bandage over her face because she had no nose, I raced into the bathroom for the razor. There didn't seem to be any difference between what was terrible in the world and what was terrible in me. I had no skin, there was no buffer, I was a spongy mass of tissue that soaked up pain, terror, suffering, despair, and defeat from everything around me. The razor made a safe, straight mark, and suddenly, because I had cut myself, there was a membrane between me and the world, and it was bleeding.

When confusion seized me in its feverish chill, and my teeth chattered violently with wanting to grow up, not knowing how I could possibly do it; when I felt ugly and stupid and wished I had never been born; when my limbs trembled in desperation because I wanted to be a child forever and I knew my body would betray me—when a mist of fear and doubt and dread came over my face with an overwhelming wish to kill myself so that I wouldn't have to face the changes, the razor cut my arm just deeply enough so that some of the pain could pour out and keep me from having to die.

The scars crisscrossed, were opened, grew infected, and healed, and I thought of the way that prisoners chalked the walls of their cells so they wouldn't lose track of time, so they wouldn't go mad. I could look at my arms as if they were a desperate, private calendar and say, *I have been here this many days, I was here then and then and then, I remember, I remember, I remember.* No one ever saw my arms. It was my secret. It was how I saved myself.

And so that summer in Winthrop, with the best of intentions, I lined up all the old volumes of flea-market Dickens, Jane Austen, and Flaubert on the marble-topped table in the sunroom where I slept, hoping to be swept away from myself

on beautiful tides of language. I opened the embossed leather
bindings, entranced by the marbled endpapers, but the double
columns of minuscule black print were daunting, and when I
discovered the creamy pages hadn't even been cut, I put aside
the books in defeat. When I tried to work on my novel, I discovered that the characters I had loved so fiercely in school
had left me—they seemed to have walked off into the hills of
New Hampshire without looking back. The typewriter collected dust. I couldn't face it. But in one of the wicker chairs,
under beach towels and pajamas and a straw tote bag with a
winking red lobster on it, were the gothic romances I'd bor-
rowed from the library. All that terrible summer, I read trash
and dreamed of swooning in the arms of some mysterious
stranger who would take me away from everything that
oppressed me, and in a transport of passion, I would become
his beloved child-bride. I would be cherished at last. Trashy
gothic novels did not have the word "never" in them. They had
the word "always."

Swooning in the arms of a stranger. Yes, that was what I
most desired—a surrender to love, a dissolution of the self into
the beloved, to be held safely in the arms of another until all
the trembling passed. I'd been wishing for it since I was four
years old.

My mother's family came from Fall River, Massachusetts,
near the border of Rhode Island, and my father raised holy hell
every time Mama wanted to see her mother or sister, Aunt
Peggy. There was no logic to his fury. We saw his parents
every weekend, and I spent holidays, all my school vacations,
and most of the summers with them, but for some reason he
didn't want us to see my mother's family. Mama and Daddy
argued hotly about it, but he always came to the same deci-
sion—once a year we could visit Nana Higgins in Fall River,
and Daddy would never come with us.

Nana Higgins was a devout Catholic, a widow who lived in
an attic apartment on New Boston Road, not far from her

spinster sister, Great-Aunt Genevieve. Nana had pure white, glossy hair, spectacles, rosy cheeks, plump, soft bosoms, and welcoming, freckled arms. She loved my brother and sister and me passionately and equally; there were no favorites in her house. We were cherished for ourselves, for what we thought and felt. We went to church a lot and behaved ourselves quite happily. She had a trunk full of crayons, paper, coloring books, puzzles, games, and we were allowed to have chocolate milk and even sugar on our cereal. Nana was the perfect grandmother.

One afternoon when I was four, my mother had taken my brother and sister to visit relatives in Tiverton, and Nana and I were alone under the sloping ceilings with the fat brocaded roses sewn onto the wallpaper, the banging radiators, and the steamy upholstered air. She was washing dishes in the tiny kitchen in a flowered house dress and apron. I was sitting in front of the ten-inch Zenith, feeling quite grown up in my pinafore, squirming on an embroidered hassock, piecing together a puzzle on a tray table.

The television rasped in the background, I heard Nana clinking silverware in the dish drainer, and I had in my hand the blood-colored petal of a poppy that needed to fit into my puzzle. Suddenly everything seemed to shimmer; all the sounds of the house faded and bloomed into unbearable noise. My eyes fixed on the flickering screen, and I felt my heart stop. There, in the pelting rain, wearing a long white coat, stood a woman whose head was bowed, her shoulders bent under the weight of a terrible burden. She put her hand, palm out, over her eyes and swayed. A dark-haired man came closer as she staggered under the heaviness of her suffering. The sad woman swayed again and fell to the ground with the rain coming down all around her. The dark-haired man bent on one knee, held her in his arms, and raised her up, with one hand touching her face ever so gently, her head resting on his shoulder, her eyes closed.

"Nana, Nana," I cried, leaping up from the hassock, spilling the wooden poppies to the floor. "What happened to her?"

Nana peered in from the galley kitchen at the television and said, "She fainted," and went back to work.

"What's that?" I whispered, my heart sinking down to my knees.

"It's like being dead—except you wake up," came a disembodied voice from the kitchen.

All at once I saw the brocaded roses open on the wall and turn toward me. The room spun like a carousel. The geraniums on the window seat seemed blown by some tremendous velocity. Iris embroidered on the hassock appeared to bloom and wither as I watched. Poppy petals spilled on the carpet like blood shaken from a mortal wound. A person could wake up from the dead. The man was touching the woman's face the way one would touch a flower, and then the man and woman kissed, cheating death, and when the man and woman kissed again, she awoke. She had come back to life because he had kissed her, and death like a terrible rain could not harm them. A woman in her coat of grief had fainted into death, and a man had held her lovingly in his arms, and she was alive again. They stood together in the rain and kissed, and death could not harm them.

I didn't know that thunderbolts could strike inside the body. There was a roaring in my ears and the daisies of Nana's dress were waving in a field where a great wind was passing over. She was holding a glass of water to my lips. It was cold. I didn't want to drink it. I was lying quietly in her bedroom on the crocheted leaves of the bedspread, my fingers curled into the shape of a stitched tulip with petals the color of blood. The shades were drawn as though someone had died.

What could I possibly have understood then at four, trembling from head to foot, about the mysteries of love and death? But I could never unsee what I had seen. I knew it was a film, and later, that the figures were not Sorrow and Love, but Jean Arthur and Gary Cooper, and yet I felt myself sliding away from the world. I felt myself fainting.

The wish to faint, to die and be loved back to life, became my most private secret, an idea I could not speak about for years, but one I thought of constantly, embroidering it carefully until the picture was as beautiful and complex as a tapestry. Though I could not have said then what I saw, I later believed that sorrow and love had come to reside in a visible action of the body, the violent death and gentle resurrection of the soul before the magnitude of everything sacred; all the mystery of life condensed into the verb "faint." The word and the thing were the same to me after that, all of my life. It made me delirious to come across the word in print. It leaped off the page and struck my heart like a bell, turning my knees to water, and the world would start to tilt from my hands. I'd drop the ballast of the book and reach for something larger, something stationary to hold me up. To faint was to die, to fall out of this world into the dark radiance of the next. To faint was to feel the greatness of death. To faint was to know the tenderness of human love, its power to revive the white butterfly of the soul that clung to love's forefinger as it gently patted my cheek to wake me up. To faint was to feel the awful annihilation of the spirit and the hand of God on my hair like a whisper, "No, child, not yet, go back," and to slip down into my body once more like a ghost returning to its house.

Faint became too sacred to speak, too holy to whisper; it became a seduction of the spirit I couldn't resist in my dreams and couldn't spoil by saying aloud. During Glee Club, a fat sixth-grade boy turned white, collapsed at the knee, and fell with a great crash from his tier on the risers. I was shocked. Sweat stood out in beads on my forehead and ran down the trellis of my spine. I saw another child, like a winged messenger, fly through the auditorium to fetch the principal. I saw our music teacher, Mr. Viggiano, take off his coat with infinite patience, fold it inside-out, in half, and then place it under the heavy head of the pale-faced boy who seemed to be sleeping. Kneeling at his side, our teacher wiped the boy's face with his handkerchief, and then his own.

I knew the boy would wake up, that his eyes would flutter and search the faces of adults for an explanation. But I was furious. I wanted to say, *Why was it wasted on you? I know what fainting means. It should have happened to me!* I saw the white wing of the Holy Ghost fly through the golden shaft of dust motes pouring from the high gymnasium windows, and I wanted to rush to the boy's side and ask urgently, *What was it like to die? Tell me about love.*

Somehow the word "faint" came into my lexicon as inseparable from other signs of maturity—the newly budded breasts, the rose petals of blood on the sheets. I thought that one day when my body had stopped its anxious growing, my heart would become a woman's heart, and I would be the figure of Sorrow who, overcome by the darkness of death, would wake to feel the hand of Love on her cheek. But the breasts came and the blood, and it was not as I'd imagined.

Trashy novels trivialized what was holy to me—the silly heroines seemed to faint at the most inconsequential moments—but the arc of the stories was still compelling, even if the details were inane. So I read romantic fiction with a kind of desperation, watching each heroine fly across the fields of innocence, running from as well as toward the darkness of her womanhood. I kept searching for clues to help me write my own life. While the heroine ran, breathless with excitement and fear, into the arms of danger, her lover, I waited for the privilege of entering a world where suffering was followed by unconditional love.

Young women in these books seemed not so much inexperienced as stupid; not innocent, but naive. Their heaving bosoms, their stays, their too-pale cheeks made them not creatures of passion but statues of passivity. Frightened like deer into a corner of the grotto, they saw, not the Virgin fainting into the arms of John, but themselves, unable to bear their own sexuality. Rescue by their Byronic heroes was nothing more than being saved from their own insipid hearts. And I hated them because they were timid and afraid—and to my utter disgust, I was just like them.

I read these books over and over, interchangeable in plot and detail, down to the sprigged muslin of the heroines' too-tight gowns. I even tried to write a spoof of one, they were so formulaic. My heroine's name was Dimity Witte, an orphan, who came as a governess at the request of Roderick Grange, the dour and darkly tormented master of Grange Grange. There were a few strange and probably deranged minor characters—Flummox, the cook, and the butler, Diddit, and the resident handsome wastrel, Cousin James Ne'er-do-well. Howling at my own cleverness, I wrote a few chapters, with a lot of macabre midnight comings-and-goings, mysterious candles burning, screams from the scullery, near-fatal accidents, and long languorous kisses in the conservatory, but boredom set in very quickly, so I went back to reading romances rather than trying to write one, even though I knew how everything would turn out in the end.

And yet I knew this was precisely why I was reading cheap romances, why I couldn't turn to Austen or Flaubert. Gothic novels were the watered-down, palatable version of a greatness I could not bear to witness. Romances were artifice, the shadow of art, and all I could look at then. I could not have survived the ancient, time-heavy language of Homer. I could not have stood up under Virgil's marble-brightness. Whispering Greek in the horse's womb, I would have fallen with the soldiers in Troy.

With every paperback I read, I waded toward the misty, vapid world of Romance and away from the profound, deep world of Love, a glory that I knew would blind me. I was trying to grow not only into a woman, but into a woman who writes. In place of a ruffled half-laced bodice, I wanted to draw a coat of grief. I was struggling out of girlhood so I could stop whispering the frightened word "lover" into the grotto. Deep sorrow could make the soul die, and the greatest of all words—love—could awaken it. To say the holy word "faint," clearly and aloud, would mean that I had grown into my full voice at last. But I could not do it yet. I did not know enough. I wanted to faint, not like a cardboard, storybook girl, but like a woman who saw and understood and could not bear life's sorrow. I wanted to believe that Love would carry me back to the world, truly awake and truly alive.

✻

There were photographs of my father in every room of Granny's house, but the longer I looked at them over the years, the less I felt I knew my own father. The sad child I saw in Winthrop bore no resemblance to the roaring, unpredictable force that threatened our lives at the farm. Above the delicate Wurlitzer in the front room, the one-year-old boy in a white lace gown and golden hair cut in the shape of a bowl sat on a rug with his hand in the open fangs of a lifelike, child-sized grizzly bear. In the foyer, under a mirror, the two-year-old boy sat humiliated and naked on a chamber pot, his chin resting in his hands, elbows on his bony knees, clenched together for modesty, a summer straw hat cocked over one eye. He was squinting into the sun, expressionless. On the mahogany table under the globed lamp in the bay window, the four-year-old Richie stared out of a gold-leaf frame, the saddest face I ever saw, his hair parted in the middle, wearing a bow tie and a coat with a fox-fur collar, his luminous dark eyes brimming with an understanding about life that no child should ever know. In the hallway, his sweet girlish features above an argyle sweater at sixteen took my breath away. He was so handsome. On the radiator behind the sofa, he sat in his officer's uniform with dark pomaded hair, a somber profile, soft plumes of smoke curling from his cigarette. Granny thought he looked like a movie star. It was the kind of photo where you'd expect to find an elegantly scrawled signature in the bottom right-hand corner, *To my dearest* ———, *All My Love*. As we watched "Perry Mason" and "Bonanza" my father stared down at us quizzically in his officer's cap and stripes and bars. His death mask was in Granny's bedroom.

"All the girls wanted to marry Richie," Granny often said. "And I took him out to Hollywood to see if I could get him into the movies." Sometimes it was hard to know what to believe.

And then there were the photographs of me: at one, in curls; at two, in a pinafore and a pool of crinoline in a round gold-leaf frame as big as a platter hanging over the sofa; at four and five and six, my growing face was scattered through the front room with photos of my father like holy pictures in a shrine. There was not a single photograph of my mother or of my parents together, as if my mother did not exist, as though I had not needed a mother. As an extension of Granny, I needed only to have been part of my father to be part of her.

Nana Higgins had given me a single picture of my mother that Mama didn't know I had, and had told me about the day it was taken. My mother was standing on the steps at the Academy of the Sacred Heart in a white dress with a lot of other girls on their way to sing at the Rose Hawthorne Lathrop Cancer Home. It was a hospice founded by Nathaniel Hawthorne's daughter, and the girls stood in a circle like lilies in the dayroom. The nurses and nuns crowded the patients in wheelchairs and beds as close to the girls as they could—mortality of the body and immortality of the soul being a lesson no one could learn too much about. The girls sang "Dies Irae" and "Lo, How a Rose Ere Blooming" to women without faces, some without breasts, legs, arms; patients who oozed disease, whose bandages reeked of death and infection. The young girls in their white dresses opened their mouths and breathed their sweet, uncorrupted breath into the air over the mouths of the incurable women who sucked each clear note into their own decaying bodies. The girls grew paler and paler as the afternoon wore on. One of the crones with pus running from what once were her eyes took my mother's arm in her fleshless claw, and while trying to talk, she had coughed green sputum onto my mother's dress. Nana said Mama had never been able to wear the dress again and couldn't get the smell of cancer out of her nose for weeks.

The summer I was twelve, I lay out on the cot in Granny's sunroom and thought a lot about my mother and father. Had they loved each other, passionately, like in my romances? Had they laughed and snuggled in the front seat of the '41 Cadillac, driving through Pinkham Notch in the White Mountains on their honeymoon? Now they could barely stand to be in the same room. I don't remember ever seeing them touch each another, even by accident. Why were there no pictures of my mother in a long white gown and veil, smiling radiantly above her gossamer and orange blossoms? It seemed like a terrible secret that no one would talk about. Sometimes I thought that my parents had to get married because my mother was carrying me, and that if I hadn't been conceived, our unhappy family would not have been brought together at all.

I sighed and turned over on my stomach, scrunching the dusty feather pillow with the crocheted laced edges under my head, watching the soft summer rain trickle down the glass and catch in little pockets on the screen. It always surprised me to smell the rain in Winthrop. I never got used to the heaviness of the air, how dense it was with salt. It was not the clear, cleansing, new-green summer rain of the farm that fell purposefully and quietly, simply to replenish the earth. In Winthrop it was an older rain, a sadder rain, as if the sky were so saturated with sorrow that it could not help but overbrim itself. Then the fog would wander in like a spectral creature half-bewildered by grief, and thread its way blindly through the houses and trees as though in search of something, its soft fingers feeling at window latches and anchor-shaped door knockers, slipping through wicker porch furniture and the drenched red heads of geraniums, hanging heavy with rain, fog with tears on its face trying to find the place where it belonged.

No, you jerk, I scolded myself furiously, *it's just a coastal storm, ordinary fog, a run-of-the-mill rain*. Instead of water tapping gently on the glass, I was hearing the hammering voices of my family, beating on my brain like a drum: *You're being melodramatic again. Living in fairyland. In dreamland. Your head's in the clouds. You're being ridiculous. Being stupid. Acting weird. Acting crazy. In a world of your own.*

In a world of my own. I felt like Archimedes in his bath. That was it! My family couldn't stand that I could take glorious flight from the life which we all seemed to be leading together and dream myself out of the room—they couldn't, or wouldn't, or were afraid. They wanted me to be mired in their concrete world of hoarded money, old junk cars, broken pipes, peeling paint, stopped-up septic tanks, and an attic, cellar, and shed chamber strewn with debris. They wanted my allegiance to their "real world." They didn't want to know that *The Great Gatsby*, *Guernica*, Tchaikovsky's 1812 *Overture* and Michelangelo's *David* existed for them as much as for me. They wouldn't have understood, nor could I have explained that language was the only thing that truly mattered to me. Language was a sun-struck, white-water river, full of aquamarine lagoons and dizzying whirlpools. The mountains of my imagination were brooding and immense, glinting with the quicksilver of moonlight and starlight; my dreams were the rich grasslands of the Serengeti running with metaphors, beautiful and swift as cheetahs or graceful as the delicate gazelles; images filled the landscape like a pride of lions sunning themselves in a fly-heavy noon, a rustling Kikuyu settlement at dusk when the first nightfires were lit, or snow falling gently, densely into an emerald lake high in the magenta hills.

I had a sudden picture of my family squatting in the doorway of a primitive cave, dressed in ragged skins, huddling near the embers where they'd half-cooked their meat, a tribe of primates fearfully scanning the horizon for roving bands of predators. Piled up, higher than a man, on either side of the cave were saber-toothed-tiger bones, the gargantuan femurs of mastodons, the skulls of orynxes—a treasure trove of dead bones that they would defend with their lives. And deep in the womb of the cave, the flame of an animal-fat torch cast shadows on a half-naked child—myself, trembling with the cold and the blaze of discovery, dipping her hand in red pigment and painting a bison on the wall.

"Come on, pieface," Granny called through the window that opened onto the sunporch from her bedroom. "I'm packing my suitcase. Come in and talk to me while I get ready."

I sighed. It was still raining. Granny was still interrupting.

I padded through the kitchen and sat on the edge of her bed. Granny never went away when she had me in her clutches, but she had decided to go by herself to the White Mountains to spend a few days with her old friends Jack and Lena Childs. Lena was a stout, bespectacled hairdresser who worked in a little resort town near the Presidential Range and boasted that Bette Davis was one of her clients. Her husband, Jack—"my onion-eyed bastard" she always called him—was a judge. Granny made a fuss about me going with her, but I couldn't think of anything I'd rather do less.

"I want to stay home and read, Granny," I said sourly.

"You can read in New Hampshire just as well as you can read here," she replied, tucking jars of cold cream into the pockets of her suitcase. I made a face and flopped back on the pillows of the sleigh bed. *No, I can't,* I snarled to myself, *because YOU'LL be there.* And I'd be subjected to stupefying boredom, plus a week of being trotted out in public like a trained monkey. Fortunately, my grandfather stepped in to rescue me.

"For Chrissake, Ma, leave the little kid alone. If she wants to stay home, let her stay home. I'll be here to look after her."

And for once, Boppa had the last word.

Then I asked meekly, "Granny, can Joycie Nolan sleep over tonight?"

I had known Joyce since we were in baby carriages together, sitting on the beach in our ruffled suits and bonnets and plastic cat's-eye sunglasses with our red shovels and pails. Her parents, Rommie and John Nolan, had been best friends with mine, and were my brother's godparents. Joyce and I had been planning that we would have supper at her house, and afterward she would sleep over at mine.

"I suppose it's all right," Granny said distractedly. Ordinarily I was never allowed to play with other kids, much less have them sleep over, because Granny couldn't stand to share me with anyone. Even her own friends knew enough not to call or visit when I was staying there because Granny would be rude and make it clear that she wanted them to go home so she could have me all to herself. But this time was different—she was going out of town.

"Go tell Rommie I said Joyce can come," Granny said with a jealous sniff.

I whooped silently as I raced down the rose-and-black runner and slammed out the front door. I stood on the porch, breathing deeply, relishing the delicious, all-too-infrequent freedom and the lovely salt rain on my cramped body.

The sea was battleship gray and rough as I ran past the turrets and high windows of the Cliff House, past the beach roses rioting over the old wooden fence at the crest of the undercliff, and down the long wooden steps to the beach. Rommie and John's house looked out over the lighthouses of Boston Harbor and the long curved boulevard shaped like a shield. Beyond their house in the waist-high grass behind a rusting, padlocked cyclone fence were the remains of an old army fort. Perched on a corroding iron structure like the Eiffel Tower cut in half was a radar station shaped like an enormous golf ball, including the dimpled surface. No one was sure what kind of rays were emitted there. A lot of people in the neighborhood got cancer and died.

When I rang the bell at Rommie's, I heard the vacuum running upstairs, so I went around the deep side porch to let myself in through the back door which was never locked. I had to smile—you could never go into Rommie's house without hearing the vacuum cleaner sucking up invisible specks of dust, germs, viruses, the microscopic filaments of nothingness that might cause plagues and epidemics and God-knows-what kinds of disease. Rommie Nolan was the best person we knew—truly kind, generous, pious, and good to a fault—but her fetish for cleanliness made us laugh because it was proof that she was a human being after all and not a saint.

Nobody else seemed to be home. I went into the shining kitchen and helped myself to a glass of lemonade. This was the one place in the world where I could help myself to whatever I wanted, without fear, without hollering. The miracle was that I could choose, I could decide for myself, without recriminations on my judgment, my gluttony, or my self. Something as simple as pouring a glass of lemonade made me feel like a real person. I loved coming here where every grown-up called me "darling." It was like going to Heaven for the weekend.

There had been so many happy times at this house for my brother and sister and me—Labor Day barbecues, Memorial Day picnics out in the backyard, Fourth of July fireworks over lobster tails and corn on the cob, summer evening cocktail parties where the children were permitted to stay up and drink Shirley Temples with maraschino cherries. Sometimes John would take us all out in his brother's boat, the beautiful *Lord Fox*. The grown-ups would drink and get silly, and we would bounce delightedly in our life jackets, growing pinker by the hour, as the boat sped between the islands of Boston Harbor across the rough wakes of other boats. And before we were born, Mama, Daddy, Rommie, and John had gathered here with their friends to feast, play cards, and drink, the record player blaring Benny Goodman, Paul Whiteman, and Cab Calloway. Everybody smoked cigarettes and drank John Nolan's famous cocktails. Someone, often my father, would stumble over to the piano and bang out some ragtime or some tune they loved like "Chattanooga Choo-Choo," "A Nightingale Sang in Berkeley Square," and "White Christmas." They'd roll back the rug in the front parlor and dance, so young and beautiful in their long, tightly-cinched evening skirts, tuxedo coats, and uniforms, while glasses of champagne were smeared with Mata Hari red lipstick and the boys scandalized Rommie by standing on the stairs and peeing into the lilacs.

I sat on the red leather sofa in the family room that faced the sea on two sides. Joyce must still be at dancing school, I thought. The vacuum roared in the upstairs hall. I was dying to sneak a couple of cigarettes out of the jade box on the coffee table—Rommie and John both smoked like fiends—but I knew I'd get caught and be lectured severely. Between two platter-sized amber ashtrays was a black leather Guest Book that I didn't remember having seen before, so I picked it up and started from the back, finding the names of my parents' friends, including those who had died, dates of parties, christenings, showers, masses, funerals that had all happened before I was born. It was thrilling to imagine their lives before they had me. I read the signatures I knew with a kind of love, because they had known my parents when they were happier: Kay Wainwright, Russell Bergman, Eddie and Mary Lou Novak, Onnie Davis, Hank Remby, Lois and Hugh Lyons, Bob and Terry Stewart, Danny Grady, Bill and Elaine Tunis. They had all been hopeful together—except for tall, dark, funny, handsome Archie Stewart, my father's best friend, who had been captured by the Germans when the Nazis knew that the war was about to end and had force-marched their prisoners toward the Russian front for weeks. Archie Stewart had starved to death only weeks before the war was over, paper-frail skin fluttering off the bones that his buddies had no strength to bury. I couldn't comprehend it. For years his poor mother Mims would raise a spoonful of food to her mouth and be unable to eat a thing, because such a morsel would have saved his life.

I flipped to the beginning of the book to see if there was a date when all the parties had begun to be recorded, and there, on the front page, the very first signature made me slam the book shut and run out of the house for air. I squeezed my eyes tightly, tears creeping between the lashes, trying to unsee what I'd just seen. But the handwriting could not be mistaken for any other. I knew what it meant but I wouldn't let it register. It just couldn't be true. It had to be a mistake. I kept swallowing something hard in my throat, hanging over the porch rail in case I had to throw up into the petunias.

Suddenly Rommie came out onto the porch.

"Melissa, I didn't hear you come in. What is it, darling? Are you feeling sick?"

I could only look at her. My stomach was in spasms.

"Come into the house. I'll get you an Alka-Seltzer."

She sat me in John's red leather recliner and brought me a glass of fizzing water, two tablets evaporating into bubbles at the bottom. I gagged it down, wishing it was arsenic.

Rommie was tender with all children, her own and anybody else's who wandered into the apron of her full skirt. When she was dressed for a party, she wore Capri pants, long colorful tunics, sparkling bracelets and earrings. Her face was powdered, penciled, rouged, and lipsticked so perfectly that she looked like a model. But in her Saturday morning vacuuming clothes without a hint of makeup—I might have laughed out loud if I hadn't been so upset—our Rommie, the best person we knew, was not wearing makeup, and damned if she didn't look like a hard-boiled egg.

"What is it, darling?"

Without a word, my stomach heaving, I brought the Guest Book to her and put it in her lap. She looked at me, puzzled.

"The first page," I croaked, and sat down with a thump

into the recliner. "Aunt Rommie, read the first signature for me."

She opened it and blushed, licked her lips nervously, and gently shut the book.

"Aunt Rommie, tell me what it means."

She coughed and reached for a cigarette, then lit it with hands that trembled slightly.

"Hadn't you better ask about this at home?" she said softly.

"No," I cried in a panic. "I have to know now, you have to tell me, I know what it means anyway, but you have to tell me the truth, you have to tell me, please!" I slumped back into the red chair, sobbing.

My mother's handwriting was clear. The long-dried fountain-pen ink said, "Anna and Tom Murphy." I had never heard of Tom Murphy, but in a flash I understood. My mother had been married before. I remembered the set of battered suitcases I'd seen in the shed chamber with the initials AHM. Now I knew they had belonged to my mother when she was Mrs. Thomas Murphy, Mrs. Anna Higgins Murphy.

"Mama was married to him, wasn't she?" I sobbed. "Why didn't somebody tell me?" This was more than even I could imagine. Who was he? How long had they been married? Where had they lived? Did my mother have any children before she had me? I was hysterical. "Rommie, Rommie, please tell me. Mama was married before she met Daddy, wasn't she? Tell me! Tell me what happened."

Rommie sighed. "Your mother should really be telling you this. If she'd wanted you to know, she would have told you herself."

"But I know now. You have to tell me."

She stubbed out her cigarette and reached for another. "Your mother was a stewardess for American Airlines during the war, you know."

I nodded. Stewardesses once had to be nurses before they could fly, but all the nurses were needed in the war, so my mother was one of the first stewardesses who wasn't a nurse. In those days if you were young and beautiful, it was considered glamorous to fly in a twenty-one-seat DC-3 that rattled and pitched, barely clearing the treetops.

"She was lovely then," Rommie continued. "Reddish curls, her beautiful smile, an hourglass figure. I guess she met Tom on one of her flights to New York or Nashville. They were married in 1943 and lived on Sewall Avenue—you know the little gray house at the end of Back Beach? That's where they lived."

I gasped. I swam there most of the summer because it was shallow for a long way out and the waves were gentle. I had seen that silver cottage with the sunporch and the lilac branches tapping on the windowpanes—I'd always loved it because you could see straight through the house to the sea. I used to dream that I would live in it someday. It was a perfect writer's house. To find out that my mother had been a bride there and I didn't know it made me sick to my stomach.

"Were they happy?" I asked, afraid to hear and not to hear.

"They were happy on their honeymoon, as far as I could tell, but it . . . it got difficult after that. Your mother should really be telling you this."

"Please?" I had to know or I thought I would jump off the sea wall.

"The cottage belonged to Tom's father, who lived in an old sea-captain's house with a widow's walk on it in Somerville and ran a liquor store with both of his sons in Charlestown next to the Navy Yard. Tom began coming home drunk every night. Finally Anne had to get a job because Tom was drinking up his salary. He'd be sober for a while, promise to reform, to stop drinking, but then he'd be right back at it in no time. He . . . I guess, pretty early on, he . . . he used to mistreat her. They stopped coming to our parties. I saw her in the market a couple of times with a black eye—she said she'd run into a door. And she began to drink with him too, I think, though she never said. She was so ashamed, I guess, she couldn't tell any of us."

Rommie had been scratching at the eczema on her elbow. It was hurting her to tell me this story, but I had to know.

"Did they have any children?"

"No," she sighed. "A good thing, too. She was married to him for eight years, and then she filed for divorce."

She winced as she said the word, and I shuddered. Divorce was wicked. If your soul was a clean white cloth, then divorce was some kind of deadly tarantula with black furry legs, crawling across it for eternity. Good Catholic wives did not divorce their husbands, no matter how miserable they were, even I knew that. My mother—divorced? I thought of Nana Higgins and how she must have felt when her perfect, brilliant daughter was divorced. And then she married my father? A divorced woman was criminal enough, but to turn around and marry another man, and one who wasn't even Catholic? No wonder Mama never took communion at Sunday Mass—she must have been excommunicated. It was like being dead to the Church, erased, annihilated, an exile so complete that it was as if she had never existed. I didn't say that my father had turned out to be a drunk too.

I had to see Granny. She would know the story. I had to get away.

"Rommie, I can't have dinner here tonight, tell Joyce she'll have to sleep over another time—I don't feel very well," I hollered rudely over my shoulder as I ran pell-mell through the front door and out of the house.

I raced home in the pouring rain. Granny would tell me about Mama and Tom Murphy. She would tell me what really happened. I ran up the front steps and banged loudly on the knocker, slipping out of my sopping Keds and shaking my wet hair. I was cold, chilled to the bone, but it wasn't the warm summer rain that was making me shiver. I felt as though I'd seen an uncovered grave and couldn't get the creepy feeling off my flesh. Granny had to tell me everything.

She was still half-dressed when she opened the door.

"What's the matter now?" she snapped.

"Joyce can't come over tonight—she's sick," I lied, hanging my socks over the radiator.

"Too bad," Granny cooed, visibly triumphant. She pulled up her slip in the front hallway to refasten a garter and straighten a seam in her stocking. "Come eat lunch. We'll have to hurry—my train's at two, and Dick has to drive us to the station."

I washed my hands at the kitchen sink and sat at the table. Baloney and cheese again. My stomach turned. I sipped cautiously at my tea, wondering how to bring up the subject of Tom Murphy and my mother's other unhappy marriage to a drunk.

"Granny," I plunged in. "Did you know Mama before she and Daddy were married?"

She wiped a feather of mayonnaise from the corner of her mouth.

"I used to see your mother walking by the house every morning on her way to work. She was a pretty little thing with bright red cheeks and lovely curls. She made her own clothes—handsome wool suits and coats. She had a stunning figure. She had real . . ." she chewed thoughtfully, "real carriage. And a smile that could light up a ballroom."

"Was she married to Tom Murphy then?" I asked casually, biting nonchalantly into my sandwich. Granny didn't bat an eyelash.

"You'd never guess he was a drunk to look at him. He was good looking, in a coarse sort of way. A lot older than she was, you understand. He worked in his father's store, so he could get his hands on all the booze he wanted. And then he'd go home and thrash that poor girl. It's a wonder she stayed with him as long as she did."

"Do you think they ever loved each other?"

"Who knows? She was a young girl, sheltered—you know how the Catholics are. I doubt she knew what love was. She stood there in the church in her white gown, and Murphy's brother—the best man—passed out dead drunk at the altar, and they had to slap him awake before they could fish the ring out of his pocket so Tom could put it on her finger. That's how that marriage started. Then she had to live in that ramshackle little cottage and try to make a home there. She told me once the old place was so drafty during a hurricane that the candles on the dining-room table wouldn't stay lit. They never had two nickels to rub together. He guzzled up every penny they ever had."

It's not a shack, I wanted to say. It's a pretty silver cottage with dormers and windows on all sides looking out at the sea, with lilacs and beach roses growing in the field.

"Are you sure he hit her?" I asked, praying for it not to be true.

"God, yes, I know he did!" Granny snorted. "One day I was out sweeping leaves off the porch steps, and your mother came rushing up the street, crying—no coat, no hat, her blouse was torn, and she'd lost one of her shoes. She didn't seem to know where she was going. She must have been in shock and just wanted to get away. God knows, I didn't know her very well, but I called to her and went down the steps to meet her. She blanched when she saw the broom, the way a dog will flinch if it's been beaten. I brought her inside, wrapped her in a blanket, gave her some tea to calm her down. She had a bump on her forehead the size of a golf ball and when I gave her some ice for her head, the blanket slipped from her shoulders, and I saw the bruises. He'd put both hands around her throat—I could see the dark prints where his fingers had been. And then she told me—after he'd tried to strangle her, he'd thrown an ax at her."

My mouth dropped open. Tears rushed to my eyes as if to her defense. Granny got up to clear the table and I grabbed her arm.

"Then what happened?" I asked, meaning her marriage, her heart, her life.

"I gave her a coat, some ration coupons, and a pair of your

father's work boots—my shoes were much too small—and walked her down to Rommie's. After a while I heard that she was living in an apartment on Mermaid Avenue with a little dog named Dusty she used to have. She'd snuck into the house when Tom was at work one day, grabbed her purse, the dog, and an armful of clothes and never went back. When she and your father started going out together, she was still a married woman. Come on, help me get dressed."

End of subject. A little man with a jackhammer was drilling at a tiny vein of ore inside my skull.

Granny sat before the mirror putting on her face while I patted her back and shoulders with powder. She wriggled into a blue and white seersucker sundress, I zipped her up and rummaged in the closet for her spectator pumps. Two large hands were pressing into my heart like a balloon.

Then she looked at me and said, "You can't go to the train station in that. Get dressed."

"I . . . no, I don't want to go. I want to stay home." My heart was like a ragged shirt being torn in my chest.

"You're coming to the station to say goodbye to me," she said matter-of-factly, turning to the mirror to pull down the fairy-blue mesh of her veil.

"No, Granny, I can't. I have to stay home. I'm sick."

"Sick?" Her voice rose in alarm.

No, no, if I say I'm sick, she'll postpone her trip. Think fast. Not sick—

"Not sick, Granny, I'm just tired—sleepy. I need to take a nap. I'm not sick at all." I smiled brilliantly and gave her a ferocious hug. "I'll say goodbye to you here. I'll miss you so much, Granny," I said, with enough treacle in my voice to make Shirley Temple throw up.

Granny peppered my face and neck and mouth with her sticky coral lips, her eyes brimming with my betrayal.

"Come on, Ma, we're going to be late. Let's get a move on," barked my grandfather from the doorway.

My heart was fluttering like a bird's. Granny was so damn

nervous, she drove me crazy. She checked the stove to make
sure it was off. She had to see that the cellar door was bolted.
She checked for keys, money, tickets, cigarettes, handkerchiefs, and had to pee one last time. I was hopping back and
forth on one foot, waiting for her to leave—feverish kisses,
hugs, Granny pulling on her gloves, the key turning the tumblers as my grandfather locked the front door, Granny's plain-
tive voice calling my name through the door's glass panels as
if she were going to Siberia for the rest of her life. I heard the
car start up and then I raced for the kitchen, my body running
with sweat.

I had to hurry. My mind was clicking like an adding
machine—how long would it take for them to get to the station, park, wait in line, Boppa standing patiently, twirling his
hat, while Granny ransacked the shops for the *Ladies Home Journal*, *Yankee* magazine, stamps, postcards, and chocolate-covered
cherries. She already had a cheese sandwich in her pocketbook, but bonbons were a traveling necessity. Boppa would
drive back alone, fill the car with gas, come home, park, wash
up, and turn on the radio to hear the Red Sox game. I had to
hurry, there wasn't much time.

My hands were in the washtub, the faucet running hot over
the skitterish bar of Ivory as I slammed through the dishes. I
swept the crumbs off the table, pushed in the chairs, filled the
teapot with an inch of water, then shook out the tea leaves
over the roots of the lilac bush outside. I had managed to finish
my chores. But now the pulse in my head was like a Mexican
jumping bean. I ran down the hall and locked myself in the
bathroom, sat on the floor in a knot, my back against the rungs
of the stone-cold radiator, my head on my knees. I was shivering. I had to stay calm. I had to try and understand.

My beautiful mother. A scholarship to Emmanuel College
when she was sixteen. An offer from Radcliffe to pay for her
graduate work. An invitation from *Time* magazine to write for
them in New York. A glamorous stewardess who'd once

danced with a duke at a Christmas party on Beacon Hill in a
candlelit ballroom in Louisbourg Square. My mother was a
golden girl, and everything good should have come to her.
What had gone so terribly, terribly wrong?

Pictures ran through my head like a film that's slipped its
sprockets, images flapping wildly one after another. I put my
head between my knees, my arms protecting my head as
though I were being shot at. The ivory bride. A death at the
altar. Wartime sunlight streaming through yellow dotted swiss
curtains made to brighten up a gray house, like the garish dye
they gave you to add to oleo so you could pretend it was butter. Meals warming till dawn in the oven. Sleepless pacing.
Charred scraps tossed out to the gulls as the sun broke over
the water. Arguments. Accusations. A chair thrown against the
wall, and splintering. Bottles of whiskey, bourbon, and rye
smashed one by one onto the rocks at low tide by a woman
beaten about the head, my mother trembling until her teeth
rattled, her husband begging and weeping against her check-
ered apron, falling to his knees in self-pity. A door slammed,
kicked in, then torn off its hinges. A mirror crashing into jag-
ged shards. Her blouse tearing. The cry of an animal, his hands
at her throat. The ax. The man. The silver edge. The arc. The
ax. The blade, falling.

I was screaming, my forehead pressed into my knees, thunder rocketing through my body, my skin crying out to be cut—
to save her, to stop him, to deaden the pain, to stop the noise,
the crawling scream, *Get out, get out, get out!* I was standing over
the sink, twisting the neck of my grandfather's razor, the blade
in its silver crib, shining with the murderous rage of a child for
its mother. Blood calling for blood. The blade moved like a
silver flame. The flash of a fruit knife slicing the flesh of a
summer melon, and my wrist was running with light and sweet
red juice, and tears fell through my lashes at last, my knees
gave way, and I could breathe again. Her anguish was leaving
my body, the panic pounding out of my lungs like a thief.
Someone's pain had fled. Someone was free.

I lifted my head. For a minute, I was lost. The bathroom. Razor. Blood. Like an automaton, I rinsed off the blade, dried it on a facecloth, slipped it into the holder, and twisted the razor's neck. I pressed on my arm with the washrag, and it came away soaked with blood. I pressed it back on the cut and held it up against my chest while I cleaned up the sink. I would stop bleeding in a minute. I pulled down the gauze and the bandages and waited.

My mother. My poor mother. How frightened and alone she must have been. If I ever saw Tom Murphy, I'd kill him.

The facecloth was drenched, blood was running into the cuff of my blouse tucked up at my elbow. It wasn't going to stop. I wrapped it tighter and pressed on it hard. It was going to stop. It had to stop. My grandfather would be home soon.

But it wasn't stopping. Blood raced down my arm like a river flooding its banks. I couldn't tell Boppa. I'd have to go to the hospital for stitches. He couldn't know. He would not understand. He couldn't know. I'd have to explain. Oh, Christ. I'd have to sew it myself.

This is a dream, I thought, swimming like a fish through the slow, watery light. I found a torn bedsheet in the bottom of the hamper and tied part of it around my arm, stepping on one end of the rag and pulling it into a knot with my good hand. My left arm didn't belong to me. I pawed calmly through Granny's sewing basket—*where are the needles?* There were needles for her Singer, tiny ones for embroidery, nothing for sewing up wrists. I found the chocolate box cover with the ladies in their ballgowns around the spinet that Winslow Gates had given Granny when he asked for her hand in marriage. *Needles, needles, where is the right needle?* I found a card holding upholstery needles and picked out a curved one that looked strong enough. But there was only cotton thread in the basket—mostly blue, some black and white, but cotton thread would break. It wouldn't hold my bleeding wrist together. *Think, think!*

Boppa's tackle box! I went into the kitchen and pulled everything out of the cupboard beside the sink until I put my hand on the blue tin box and found a spool of fishing line. But could I do it? Sew myself? The room was beginning to speckle. I put my face under the cold-water tap and let it run over my cheeks and the back of my neck. I had to hurry.

I ran back to the bathroom and locked the door. I lay a towel on the toilet seat, got the nail scissors, and knelt before my makeshift operating table. The sheet was soaked. I tore it off and threaded the upholstery needle. My hands were shaking. I felt weak. I had to do this. I didn't know if I could.

There was so much blood. I let the water run in the sink and kept rinsing off my arm while I sewed. It was hard to push a needle through skin. It didn't hurt—I was numb—but the skin kept moving, and I had to run my arm under cold water between stitches. One, two. How many would it take? French knots. Three, four, five. I kept rinsing my arm. It was so cold now that it was paralyzed. Six, seven, eight. It seemed to be holding. I cut the fishing line with the nail scissors, pressed the wet rag to my wrist, held it to my chest. With my good arm, I rinsed the sink, scrubbed it with Bon Ami, and wiped away the blood. The stitches seemed to be holding.

I dried my arm with a towel, wrapped it quickly in gauze, and started to put everything away. I rolled the bloody towel and my shirt in newspaper and stuffed it into the wastebasket in the pantry, burying it under the other rubbish. I put away the tackle box and changed my clothes, buttoning my sleeve tightly over the gauze. Boppa would want tea when he came home. I was just filling the kettle when the key turned in the lock. A bright blade of pain went through my skull.

I brought Boppa his tea on a tray table while he turned on the Red Sox. I kissed his broad, innocent forehead. I couldn't look at him, much less tell him what I had done. I crawled into my cot in the sunroom and pulled the covers over my head, my wounded wrist tucked between two pillows and a towel, in case it started bleeding again. I was exhausted. I was crying when I fell asleep.

Someone was shaking me and calling my name. It was dark.

I didn't know where I was. I sat up quickly as a corona of fire danced in front of my eyes, and squinting, I saw Boppa, and then lamplight, but a chisel of pain went through my skull, exploding in fireworks, and I slid back onto the pillow, holding my head.

"Were you having a nighthorse?" My grandfather asked gently. "I heard you crying from the other room."

My teeth hurt. My skin hurt. Light shining on the marble table blistered my eyes so I shut them. The whole right side of my head was in a vice. I thought I was going to die.

"I'm sick, Boppa. My head hurts. It hurts so much." Suddenly my voice was a little girl's, and I didn't recognize it. The pain was everywhere. I couldn't escape it.

"A headache?" he said. "Show me where." His gentle hands touched my forehead for fever, touched my hair.

"It's here," I moaned, holding the right side of my head. "I'm going to throw up." He pulled up a wastebasket and I hung, retching, over the side of the bed.

I heard Boppa walking into the kitchen. I was going to die. When he came back, he laid a cold cloth on my forehead and put an ice bag against my temple.

"I think you have a migraine, sweetheart. They run in our family. I used to get them. Your father got them. Your Uncle Ollie would stay in bed with them for three or four days. It's a very bad head, I know, but you'll be all right. I'll sit with you for a while."

I had never heard of migraines. I thought it must be a brain tumor. I tried to lie still but the ice only made the pain colder. I kept crying and turning my head because a glacier was bearing down on me, an ache so fierce that I thought I was breaking in half. Boppa held my hand. I slept a little, but when a sword-point of pain went through my brain, I sat up and screamed.

"Boppa, Boppa, I'm going to die, please don't let me die!" I pleaded. I was shivering and feverish.

He put a blanket over me and left the room. I began to make my last confession, but I couldn't remember any of the church's words. I wept, wondering if when I finally crossed this threshold of agony, I would see God. *Please forgive me, Lord, for being so rotten, so mean, selfish, lazy, and spoiled. I'm sorry I hate my sister. I don't hate her now. I'll never see Daddy again. Do they know I love them? Please let them know. Don't let me die.* Then a bayonet pierced my head so deeply, my mind shattered like glass.

When I opened my eyes, another man was standing next to my grandfather. Was it the undertaker? I barely opened my eyes, peering between my lashes because the light was so bright. It was Dr. Conrad, our family doctor, who still made house calls. He sat on the edge of my bed and took my hand. He was wearing his white hospital coat.

"You'll be all right," he said kindly. "I'm going to give you some medicine to take away the pain and help you sleep."

He looked in my eyes with a little flashlight, which felt like torture, then put a hand on my forehead, placed a thermometer in my mouth, and talked quietly to Boppa while he waited to see if I had a fever. He pulled my wrist out from under the pillow to take my pulse, but I yanked it away and bit down on the thermometer so hard that it broke in my mouth. His eyes met mine and I knew that he'd already seen the stitches under the sleep-strangled gauze.

I spit the thermometer pieces into a tissue he held out for me. My mouth was not cut. He stood up and reached into his black doctor's bag for a pad of paper, then wrote quickly with a black fountain pen.

"Here," he said to my grandfather. "I want you to get this prescription filled. It's for codeine. It'll numb the pain enough for her to sleep. She should be feeling a lot better tomorrow."

Boppa was gone. I heard the front door close. Oh, God, what was Dr. Conrad going to do to me? I didn't want to look at him. I felt the gauze untangling and his fingertips touching the wound and the knotted fishing line. He spoke to me gently.

"You must have been very unhappy to have cut yourself." He paused. "Did you use a razor?"

I opened my eyes in surprise. How did he know? He looked down at me over his half-glasses. His brow was furrowed, his face full of concern, but he was not angry, he wasn't going to punish me for anything. He had seen the other scars. Did he understand?

"It feels better . . . when I cut myself," I said. "But I didn't know it would be so deep."

"What made you think of stitching it up yourself?"

I looked away. The light was too bright. It was still raining. "I couldn't let anyone know I'd done it. If my grandfather had seen it, I would have had to go to the hospital and explain . . ." I stopped. *Explain what couldn't be explained—that cutting made me feel better, that the pain was made bearable, that cutting meant I could stay alive.*

"This is a very deep cut, the kind of thing people do when they want to kill themselves." The doctor held my face carefully with one hand and looked straight into my eyes. "Were you trying to kill yourself?"

I couldn't answer for a minute. I did want to be dead, so much of the time. I kept waiting for my life to be over, but it just went on and on. I didn't know how to answer him. I started to cry. Is that why I cut myself? To die? I thought it was to keep from dying.

"I . . . I just wanted . . . the pain to . . . stop."

He held my chin gently, examining my face as though he'd never seen it before. He was thinking hard about something, but I couldn't guess what it was. Finally he cleared his throat.

"Well," he said. "You did a pretty fair job of stitching this. Do you want to go to medical school when you grow up?"

I tried to smile. "No, I want to be a writer."

"In that case, you have to be alive and well, don't you? I'm just going to take out this fishing line and suture it properly so you won't get an infection, all right?"

I felt the cool blade of the scissors snipping at the stitches. He rubbed something cold over the wound. His needle was

warm and quick, and I hardly felt anything more than pin-
pricks. He painted over the stitches, then wrapped my arm
tenderly with gauze.

"There," he said, putting back the scissors and gauze into his
doctor's bag."That should do it." He paused again and gazed
down at me. "You must stop cutting yourself. You could be in
real danger, you know. No one wants you to die."

A lump came into my throat. No one? No one but me?

"Are you going to tell my grandfather?" I asked, the pounding in my head still like rifle shots.

"Should I tell him?"

"I won't cut myself anymore, Dr. Conrad," I promised,
though I knew I was lying. I didn't want to make a mockery of
his kindness. "Please don't tell anyone. I'll stop." But I knew I
couldn't stop. He searched my face again and seemed to
believe me. He would not tell Boppa.

Dr. Conrad tucked my wrist under the blanket and pressed
the ice bag softly against my head. When my grandfather came
in the front door with my medicine, he got up and went out
to meet him. I heard their steps in the hallway, their quiet
voices in the kitchen. I didn't deserve such attention, such
worry. It was so wonderful and complete that it hurt, like a
knife.

I swallowed two yellow pills and sipped a glass of hot milk
with honey and cinnamon in it. I tried to imagine those two
tall men with white hair fussing over hot milk on the stove. I
began to feel warm, as if I were rocking in the sunlit summer
waves on Back Beach by a silver-gray cottage with yellow curtains blowing at the windows. The last thing I remember was
Dr. Conrad sitting on the edge of the bed, holding my hand,
and my grandfather, in the wicker chair beyond him, chewing
on his unlit pipe.

Fog, more like lace than mist, rushed past my face, pulling veils
of silk over my streaming hair, my weightless body. In my

dream I was sailing effortlessly under a canopy of trees, and
through their fretted branches a blue-black sky was knotted
with stars. I could smell the sea and soon was upon it, thousands of stars adrift on bright waves. I came to the yellow
house at 56 Floyd Street and rose up the long front stairs without touching the bricks with my feet. The door was open. I
knew Cap Bergman would be waiting, and tears came to my
eyes because he'd been dead for some time, and I missed him
terribly.

I floated into his study, the mahogany and brightwork, and
found him standing by the window in his blue uniform with
brass buttons and a gold braid on his broad-billed hat. He was
immaculate and trim, and happy to see me.

"I've been waiting on you, daughter," he said fondly. "Come
here."

I saw the shelves of ships in bottles, the beautiful *Star of India*,
the three-masted, square-rigged bark that I'd helped him build
so long ago. In the glowing bottles around the room were frig-
ates, ketches, schooners, yawls, all tenderly preserved in their
glass sarcophagi.

He motioned me over to a shelf I hadn't noticed, where five
bottles were cradled on their sides, moonlight filling the glass
with an eerie brightness, lighting the bowsprits, capstans, halyards, and spars of the ships inside, bleaching the billowing
sails.

I bent closer to the bottles and read out the names of the
vessels. The *Girl Aurelia* tossed in heavy Irish seas, water like
steel, no land in sight—the ship on which Jeremiah and his
mother had come to America. *Maria Consuela* shone, a ribbon of
moonlight gilding the placid clay deeps at the sky-blue horse
latitudes, a tiny figure—the young Jeremiah—suspended by
fishing line falling from Jacob's ladder. The swift sloop *Louise*—
my grandfather's boat named after his mother, Emma Beckett—fully crewed, leaned into the wind by Graves Light, waiting for the sails to come about. John Nolan's brother's little

cabin cruiser, the *Lord Fox*, zigzagged dangerously between shoals and sandbars in Cape Cod Bay. The peeling shutter-green rowboat that hung on the wall of the cooperage at the farm, the *Chick-a-Biddy*, was hauled up on a bank of the Squani-cook, two bamboo poles askew at the bow when Flap, Daddy, or Boppa had taken it out fishing.

Then I looked at Cap Bergman and asked, "Did you ever see these boats?"

"Nah, m' dear. Didn't need to. D'ye understand yet? Ships built in bottles can never sail. They're destined to be trapped in a dream of sailing. These are whiskey bottles, child, all my ships are built in whiskey bottles. When your great-grandpa came from Ireland on the *Girl Aurelia*, he brought the seed with him. A life he thought was free was no more the open sea than the frigate in this bottle. And every generation after him leaped upon their decks, raised the sails, and cast off, not knowing that their anchor, so light a thing as a bottle of whiskey, would never let them sail."

"Glass rooms—ships in bottles—coffins of glass," I was crying out when my grandfather shook me awake.

He gave me a yellow pill, but my hands were trembling so hard that I couldn't hold the milk cup. He cradled me in his arms and rocked me like a baby while I tried to tell him about my dream. But there was something wrong with my tongue. I sank back under the whitecaps beating against the seawall of my glass heart, and dreamed again.

It was the deepest part of winter. I was on a train in Winthrop, and as the snowy fields fled past, the windows dealt out squares of light like playing cards. Along the boulevard, the surf was high, the roiling waves racing in from the horizon and crashing over the ice-bearded rocks, spume flying fifty feet into the air before it fell. The train was steaming hard as we rounded the trestle at Great Head, washed away hundreds of storms ago. Then the train turned past Short Beach toward Point Shirley, and suddenly it was summer, and the sea breeze

smelled of salt, sunshine, and beach roses. I could see Colum-
bia Cottage, the Crest Hall Hotel, the Elsmere, the Hawthorne, the Hazelhurst, Lawrence Cottage, the Leeds, the
Leighton House, the Ocean Spray Hotel, Mrs. Palfrey's, the
Phoenix, St. Leonard's, the Taft Inn, and Young's Hotel. The
water was calm and tourmaline. People were peppering the
beach in their wool knickers, skirted bathing suits, and enormous striped umbrellas.

There was no sound and everything moved as if it were
underwater. Waves took minutes to crest and crash, guests in
wicker chairs fluttering white handkerchiefs from the wide
white porches of the hotels seemed like birds riding the invisible wings of the wind. The train curved through the marsh
toward the Highlands, no longer following its Narrow Gauge
track through town, but steaming past all the places I knew in
my dreams.

I saw Emma hitching Jingo to the pony cart, hoisting her
three children into the back with the picnic hamper, and leading them down Cliff Avenue toward the field at the end of the
bluff. I saw the silver-gray cottage on Sewall Avenue with my
mother frozen in the front parlor, her husband's hands around
her neck. We traveled past the Highland Garage where my
grandfather in greasy rags was bending to tie his boots, done
up with butcher's string. The train went up Revere Street to
Summit Avenue, and I saw ten-year-old Philip Lincoln Flynn
being thrashed by his mother with a fireplace poker, his
drunken grandmother looking on, past the school where Miss
Cochran made my father recite, "I was befallen by a snowstorm," past the white house with the glass entranceway where
little Anna was riding frantically over the head of a carved
wooden horse, past the black house where my drunken grandfather had put his wrist in a vice for hitting his son and hammered four knuckles flat, past Granny standing on the porch
in a cloche hat, a monkey-fur suit, and a black blouse printed
with red lips, holding a suitcase in her hand, past Rommie and

John's, past Cap Bergman's, down the boulevard beside the sea, past all the pain of the past, watching it happen again and again as if it would go on and on, whether I rode the train or not. I wanted to get off that train. Forever.

The Narrow Gauge chugged softly into a station, and I saw that it was the dock where I could take the ferry and leave Winthrop behind. The brass and mahogany door opened, and I leaped over the steps and fell to my knees in excitement. A gloved hand took my elbow and raised me up. I squinted into the sun and saw that it was Archie Stewart, my father's best friend, smiling and handsome and young in his full dress uniform. He would be my escort to the ferry. He was so tall and strong and beautiful in death, as if he'd never been starved in life. I was wearing the dress that my mother wore when she had sung at the Rose Hawthorne Lathrop Cancer Home, and it was as pristine as the tide's hem of lace. I had washed it clean with my tears.

At the ferry I reached up to kiss Archie Stewart on his smooth cheek.

"I will always think of you," I said. "I'll remember everything." Archie winked and saluted, then gave my hand to Cap Bergman who was standing on deck.

Cap Bergman helped me on board. He threw a black oilskin over my shoulders, as big as a shiny tarpaulin. The sun was bright.

"I won't be cold," I said bravely.

"Nay, not you, m' dear. But you must think of the child."

He put a white bundle into my arms, a baby wrapped in bunting, and I pulled the oilskin closer so the spindrift would not touch her face. The ferry started. Archie Stewart stood at attention on the landing. Cap Bergman drew up the anchor, and we started across the wide waters toward Rowe's Wharf, toward Boston, toward Beth Israel Hospital, where the child I was holding so carefully in my arms would be born and be named Melissa.

Epilogue

I hated her fiercely all my life.

I kept my distance whenever possible. I did not offer kindness when it might have mattered, I did not console her when it might have held back her tears. I castigated and tormented her. She alone bore the brunt of my rages, my childish tantrums, my wildest fury, and she never once reproached me. I hated her passive face. I hated the way she took punishment and criticism seemingly from the air itself and fed on it, as though it were her meat and drink. She dogged me all through childhood like a shadow I could not escape. I hated her and wished she would die. I despised her frailty, her fevers, her soft teeth, her headaches, her toxic blood and saliva. I turned my back on her, pretending that she was a war in another country that had no bearing on my life. And now she is still beside me, lying quietly on her back in our bed, her arms calmly folded across her belly, hiding her navel, as if she too wished that she had never been born. I have my face to the wall.

It is so quiet tonight. Venus stands very near the new moon. The trees are rustling with snow in their branches. I cannot sleep.

She sighs. Perhaps it's not a sigh after all but the sound of the surf sinking into the sand. I turn to look at her. I have not really looked at her for years.

She's grown so much older. I'd forgotten how much time has passed. The golden barley-sugar curls are gone, and the sepia fall of hair to her waist. Now it is short and dark. I hesitate to touch it, she is so motionless, but I tentatively finger the silver filaments that run through its waves. She lies as still as a corpse in her nakedness. I did not know she would be so pale. She is breathing softly, sienna half-moon shadows under heavy lashes, closed for the night. Her face is like the moon, bright but pitted with scars, each one a touchstone for some ancient pain, marks of passion and shame, disfigurements that have buried long-forgotten injuries, except for the traces of self-loathing. Her features are smaller than I thought—a short nose, bent slightly to one side, small lips, a square but delicate jaw. I learned today the name of the smallest bone in the face, the lacrimal bone, the bone meaning "tear." I want to touch her eyes, but I cannot.

Her earlobes are pierced, but she never wears earrings. She once envisioned gold medallions, sparkling silver stars, heart-shaped rubies, feathers, chains of frost and fire, but she's allergic to everything and goes about the world unadorned. Her shoulders are strong like a swimmer's, and if I look closely I can see the white wheals of old belt marks, faint as the shadows of winter grass on old snow. Her breasts—I remember her sprinting through the orchard and they were no bigger than mushrooms as she ran. They were like a young girl's breasts for most of her life. She used to be slender, but now she is middle-aged, and her breasts are as full as casaba melons with large, dark nipples, the nipples of a woman who will never bear a child.

Her hands are still small, held like a baby's in prayer, the same hands that made her First Communion, pressed fearfully against the waist-ribbon of a white lace dress and petticoat, touching but not believing the beauty of her gossamer veil. When our father died, I put his signet ring on her wedding finger, knowing that she would never marry, but wanting to put something of love on her thin white hands. I turn over her wrist. The scars are deep. I'd forgotten there were so many. She once knew the number of stitches that it took to close up each wound, but now she no longer remembers. They don't look painful anymore, as though they were carved on her skin the way a scallop shell gently sculpts the sand.

Her belly has always been round. Her hands rest there to protect it from harm. As a little girl she had nightmares that her appendix would burst inside her, and when the surgeon cut her open with his sharp knife and parted the lips of the wound, maggots, not blood, would boil out. There are hundreds of scars on her ribs, on her sides, on her stomach, even she doesn't know how they got there. Down at the pelvic bone, her hair is very soft, the labia damp and rosy like a child roused unwillingly from sleep. She has forgotten that her sex existed, the unspeakable things that were done to her there. Her thighs are strong, veined like marble columns, flecked with impurities and the shadows of punishments. Her knees are scarred, but her calves and ankles are still like a young girl's.

She sighs and opens her eyes. I did not know they contained such sorrow. The lines around them are from thinking too deeply and finding no solution, from despairing and finding no hope, from weeping and finding no solace. How could I have thought she was my enemy? She was not loved. I hated her more than anyone, and yet she did not deserve to be abandoned, especially by me. I look deeply into her eyes and see for the first time that they are gray-blue and flecked with specks of gold. She is so sad. I don't know how to beg her forgiveness. I touch her inner cheek, wanting to find the smallest bone in her face, the lacrimal bone, the bone of suffering. I put my lips on hers, and it is like a seal, hot as wax, and permanent. Shyly I embrace her, and she puts her strong arms around me and I feel her pulse, clear and calm. I hear the sound of a beating heart, and suddenly I understand—it is my heart beating. I have become myself at last, a body and soul, fused together as nature intended, and I stretch like a cat to feel my muscle and tissue respond. I am exhausted. I am whole.

Venus stands very near the new moon. The trees are rustling with snow in their branches. I wipe my eyes, wet for a thousand years, and think, *Now I can begin my life.*